Transitional justice in process

MANCHESTER
1824

Manchester University Press

Identities and Geopolitics in the Middle East

Series editors: Simon Mabon, Edward Wastnidge and May Darwich

After the Arab Uprisings and the ensuing fragmentation of regime-society relations across the Middle East, identities and geopolitics have become increasingly contested, with serious implications for the ordering of political life at domestic, regional and international levels, best seen in conflicts in Syria and Yemen. The Middle East is the most militarised region in the world where geopolitical factors remain predominant factor in shaping political dynamics. Another common feature of the regional landscape is the continued degeneration of communal relations as societal actors retreat into sub-state identities, whilst difference becomes increasingly violent, spilling out beyond state borders. The power of religion – and trans-state nature of religious views and linkages – thus provides the means for regional actors (such as Saudi Arabia and Iran) to exert influence over a number of groups across the region and beyond. This series provides space for the engagement with these ideas and the broader political, legal and theological factors to create space for an intellectual re-imagining of socio-political life in the Middle East.

Originating from the SEPAD project (www.sepad.org.uk), this series facilitates the re-imagining of political ideas, identities and organisation across the Middle East, moving beyond the exclusionary and binary forms of identity to reveal the contingent factors that shape and order life across the region.

Previously published titles

Houses built on sand: Violence, sectarianism and revolution in the Middle East
Simon Mabon

The Gulf States and the Horn of Africa: Interests, influences and instability
Robert Mason and Simon Mabon (eds)

The labour movement in Lebanon: Power on hold   *Lea Bou Khater*

Surviving repression: The Egyptian Muslim Brotherhood after the 2013 *coup*
Lucia Ardovini

Transitional justice in process

Plans and politics in Tunisia

Mariam Salehi

MANCHESTER UNIVERSITY PRESS

The right of Mariam Salehi to be identified as the author of
this work has been asserted by them in accordance with the
Copyright, Designs and Patents Act 1988.

Published by Manchester University Press
Altrincham Street, Manchester M1 7JA
www.manchesteruniversitypress.co.uk

British Library Cataloguing-in-Publication Data
A catalogue record for this book is available from the
British Library

ISBN   978 1 5261 5538 2   hardback

First published 2022

The publisher has no responsibility for the persistence or
accuracy of URLs for any external or third-party internet
websites referred to in this book, and does not guarantee
that any content on such websites is, or will remain,
accurate or appropriate.

Typeset
by New Best-set Typesetters Ltd

Contents

List of figures   vi
List of tables   vii
Acknowledgements   viii
List of abbreviations   xi
Preface   xii

Introduction   1
1 The past is not another country: Tunisia background chapter   21
2 Transitional justice in process: developments and dynamics   44
3 Initiating transitional justice   70
4 Designing transitional justice   95
5 Performing transitional justice   127
Conclusion   167
Appendix   188

References   191
Index   208

List of figures

0.1 Schematic timeline of political developments and
transitional justice in Tunisia since 2011 (author's
illustration)   4
0.2 Uneven double helix depicting the dynamic research
process and the researcher's position in it (author's
illustration)   13

List of tables

3.1 Table summarising measures and purpose for the stage of
    initiating transitional justice   75
4.1 Table summarising measures and purpose for the stage of
    designing transitional justice   100
5.1 Table summarising measures and purpose for the stage of
    performing transitional justice   131

Acknowledgements

This book would never have come into being without the cooperation and support of many other people, not least my interview partners, who willingly and generously shared their time and insights. Tunisia offered an exceptionally welcoming research environment, and especially when I was still 'new,' my interview partners were very patient with me figuring things out, but also challenged me to get – in their opinion – the story right.

The major part of the research for this book was done in the framework of the research network Re-Configurations: History, Remembrance, and Transformation Processes in the Middle East and North Africa at the University of Marburg, where I was a research fellow from 2013 to 2017. I thank the German Ministry of Education and Research for generously funding the project and my research, as well as my colleagues at Re-Configurations – Amira Augustin, Andrea Fischer-Tahir, Igor Johannsen, Perrine Lachenal, Laura Ruiz de Elvira Carrascal, Christoph Schwarz, Dimitris Soudias, Alena Strohmaier, Steffen Wippel, and in particular Irene Weipert-Fenner, the best office mate one could wish for – for both the challenging discussions and the fun we had. Rachid Ouaissa encouraged me to work on Tunisia, for which I am very grateful. Felix Wiedemann and Sihem Hamlaoui did an excellent job transcribing the bulk of my interviews, and without their support I would probably still be occupied with transcribing interviews instead of writing acknowledgements.

I am grateful to my colleagues at the Center for Conflict Studies at the University of Marburg for making the centre such a positive research environment. I am extremely grateful to Susanne Buckley-Zistel for her guidance and support. She was there all the way and offered excellent advice – from the first field research to the last stretch before submission. She also created a great environment for fruitful exchange in the team colloquium of the 'Best Team in the FuK,' which really made a difference. I also thank Annika Björkdahl for agreeing to act as second examiner and Thorsten Bonacker for being part of my committee. Kristine Avram, Julie Bernath, Julius Dihstelhoff, Alexandra Engelsdorfer, Alina Giesen, Melanie Hartmann, Maria

Ketzmerick, Nele Kortendiek, Ulrike Krause, Philipp Schultheiss, Katrin Sold, and especially Anne Menzel and Timothy Williams commented at different stages on different parts of the manuscript. Their insightful comments always came at the right time and greatly improved the study. The centre would not have been the same without Werner Distler and Judith von Heusinger.

As well as my interview partners, I would also like to thank many people in Tunisia who generously shared their insights, contacts, or flats. Eileen Byrne, Sarah Mersch, and Yasmine Ryan shared their journalistic insights and were extremely helpful in pointing me to interesting people to talk to and in sharing their contacts. I also thank Eileen for initial language editing and putting my analysis under scrutiny along the way. Lorenzo Feltrin was a great travel partner to Gafsa, and Leyla Slama and Philip Jain let me crash at their places in Tunis/La Marsa at different points in time.

I finalised the book manuscript at the Global Governance unit of the WZB Berlin Social Science Center and am grateful to the A.SK Foundation for the postdoctoral fellowship and to Michael Zürn for hosting me at the unit. For the challenging and productive academic environment, the stimulating political discussions, and lots of fun, I thank Luis Aue, Robert Benson, Jelena Cupać, İrem Ebetürk, Julia Fuß, Johannes Gerschewski, Sassan Gholiagha, Tine Hanrieder, Cédric Koch, Christian Rauh, Nieves Fernández Rodríguez, Lena Röllicke, Johannes Scherzinger, Hendrik Schopmans, Mitja Sienknecht, Matthew Stephen, Alexandros Tokhi, Editha von Colberg, Katinka von Kovatsits and Maximilian Weckemann. I also thank Paul Collins and Martha van Bakel for proofreading my sample materials.

I am delighted that the book has found such a great home in the Identities and Geopolitics in the Middle East series at Manchester University Press. I would like to thank Marc Lynch and Bassel Salloukh for inviting me to the Carnegie Workshop in Beirut in September 2019, where I first met Simon Mabon, whom I saw again a couple of weeks later at the annual conference of the German Middle East Studies Association in Hamburg, where I was awarded the 2019 dissertation award. Simon and Edward Wastnidge had just started the series and invited me to send over my book proposal. Simon offered constant support throughout the process, for which I am most grateful. I would also like to thank Robert Byron at Manchester University Press who was excited about the project from the start and found reviewers who provided timely and constructive feedback.

Last but not least, I thank Lotte Kirch and Paula Quentin for their friendship and for transforming my ideas into beautiful designs. I don't know how I would have made it through the pandemic without Friday dinners with Lina Behrens and Johann Voss, Janis Zöll's Chinese cooking, and runs with Hanna Klein.

I am most grateful to my mother, Sigrid Salehi, for all her support. And to Nicolas Merz for making my life much happier.

While I really hope that I haven't forgotten to thank anyone, in the end, of course, all errors remain my own.

List of abbreviations

ARP	Assembly of the Representatives of the People
CPR	Congrès pour la République; Congress for the Republic
ICC	International Criminal Court
ICTJ	International Center for Transitional Justice
IMF	International Monetary Fund
INLUCC	Instance Nationale de Lutte Contre la Corruption; National Instance to Fight Corruption
ISIE	Instance Supérieure Indépendante pour les Élections; Independent High Authority for Elections
LTDH	Ligue Tunisienne des Droits de l'Homme; Tunisian Human Rights League
MENA	Middle East and North Africa
MP	Member of Parliament
NCA	National Constituent Assembly
NGO	Non-Governmental Organisation
OHCHR	Office of the High Commissioner for Human Rights
RCD	Rassemblement Constitutionnel Démocratique; Democratic Constitutional Rally
SWP	Stiftung Wissenschaft und Politik; German Institute for International and Security Affairs
TDC	Truth and Dignity Commission
UGTT	Union Générale Tunisienne du Travail; Tunisian General Labour Union
UN	United Nations
UNDP	United Nations Development Programme
UTICA	Union Tunisienne de l'Industrie, du Commerce et de l'Artisanat; Tunisian Confederation of Industry, Trade and Handicrafts

Preface

29 July 2021

As I review the copy-edits for this book, the political situation in Tunisia is once again in flux. On the evening of 25 July, President Kais Saied dismissed the Prime Minister, froze the activities of the parliament, and revoked parliamentarians' immunity from prosecution. In doing so, he invoked Article 80 of the Tunisian Constitution of 2014, which allows the president to take emergency measures in situations of "imminent danger." Whether his actions are fully in line with the constitution is questionable: Article 80 states that parliament should be "deemed to be in a state of continuous session" throughout any such exceptional period. Moreover, it also requires the president to consult with the prime minister and the president of the Assembly of Representatives (ARP) (parliament) before taking exceptional measures. He is also required to inform the president of the Constitutional Court of his decision. While there have been contradictory statements on whether he consulted with the Prime Minister and the assembly, there was no president of the Constitutional Court to inform since the Constitutional Court (due to have been created by 2015) has not yet been established. Parliament had so far failed to agree on which judges should be appointed to it. The article further states that thirty days after the special measures come into force, or any time thereafter, parliamentarians may ask the Constitutional Court to rule on whether the circumstances are still "exceptional." Therefore, it is not clear at the time of writing when and how things will return back to "normal functioning of state institutions and services" (Article 80).

An opinion poll published on 28 July by a local consulting firm indicates that the President's move is popular with the Tunisian public, which has been suffering due to the poor state of the economy, a catastrophic pandemic situation, and has generally been upset about nepotism and corruption among the political class. The next days and weeks will show whether Saied proceeds to nominate a new government and whether he allows parliament to go back to work. They will also reveal whether it is justified to call this power grab, which he claims to be temporary, a 'coup.'

In my introduction to this book, I point to a trope of 'success': Tunisia as a 'poster-child' for the so-called Arab Spring. In the same paragraph, I speak of the country as "the only nascent democracy remaining from the eventful year of 2011." I indicate that this is only one option for telling the story of Tunisia's political developments over the past decade, and that I hope my book will tell a more nuanced story.

I decided to leave these comments unchanged for the following reasons: first, this trope is still very much part of the story; second, the situation is still very much in development; and third, I want to avoid contributing to (re)producing another trope such as the 'fallen poster-child,' the inevitability of democracy 'failing in the Arab World,' or 'Egypt 2.0' – to name just a few that have been floating around the social media landscape in recent days. As for the term 'nascent democracy,' I already publicly pondered about its appropriateness when I was preparing the manuscript for final review in late 2020. At that point in time, however, I was more concerned about the possibility of downplaying achievements and manifesting terminology that may no longer have been appropriate ten years after the revolution. I decided to stick with the term because my impression was that things were not settled (whatever that would mean), not least from an institutional perspective, in particular since the Constitutional Court, which is foreseen in the constitution, had still not been established. As we can see now, the absence of a Constitutional Court has provided an essential loophole for the President's move to assume extraordinary executive powers.

This book aims to emphasise non-linearity and complexity. Therefore, the current developments do not appear to contradict its narrative – rather the contrary.

Introduction

The truth, whatever we do, is revolutionary.
Writer Gilbert Naccache at the first public hearings of the Tunisian Truth and Dignity Commission, November 2016[1]

The truth is rarely pure and never simple.
Oscar Wilde, *The Importance of Being Earnest*[2]

Tunisia is often presented as a 'poster child' for the so-called Arab Spring.[3] It is the country where the region-wide uprisings against authoritarian leaders first started, in December 2010, with small protests following street-vendor Mohamed Bouazizi's self-immolation. These events snowballed in the weeks that followed, eventually bringing down the authoritarian regime of Zine el-Abidine Ben Ali. Moreover, Tunisia is the only nascent democracy remaining from the eventful year of 2011.[4]

After the fall of the Ben Ali regime in January 2011, Tunisia began to develop new political rules and institutions,[5] nourishing hopes for democratic developments that would go beyond lip-service. "We have a new political architecture in Tunisia. Everything has to be reinvented," a ministerial staff member told me in a research interview.[6] The country held elections in 2011 and again in 2014, which were generally seen as free and fair, and adopted a new constitution at the end of January 2014 in the period between the two votes. It also started to deal with its authoritarian past by introducing transitional justice measures aimed at paving the way to sustainable peace, democracy, and political rule based on respect for human rights and the rule of law.

And yet on closer examination one could tell the story of post-revolutionary Tunisia in at least three ways.[7] The first would be a story of ongoing success, of transformation from authoritarianism to democracy, of a country that fought back fiercely against radical Islamist terrorism and defied economic hardship. The second would be a grim story of a country marked by Islamic extremism, economic failure, and an authoritarian backlash. The third story, as it is told in this book, paints a more complex and nuanced picture of a political context in flux, in which the above features can exist alongside each other, either in parallel or as results of feedback loops in non-linear processes of change. To do so, this story concentrates on one element in the Tunisian transition – transitional justice – and connects it with the 'bigger picture' of political developments. This book therefore analyses transitional justice in connection with the 'transition' it relates to.

Transitional justice after the revolution

After Ben Ali was ousted, Tunisia started dealing with its repressive past very early on. It introduced measures that aimed at seeking accountability, established a record of practices and events where egregious human rights violations or atrocities had taken place, and sought to rectify past wrongs such as human rights violations, the curtailing of civil and political liberties, nepotism, and socio-economic deprivation. This initially happened in the framework of existing legislation and later with the development of a planned transitional justice process.

Like the story of the overall transition, the story of transitional justice could also be told in three ways: the first would be a story of success, in which the country introduced a far-reaching transitional justice project with a truth commission that was well resourced, had extensive powers, and delivered a final report at the end of its mandate. The second story would be a story of failure, of declining political support, of a truth commission that worked inefficiently and non-transparently, was marked by conflict, and did not get anything done. The third story, as I would like to tell it in this book, is a more complex one, in which the above features can exist alongside each other.

The planned transitional justice process in Tunisia has been deeply internationalised. Thus, the third, more complex post-revolutionary storyline presented here is essentially also one of international politics. Consequently, to fully understand the transitional justice that has been in process in Tunisia, this study needs to be as much a study of internationalised transitional justice as a study about the Tunisian transition.

Under dictatorship, international political engagement, especially in areas related to human rights, was highly restricted in Tunisia (Kausch 2013, 1; Bush 2015, 188ff.). But after the fall of the Ben Ali regime there was a dramatic boost in international engagement (Bush 2015, 19), with a range of agencies providing financial and technical/professional support. International organisations and NGOs were active in advising on development, political reform, conflict resolution, human rights, and so forth. The processes shaped by international efforts to induce or support change are termed *internationalised processes of change* in this book. In line with findings that international advocacy for, and professional engagement in, transitional justice has greatly expanded in "size, reach and consequences" (Subotić 2012, 106), the international community – most notably the International Center for Transitional Justice (ICTJ), the United Nations Development Programme (UNDP), and the Office of the High Commissioner for Human Rights (OHCHR) – was also highly proactive in establishing a transitional justice project in Tunisia (Nassar 2014, 2020; Andrieu 2016, 264).

In December 2013, the Tunisian National Constituent Assembly (NCA) passed a much-lauded transitional justice law. The law provided for an extensive transitional justice project that was to deal with almost six decades of authoritarian rule and was prepared with major international support. It provided for the establishment of a Truth and Dignity Commission (TDC) in 2014, the central institution of the project, equipped with strong investigative powers to uncover the 'truth' about violent, repressive, and marginalising practices under dictatorship. Transitional justice, of which truth-seeking is an integral part, is consequently an essential element in Tunisia's transition.

Less than four-and-a-half years after the adoption of the transitional justice law, in March 2018, the ARP, the NCA's successor as Tunisia's legislative body, took a controversial vote[8] to deny the TDC a prolongation of its mandate – although this was in fact provided for in the law. Hence parliament voted to disband the body before it could finish its work. However, the vote took place in a late-night session and with less than a third of the Members of Parliament (MPs) present – which would normally not have met the quorum needed to maintain the session and for a vote to go forward. Domestic and international civil society organisations viewed this vote as a major setback to Tunisia's democratic transition and a "'yes' for impunity" (Human Rights Watch 2018; see also Middle East Monitor 2018a). Yet in late May 2018, transitional justice in Tunisia developed in a different direction. The Ministry for Relations with Constitutional Bodies, Civil Society, and Human Rights granted the TDC an extension of its mandate until the end of the year. Moreover, the specialised chambers in the Tunisian court system, which had also been established within the framework of the transitional justice law, heard the first human rights case that had been transferred to them by the truth commission. Thus, the 'yes for impunity' seemed much less definite by then. The truth commission, plagued by internal struggles, defections, and an enormous mandate to begin with, did not manage to complete all its tasks before the termination of its operations but handed over a final report to the 'three presidencies' of the republic, the government, and parliament by the end of 2018, and a version was published on its website in March 2019. Afterwards the report was shelved, and Tunisians had to wait for a new government and until

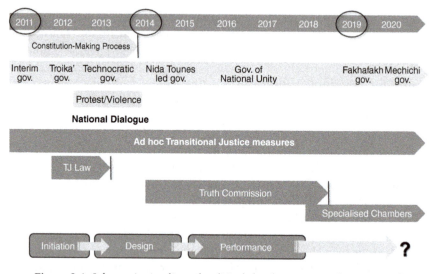

Figure 0.1 Schematic timeline of political developments and transitional justice in Tunisia since 2011. Encircled dates depict years with presidential/parliamentary elections

mid-2020 to see the report published in the country's official gazette and thereby recognised by the state.

Notwithstanding this chronological presentation of developments (see also fig. 0.1), these events illustrate the non-linearity of transitional justice and raise crucial questions in need of academic research to better understand processual developments and the prospects for peace, justice, and democracy in Tunisia, as well as processual developments of planned transitional justice projects that are set up with major international involvement. This book thus contributes to those perspectives in transitional justice that put the *justice* and the *transition* part of transitional justice in conversation with each other, exploring how transitional justice relates to processes of political change. It therefore presents novel empirical insights that aim to show both a certain breadth and depth of transitional justice in Tunisia and analyses them through a process lens.

The question

In conceptual debates, transitional justice has been "associated with periods of political change" (Teitel 2003, 69) and societal transformation (Andrieu 2010, 540). It should deal with the legacy of atrocities committed by repressive regimes or during violent conflicts (Buckley-Zistel 2018, 153). Transitional justice should contribute to societal peace and democracy (De Greiff 2012), foster justice and accountability (Sikkink 2011), offer redress for past abuses (Barkan 2006), and ensure that there is no impunity for the crimes of an old political order (Arthur 2009). These goals should be achieved by, for example, trying those responsible for atrocities, seeking the truth about past wrongs, reforming state institutions, and compensating victims of violence or repression.

In Tunisia, the foundations for a comprehensive, 'holistic' transitional justice process that combines several measures in working towards the abovementioned goals were initially laid with the support of international transitional justice professionals. But transitional justice has been an arena of contention instead of bringing about peace and justice; and it has been hard for the project to deliver on its goals and promises. Against this backdrop, one is encouraged to wonder how such a thorough approach to transitional justice could evolve towards a decision to disband the central institution of the planned transitional justice project – followed by a decision not to do so after all and a subsequent oscillation between furthering and hindering the project.

In light of these puzzling processual developments,[9] which fluctuate between accountability and impunity, between the trend of pursuing a thoroughly planned, comprehensive transitional justice process and a counter-trend to override it, the central question emerges: *How did the Tunisian transitional justice process evolve and why?*

The book answers this question by combining 'process-concurrent' empirical research – studying the Tunisian transitional justice process while it was evolving – with social-theoretical approaches to analysing processes of change, drawing mainly on the process sociology of Norbert Elias (Elias 1977, 1978, [1981] 2006a, [1983] 2006, [1986] 2006).

To develop its conceptual starting points for answering the research question and to establish the global setting in which the Tunisian transitional justice process is situated, the study brings together different strands of debates that are mainly tied into the broader fields of international relations and peace and conflict studies. It thereby considers literature from different academic disciplines, such as political science, sociology, anthropology, and international law, that provide crucial contributions for understanding the tenets, developments, and dynamics of transitional justice. The vantage point of the processual analytical approach is a strong interplay between transitional justice and social and political change. This study consequently contributes to the literature focusing on the domestic and international politics of transitional justice that complement perspectives concerned with transitional justice's goals, outcomes, and effects. In an iterative interplay between theory and empirics, it aims to develop a compelling argument (Travouillon 2015, 7) that delivers a study that is both "theoretically consistent and empirically plausible" (Menzel 2015, 29; my translation). It also aims to span an arc from the global dimension of professionalised transitional justice in the emergence and developments of transitional justice in post-revolutionary Tunisia to how these characteristics and developments interact with the broader transition, of which the transitional justice process is one key component.

Transitional justice: debates and entry points

Several definitions of transitional justice can be found in the scholarly literature, as well as in policy documents and on the websites of practitioner organisations, both governmental and non-governmental. Most of them define the term in a similar way: transitional justice means dealing with a repressive and/or violent past with the help of one or several of a variety of measures, usually including trials, truth commissions, reparations or compensation measures, lustration and institutional reforms, as well as memorials and public apologies (UN Security Council 2004; UN 2010; ICTJ 2009). Initially largely legal in nature and focusing on gross human rights violations, transitional justice has since expanded in scope, and previously peripheral issues, such as socio-economic injustice and economic crimes, have moved to the centre of debate (Sharp 2013).

One prominent strand in the transitional justice literature focuses on the normative goals, outcomes, and effects of transitional justice (Crocker 1999; Olsen, Payne, and Reiter 2010a, 2010b; Wiebelhaus-Brahm 2010; De Greiff 2012; Kochanski 2020a, 2020b). Another strand calls for more attention to be paid to the role of domestic and international political dynamics and the *transition* part of transitional justice (McGrattan 2009; Subotić 2009; Jones and Bernath 2017; McAuliffe 2017b; Cronin-Furman 2020). This book contributes to the second strand and adds a decidedly processual perspective, as well as a corresponding heuristic, to transitional justice scholarship. In a nutshell, this book identifies the dominant approach shaping transitional justice in Tunisia as an internationalised, professionalised, holistic approach to transitional justice (see also Ben-Josef Hirsch 2006; Subotić 2012; Friedman and Jillions 2015; Rowen 2017; Jones 2020). This approach is inherently political and gains ground in different contexts through the circulation of international norms, knowledge, and resources. It is appropriated and reconfigured, and shaped by, but is also a driver of, frictional encounters between different actors.

The meaning of transitional justice has evolved over time, as has the way it is implemented in practice. Like any other transition, the Tunisian transition and the corresponding transitional justice efforts are situated in a particular "world-time context" (Finnemore and Sikkink 1998, 909) in history and global politics. Thus, the dominant approaches in the particular world-time context have (co-)determined how transitional justice has been done in Tunisia. In the Tunisian case, the planned transitional justice project has been informed by a holistic approach (see De Greiff 2012; critically: Friedman and Jillions 2015) that has led to a mandate covering a period of almost six decades and an array of violations and grievances, from 'classical' human rights violations to economic crimes and marginalisation and therefore leads to a large population of potential victims. The study contrasts the supposed technocratic logic of transitional justice efforts with how they emerge from political concerns, how they influence politics and power structures, and how they can be used for political ends that sometimes diverge from their original purposes. In the Tunisian case, technocratic logics and politics do not contrast each other, with the former instead being means towards political ends. The study thereby contributes to debates on the political and contested nature of transitional justice (Subotić 2009, 2014; Ottendörfer 2016; Jones and Bernath 2017; Cronin-Furman 2020; Jones 2020) and the interface of professionalisation/technocratisation and politics (Nagy 2008; Subotić 2012; Rowen 2017; Jones 2020).

Transitional justice is a normative concept insofar as it defines standards of appropriate behaviour that relate to ideas and practices and are subject to change. To examine how transitional justice gains ground and is vernacularised and appropriated in Tunisia, the study considers concepts of normative change beyond convergence. It looks at circulating value packages, knowledge, and discursive resources, as well as points of reference and resonance that eventually produce new, but necessarily contingent accounts. Thus, the study links to questions of the relationship between global norms and expertise with local contexts and appropriation (Ben-Josef Hirsch 2006; Björkdahl and Höglund 2013; Rowen 2017; Obradovic-Wochnik 2018; Jones 2020; Menzel 2020); as well as the contested nature of gaining ground and the appropriation and reconfiguration of ideas and normative concepts in different contexts (Acharya 2004; Merry 2006; Levitt and Merry 2009; Boesenecker and Vinjamuri 2011; Björkdahl and Gusic 2015; Zimmermann 2017; Moe and Geis 2020).

For transitional justice, the concept of friction has particular analytical value in conjunction with its conflictive dimension, since transitional justice emerges from conflict and can foster new conflict or friction. Friction comes about through connection across difference (Tsing 2005) and has an ambiguous character: it is both productive and disruptive. Understood in a processual sense, frictions can either hinder or foster change. In this study, frictions are understood as cross-cutting dynamics that can span across actor groups and lead to alliances beyond common categories such as civil society, politicians, or international actors. The study therefore relates to how frictional encounters drive and define internationalised processes of change, especially transitional justice (Tsing 2005; Björkdahl and Höglund 2013; Kappler 2013; Arnould 2016; Buckley-Zistel 2016).

As many of the processes covered in this book were unfolding as it was being written, it is not surprising that only a limited amount of scholarly analysis and literature is available on transitional justice in Tunisia. While there is of course extensive journalistic coverage of various stages of the process, a body of academic literature and debate is only just emerging to discuss the politics of initiating transitional justice in Tunisia (see e.g. Lamont and Boujneh 2012; Lamont 2013; Nassar 2014; Preysing 2016; Aboueldahab 2017) as well as its design and scope (see e.g. Gray and Coonan 2013; Andrieu 2016; Lamont and Pannwitz 2016; Mullin and Patel 2016; Preysing 2016; Yakinthou and Croeser 2016; Aboueldahab 2017; Kurze 2019; Sammari 2020). Scholarship analysing the performance of transitional justice in Tunisia after the process's central institution, the TDC, began its work is even scarcer (see e.g. Robinson 2015; Ketelaars 2018; Ladisch and Yakinthou 2020; Sammari 2020). Nor are there comprehensive analyses that cover the process from initiation to performance. This book therefore advances the body of academic research on Tunisia's transitional justice process beyond initiative, design, and scope. It analyses developments in performing transitional justice and examines these developments jointly with earlier developments in initiating and designing transitional justice. With such a focus on processual developments, the study is therefore able to contribute to and even shape an understanding of changing dynamics and non-linearity in transitional justice with regard to measures, political preferences, and perceptions.

The arguments and analytical framework

When analysing processes of transitional justice, it is just as important to examine the 'how' as their substance (i.e. the 'what') (Autesserre 2014, 9). Rather than focusing solely on the goals, outcomes, and effects of transitional justice (i.e. the what), the study aims to contribute to those perspectives in transitional justice that analyse the politics of transitional justice and put the *justice* and the *transition* part of transitional justice in conversation with each other, exploring how transitional justice relates to processes of political change.

Transitional justice has often been linked to a particular, teleological understanding of transition that has influenced which justice claims have been perceived as legitimate, namely those that are believed to facilitate a transition to liberal democracy. These justice claims consequently serve as commodities and enable the mobilisation of both attention and funds. They are gradually recognised or even codified as rights, determining corresponding rights violations, since rights serve as the "cultural category for justice talk" (Levitt and Merry 2011, 87).[10] The 'transition paradigm' and the corresponding justice claims, as well as the neglect of Western democracies' role in atrocities, shape "the perception of the nature of violence, victimhood and perpetration" to be considered in transitional justice and hence "skew the direction of truth, justice and reconciliation" (Nagy 2008, 277). Moreover, this teleological perspective, which assumes a linear process with a clear direction and a fixed endpoint, does not account for diversions or possible later challenges to aspects of transitional justice or to the transition itself. This book accordingly proposes a research agenda that is – in addition to the what – concerned with the *how* and *why* of initiative and development of transitional justice projects. These aspects are important to consider, because they advance our understanding of the 'in between' of goals and outcomes/effects, of contestation and contingency in transitional justice processes.

For the ease of following the analysis, I distinguish three stages in the Tunisian transitional justice process that are temporally defined but analytically informed: initiating, designing, and performing transitional justice. By harnessing Elias's theory of social processes for this area of research, this study contributes a processual perspective and a corresponding heuristic to transitional justice research. Elias's theoretical foundations (Elias [1939] 2006, 1977, 1978, [1981] 2006a, [1981] 2006b, [1983] 2006, [1986] 2006, 1992) can be used for the benefit of analysing internationalised processes of change, such as transitional justice, as they are still evolving. They allow us to put these processes at the centre of social scientific enquiry while also paying attention to the actors shaping them and the context in which they are embedded. In line with the analytical framework, the book therefore argues that internationalised processes of change, such as transitional justice, can be explained by examining the following characteristics: the interplay between socio-technological or planned processes and unplanned social and political dynamics; the non-linearity of processes of change marked by trends and counter-trends; international interconnectedness, including interdependencies between 'the global' and 'the local'; as well as conflict and friction as defining and driving components of the processes in question.

The book argues that planned transitional justice processes, despite their goal-orientation, very rarely proceed exactly as planned, since their processual development is linked to interaction with unplanned political and social dynamics (Elias 1977, [1986] 2006). This then most likely leads to processual outcomes that nobody had intended or planned. The focus on the 'how' hence allows us to not only see these developments as divergent from plans (and therefore as 'failure' rather than 'success'), but to understand them as an integral part of the process and therefore better grasp the corresponding political dynamics in the transitional context. With regard to the dominant perspective of the 'holistic approach' in scholarship and practice (see e.g. UN Security Council 2004; De Greiff 2012; Friedman and Jillions 2015) that has shaped the planned transitional justice project in Tunisia,[11] this book identifies a 'problem–capacity nexus': while the approach fits well with the justice problems that should be addressed by transitional justice in Tunisia, as well as with the capacities of international transitional justice professionals, it does not necessarily fit the capacity of the transitional institutions that are relevant to the process of bringing about this justice. The book therefore argues that a holistic approach does not necessarily fare better in delivering (a sense of) justice, as it imposes tasks that prevent transitional justice from delivering on its promises (see also Salehi 2021). However, through this constant interlocking of the planned and unplanned, processes of change can develop a limited degree of autonomy from non-linearity in power constellations and shifting political preferences, and therefore, in some instances, from the dynamics challenging them (Elias [1986] 2006, 101–3). Thus, as illustrated in this book, while there were severe challenges to the planned project, institutionalised transitional justice in Tunisia proved able to withstand these challenges to a certain extent; and in several instances it was performed almost as planned.

The analysis over time revealed the non-linearity of processual developments marked by trends and counter-trends, and how the processual developments were influenced by shifts in power relations, political preferences, and norm dynamics in the transitional figuration (Elias 1977, 1978, [1986] 2006).[12] The Tunisian case shows that what different actors understand by transitional justice and the measures they pursue can shift over time and for various reasons in a non-linear manner. The study therefore argues that transitional justice processes are non-linear and contingent, that norms of transitional justice are reversible, and that the often assumed teleological appeal of transitional justice is misleading. Even when processes of seeking truth, justice, and accountability have been initiated, they are not immune to opposing political trends, changes in their acceptance, backlashes, and reversal.

This book furthermore argues that transitional justice processes are characterised by international interconnectedness (Elias [1981] 2006a). This is because international transitional justice professionals play a significant role in determining what makes up the socio-technological offering, the 'toolbox' of those measures that are commonly applied in different contexts (see e.g. Ben-Josef Hirsch 2006; Rowen 2017). What is on offer in global professionalised transitional justice – the "'supply' mechanism" (Ben-Josef Hirsch 2006, 185) – influences the knowledge that is transferred (Jones 2020) and may consequently be appropriated and reconfigured to resonate with domestic/local ideas of what transitional justice should mean and entail. Since international transitional justice professionals were closely involved in transitional justice in Tunisia, from initiative to performance, the dominant international approach influenced what transitional justice would look like and how it would proceed in the country.

Moreover, this study argues that technocratisation and professionalisation (both on the international as well as the domestic level) do not lead to a depoliticisation of transitional justice. Nor do they contradict the political nature of the concept and the measures it entails. Rather, the technocratisation and professionalisation of transitional justice co-constitute its political nature, since these features fulfil political functions that serve the interests of some actors better than those of others (see also Ferguson 1994). Thus, transitional justice may not be political *despite* technocratisation and/or professionalisation, but exactly *because* of it.

Given that transitional justice only comes about through conflict, the political nature of transitional justice, the challenges the project is facing in a dynamic context marked by shifts in political preferences and power structures, and the interplay between the planned process and unplanned social and political dynamics, the study argues that transitional justice is driven and defined by conflict and friction (Elias 1977, 1978, [1986] 2006, [1987] 2003). These relate to developments connected to the planned, institutionalised project and unplanned developments in the political context. The book argues that frictions are cross-cutting and that alliances traverse common clusters of actors such as groups with rival political ideologies, political actors and civil society, and international and domestic actors.

The book tentatively argues that transitional justice has a performative nature that presents a constitutive element with regard to the eventual effects of transitional justice, which may indeed be different than what was initially planned. Even if planned transitional justice is reversible, and a policy intervention is characterised as 'failed' if it is not exactly executed as planned, it may still have (positive) effects. These assessments depend on perspective and interpretation, which may be obscured when only thinking in categories of 'success' and 'failure' (Mosse 2005, 18–19). The introduction of transitional justice measures and the way they are performed in practice are constitutive in that they anchor ideas of pursuing justice, accountability, and truth-seeking in 'society's mind' and offer avenues for how this could be done and achieved (see Butler 1990) – they "crack [...] the past [...] open" (Subotić 2009, xii). For example, in response to the parliamentary motion that the truth commission's mandate should not be extended further in 2018, which nearly led to the planned transitional justice project being abandoned, it can be argued that the deeply political as well as conflictive nature of this project is reiterated by the constant renegotiation of the value and significance of transitional justice among political actors. It is also reflected in the way the attempts were made to abolish the transitional justice project in Tunisia, namely by staging a controversial vote in parliament. This act of upholding the façade of democratic procedures, then, also echoes the performative character of transitional justice.

Lastly, although transitional justice is characterised by many specificities, "it is a core site through which key ideals and norms of [internationalised processes of change, such as] peacebuilding are enacted" (Obradovic-Wochnik 2018, 2). Thus, transitional justice can function as an exemplary field for an array of internationalised processes of change initiated with the help of liberal policy interventions in Tunisia after the revolution. Hence the study offers insights for other areas beyond the field of transitional justice that may also be relevant for contexts beyond Tunisia as well.

The research approach

While I researched and analysed some developments in hindsight, especially from the early transition period and after the termination of the truth commission, I directly examined others while they were unfolding. The 'process-concurrent' research process and the immediately experienced dynamic nature and perception of the research topic, as well as the context, formed an essential part of how this processual analysis could come into being and influenced the shape the study would eventually take. While the term 'process-concurrent' is cumbersome, it fits the characteristics of those research processes I want to describe better than the sometimes used 'real-time' research (see e.g. Preysing 2016). While 'real-time' usually indicates immediately,[13] process-concurrent research accompanies social and political processes over a certain amount of time. And while the approach is generally characterised by temporal proximity, data collection may not necessarily always be immediate but can vary in the level of timeliness. The period of data collection influences the perspectives evolving from the data, since processes have evolved over time. Thus, 'process-concurrent' research aims to capture the researcher's temporal proximity to evolving processes but also pays attention to the fact that the researcher may not observe everything in real-time.

In process-concurrent research and in light of constantly changing political realities, there is a need for a *dynamic* conceptualisation of the research

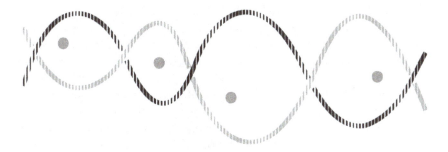

Figure 0.2 Uneven double helix depicting the dynamic research process and the researcher's position in it. Black line: (dynamic) context. Grey line: (dynamic) research topic. Dots: researcher

process. I suggest conceptualising the research process imagined as a dynamic double helix (see fig. 0.2), in which the research situation is constituted and reconfigured by the dynamic context and the dynamic research topic. The researcher's position within the research situation depends on the interplay of the two strands. In a dynamic political context, this means that the sensitivity of the research topic may change, as may the vulnerability of actors and the security situation. I therefore had to adjust my strategies as well as my ethical and security assessments over time.

The study is based on an interpretive approach (Schwartz-Shea and Yanow 2012). Interpretive research approaches allow one to research questions along the lines of "'What is going on here?'" (Schwedler 2013a, 28) and are particularly suitable for seeking to understand complex social and political processes (Schwedler 2013a, 28), such as the dynamics of transitional justice and social and political change in Tunisia.

Interpretive research can be based on a variety of theoretical underpinnings that guide what the researcher is looking for in interpretation. When researching the dynamics of the Tunisian transitional justice process, the theoretical starting points I paid particular attention to were non-linear conditions and changes, shifting knowledge paradigms and power dynamics, and what norms and ideas were invoked, by whom, and for what reasons (Foucault 1980, 84–7; Torfing 2005, 4). I also looked for 'alliances' among different actors in the transitional justice figuration in Tunisia, and thereby also at friction between actors, both of which can be cross-cutting. Moreover, actors can form part of different alliances at the same time (Hajer 2005, 303). These approaches therefore offer a valuable starting point for an interpretive, process-concurrent research project in a political context in flux. They are also mirrored in the codes attributed to the materials, as well as in the process of making sense of the empirical data. Matthew

Miles, A. M. Huberman, and Johnny Saldaña (2014) differentiate between tight and loose research designs. Tight designs are more pre-structured and delineated; they offer more guidance and clarity about how research should proceed and what data should be collected. Loose designs are emergent and less pre-structured; they spell out how research should proceed to a lesser extent, and initial data collection is less selective. Qualitative-interpretive research designs usually lie in between these two ends of the scale (Miles, Huberman, and Saldaña 2014, 19). And while interpretative research usually has some structure and guidance, it most often lies on the looser side of such a continuum, as does the design of the present study. This allows us to 'case the study' (Soss 2018) as the research develops.

Data collection and analysis

Relying on an interpretive, qualitative research approach, mainly based on loosely structured, topic-centred interviews that were adapted to the different interlocutors with interview partners drawn from politics, government and the civil service, civil society, the media, international organisations, and NGOs, complemented with (participant) observations, this study traces the processual developments in transitional justice. For this purpose, data was collected in Tunisia (mainly in Tunis and the surrounding suburbs, but also in the central towns of Gafsa and Kasserine) in several stages of field research and shorter visits over a period of four years, starting in the spring of 2014 (shortly before the nomination of truth commissioners). I also collected data during two periods of research in the United States (two and a half weeks in New York in 2015 and two months in 2019 in which I mainly stayed in Washington, DC but also conducted interviews in New York and the San Francisco Bay Area) and through phone and video interviews. The fourteen follow-up interviews I conducted in 2020 with Tunisian and international actors were all conducted by phone or video because of the coronavirus pandemic and related travel restrictions. In total, I interviewed 102 people, most of them individually and in person, some of them in groups, some of them together with another interviewer (academic or journalistic), or by phone or video call. Some of them I interviewed, or spoke with for research purposes, more than once.[14]

The setting of my research took place in what can broadly be described as the 'political scene' and comprises politicians and government representatives, truth commission members and staff, politically active civil society, as well as Tunisian and international representatives of international organisations and NGOs that were involved in the 'transition,' that is, the political reconfigurations in the country. Most of my interlocutors in Tunisia therefore formed part of the country's political and social elite.

Interview partners were chosen through a combination of different strategies. First, I sampled politically important or salient cases: interview partners were chosen because of their function or position within the political configuration (e.g. members of a certain party or civil society organisation, members of the technical committee drafting the transitional justice law, etc.). In general, there may be a bias in representation in favour of those interview partners specifically dealing with transitional justice, since these actors are usually considered salient. However, some interviews were conducted with actors who were not directly involved in the transitional justice project but who were nonetheless involved in decision-making or were in opinion-leader positions – and were therefore generally informed about the process – in order to gain a broader perspective outside of a confined 'transitional justice bubble.' Second, I used opportunistic or snowball sampling: interview partners were recommended by colleagues or other interview partners, and interview partners were chosen by convenience (e.g. they joined an ongoing interview or happened to be in the vicinity of an interview situation and offered to be interviewed as well). Conducting process-concurrent research, my sampling had "an iterative or 'rolling' quality, working in progressive waves as the study [and also the transitional justice process] progresse[d]" (Miles, Huberman, and Saldaña 2014, 33). It therefore required making decisions at each step of the way. As sampling is also investigative, new information often influenced the iterative process (Miles, Huberman, and Saldaña 2014, 33).

To prepare the data for analysis, the recorded interviews were transcribed with the support of two research assistants,[15] who transcribed the bulk of my interviews. For non-recorded interviews, I took handwritten notes and typed them afterwards, supplementing them with further information from memory. Observations and field notes were treated as complementary material, and as such were not systematically coded but consulted when necessary. The data was coded in the qualitative data analysis software MAXQDA intermittently in several partial coding cycles and in one more comprehensive coding cycle after the end of the main data collection period. The findings then informed the development of the processual heuristic and the empirical account. Follow-up research conducted remotely in 2020 followed the main logic of closing gaps but also allowed for some new issues to emerge. These findings were then integrated into the written account.

Structure of the book

Following this introduction, the book is structured in five chapters (Chapters 1–5) and a conclusion. Chapter 1 provides background on the kind of past that the Tunisian transitional justice process is meant to deal with. It first outlines the legacies of colonialism, the fight for independence, and the era of Tunisia's first president Habib Bourguiba, whose policies paved the way for the marginalisation of entire parts of the country. The chapter then turns to the systems of power defining the period when the country's second president, Ben Ali, was in office, which was marked by more violence and more accentuated nepotism. The chapter also offers some possible explanations for the fall of the Ben Ali regime before sketching out the post-revolutionary reconfigurations, political polarisation, and subsequent rapprochement that are important for the processual dynamics of transitional justice.

Chapter 2 provides the conceptual background of transitional justice, outlining the origins, developments, and dynamics of the concept and the field. The chapter looks at the characteristics that define the approaches that are currently dominant in research and practice. It then turns to the question of how transitional justice gains ground and is appropriated and reconfigured in different contexts before ending with a discussion of frictional encounters in internationalised processes of change. These aspects are crucial for understanding how and what kind of transitional justice was introduced in Tunisia.

Chapters 3, 4, and 5 map the three stages of transitional justice in Tunisia covered in this book and form the empirical centrepiece of this study. The stages are temporally defined but analytically informed. For the analytical categorisation, and therefore the naming of the stages, developments in transitional justice itself were decisive, although empirically, their interplay with broader political dynamics was also important. The characteristics, however, were developed in an iterative fashion, benefitting from the interplay between theory and empirics that is a common feature of interpretive research. For the sake of clarity, the empirical chapters all follow the same structure, and characteristics are therefore displayed in the same order, even if the inner logic of a chapter would prefer a different order. They begin with an outline of the stage's context and transitional justice activities before turning to the characteristics of interplay, non-linearity, international interconnectedness, and conflict and frictions. All stages close with a conclusion.

Chapter 3 analyses the process of *initiating transitional justice* and temporally covers the period from 2011 to 2012. From a transitional justice perspective, it mainly deals with ad hoc justice measures as well as the first steps towards a planned process of change. The chapter identifies a general trend and political willingness towards seeking justice and accountability but highlights how the initial measures were scattered, ad hoc, and based on pre-existing structures and logics. This stage was dominated by a wider transitional struggle, in which these ad hoc measures played a crucial role in co-determining who could play a role in transitional politics. First efforts towards the institutionalisation of transitional justice in this stage already indicated that supposedly technocratic measures may be political exactly because of their technocratic logic and not despite it. Both types of measures, those initiated ad hoc and the first institutionalisation efforts, were not necessarily perceived as genuine but had performative appeal. The chapter also discusses the prompt engagement of the 'justice industry' in transitional Tunisia and its role in laying the ground for the development of Tunisia's planned transitional justice project in the next stage.

Chapter 4 takes up the process of *designing transitional justice* and is temporally situated between 2012 and 2014. This chapter mainly deals with the development of a planned, institutionalised transitional justice project which was supported by international transitional justice professionals. The stage was marked by the interplay of planned processes of change, both in the wider transition and in transitional justice in particular, and unplanned political dynamics of political conflict and public unrest. While the trend towards seeking accountability continued and transitional justice was further institutionalised, a simultaneous counter-trend also emerged whereby certain accountability measures were abandoned in the process of political deal-making in the context of acute conflict resolution. Linked to the growing engagement of international transitional justice professionals was the development of the planned transitional justice project that was designed in line with a holistic approach to transitional justice. Here, the chapter identifies a problem–capacity nexus[16] that sees the applied measures as fitting the justice problems that needed to be addressed in the Tunisian context and the capacity of transitional justice professionals but not necessarily the capacity of Tunisia's transitional institutions and the context in flux. The end of this stage also saw emerging frictions between those involved in transitional justice and the political sphere.

Chapter 5, the last empirical chapter, examines the process of *performing transitional justice* from 2014 to 2020. It analyses the institutions established through the planned transitional justice project in action. Here, the focus is on the TDC, since it was the only institution of the planned transitional justice project that was operational during the main period under examination.[17] In this stage, there was a continuous interplay of socio-technological/planned and unplanned/spontaneous processes. Political support for transitional justice was non-linear in this stage, and at times the same actors that supported the process would simultaneously work against it. The trend went more into the direction of elite deal-making and political compromise, countering the trend of seeking justice and accountability and further fostering friction between transitional justice actors and the political sphere. It also influenced the dynamics of international interconnectedness insofar as the position of international actors shifted from mere support of, to advocacy for, the planned transitional justice project, even though their absolute stance towards the project did not change. Moreover, this trend showed that the development of partial autonomy of the transitional justice process from shifting political preferences and challenges. The continuous performance despite the challenges, especially of the project's outward oriented measures such as public hearings, offers prospects of constitutive effects.

The book closes with a concluding chapter that revisits the characteristics of transitional justice in process, fans out its contributions to different knowledge areas, outlines potential avenues for future research, and provides an outlook with respect to more recent political developments. Its unique contribution to research in the Tunisian case lies within the broad approach that investigates transitional justice in connection with the transition it relates to, as well as within its process-concurrent research that offers a baseline for later analyses of these processes in hindsight. It also contributes to the field of transitional justice by furthering the strand of research that deals with the domestic and international politics of transitional justice and by offering an analytical account of transitional justice *in process*. The conclusion furthermore outlines what we can learn from the findings of the study for other cases in the Middle East and North Africa (MENA) region and beyond. It closes with an outlook of recent developments in Tunisia's transitional justice process that reiterates that plans interplay with politics.

Notes

1 Personal observation, Sidi Dhrif, November 2016.
2 Yasmine Ryan (†2017), whom I got to know in Tunis, included this quote as a description in her Twitter handle, where I first saw it. Since it perfectly complements Naccache's quote for introducing this study, this stands in memory of her.
3 The use of the term 'Arab Spring' in this book is only in the sense of a common label for the assemblage of events and developments related to the uprisings in North Africa and the Middle East in 2010/11. It does not represent an analytical or political assessment of these events and developments.
4 Of the other countries that experienced uprisings during that time, Egypt is under repressive military rule and wars are being waged in Libya, Syria, and Yemen.
5 If not mentioned otherwise, this book relies on a narrower understanding of institutions that relates to formalised, rule-based structures of social order.
6 Personal interview with ministerial staff member, Tunis, March 2015.

7 While there are plenty of debates about the proper terminology for what happened in Tunisia and around the question of whether it was really a 'revolution,' this is not a discussion that this book engages in. It should therefore suffice to point out that I use the term 'revolution' alongside the less fundamental notion of 'uprising' to describe the processes of 2010/11 culminating in the ouster of Ben Ali, because 'revolution' is how the upheaval is usually termed in Tunisia.

8 See Chapter 5 for an account of the vote and the ensuing controversy.

9 I would like to note here that the puzzle could of course only be identified in hindsight, while the research process itself was more driven by questions of "'What is going on here?'" (Schwedler 2013a, 28), as outlined below.

10 Over time, novel rights and violations of rights have been recognised, for example the right to truth or to reparations.

11 The dominance of this approach was also identified by interview partners, e.g. with transitional justice professionals in New York, April 2014.

12 Figurations explain the relationship between individuals and society, and the concept should serve the purpose of avoiding a dichotomous distinction between the two spheres in the manner of "here the individual, there society" (Elias [1986] 2006, 103). Figurations therefore have decisive influence on dynamics of social processes and changing power relations. They form "[t]hrough the force of essential interdependence" (Elias [1986] 2006, 101) of the actors. Figurations have structural features and function as representatives of a particular order (Elias [1986] 2006, 100–1). They are shaped by the transmission of knowledge: actors enter specific symbolic worlds of existing figurations, which may alter those figurations. But actors also acquire specific societal symbols of knowledge or language when they enter the figuration. Actors change and figurations change, and although these processes are interwoven, they represent different kinds of processes of change on different levels (Elias [1986] 2006, 102). Figurations, and thus social processes, are shaped by interdependent and changing actor and power relations. They can form on different levels and in different sizes.

13 Real-time research usually captures much shorter timeframes. It is also often used with regard to evaluations that are aimed at immediately adjusting processes, for example with regard to emergency responses.

14 Included in this compilation of interview partners are those conversations that were conducted with a certain degree of formality (this means that the meeting was set up with the purpose of talking about my research) and with direct relevance to my research topic. Thus, while I include more general interviews on transitional justice beyond the Tunisian case, I have excluded interviews with Tunisian interlocutors that I conducted for other purposes and that did not touch on transitional justice. The latter contributed to my overall knowledge and impressions of the case and its political and social dynamics, as did the various informal conversations I had with Tunisian and foreign journalists or chance encounters with people in Tunisia, which helped tremendously but are likewise not mirrored in this list. Most interviews were conducted in French, some in English, and some with impromptu, non-professional translation from Arabic to English or French. For some of the phone interviews conducted in

2020, I worked with a professional translator. All translations of original quotes from French are my own.

15 I am very grateful to Sihem Hamlaoui and Felix Wiedemann.

16 For a more detailed discussion, see Salehi (2021).

17 The specialised chambers for transitional justice in the Tunisian court system only became functional in March 2018 and heard their first case in May of the same year.

1

The past is not another country:[1] Tunisia background chapter

Before looking at *how* Tunisia has sought to deal with its repressive past, it is important to look at *what kind of past* we are talking about, as well as the political context in which transitional justice is taking place. To this end, this chapter examines Tunisian history from the end of the colonial period to the transition following the fall of the Ben Ali regime. By giving a short overview of relevant periods and features of Tunisian history,[2] the chapter aims to identify the main societal cleavages and lines of conflict, power structures and changes to them, and the nature of the regime that people rose up against in 2010/11. Although the chapter describes historical processes 'leading up' to the transition, it does not mean to imply that transitional politics and their corresponding conflicts should be perceived as historically predetermined. The chapter instead aims to show that the Tunisian revolution did not provide a clean slate for transitional justice and that transitional justice is therefore neither neutral nor happening in a historical and political vacuum. The chapter also presents possible explanations for the regime's collapse, as discussed in the academic literature, as well as a discussion of post-revolutionary political developments, power shifts, and frictions. It thereby also outlines the political climate after the ruptures of 2011 to better understand the dynamics of transitional justice, the course it takes, the friction the transitional justice project provokes, and the challenges it faces.

The legacy of colonialism, the fight for independence, and Bourguiba's rule

Tunisia is a small country in the Maghreb – a term referring to the western part of North Africa. In its current form, as a sovereign nation-state, Tunisia has existed for just over sixty years. European colonisation had a considerable influence on some of the most recent territorial demarcations of North Africa. But beyond territorial determination, French colonialism, as well as the resulting fight for independence, has had important repercussions for the cleavages and conflictual dynamics still dominant in Tunisia today,[3] a connection that the truth commission explicitly establishes in its final report (TDC 2019, e.g. 137, 154).[4] The colonial period is briefly described below, before turning to the independence period and the conflictive dynamics that have their origins in that period.

Colonial period

Tunisia was under French colonial rule for seventy-five years, from 1881 until 1956, with the status of the French Protectorate of Tunisia. Nominally, the *Bey*, the Tunisian monarch, continued as ruler and the French ruled indirectly through them. Yet, in reality, a French *résident général* exercised de facto power. This allowed France to have "the advantages of annexation without the inconveniences" (Chouikha and Gobe 2015, 11; quoting Martin 1993; own translation). In Tunisia, elaborate administrative structures had already existed before colonisation, as well as an educational and military system, that aspired to give the central administration control over the countryside. The French were consequently able to use pre-existing administrative structures during the period of colonial rule, and the post-colonial state could also make use of them after the French had left.

One may not necessarily agree with Hatem M'rad's (2015) assessment that the colonisation of Tunisia was "soft," since I would question whether this is possible at all; however, to put the country's colonial experience into perspective, it can be described as somewhere between the Moroccan and Algerian experience: longer and more intrusive than in Morocco, but shorter and less brutal than in Algeria. Among these three North African countries, Morocco experienced the shortest period of colonisation, lasting for forty-four years from 1912 to 1956.[5] Arguably, it was also the one that affected the country the least, not only because of its shorter duration, but also because the first French *résident général* responsible for Morocco applied a "policy of minimal interference in traditional Muslim life" (Willis 2014, 22). Combined with adherence to monarchical traditions, this helped to strengthen the traditional political institutions that had emerged in Morocco before colonisation. Algeria, meanwhile, spent the longest period under colonial rule: 132 years from 1830 to 1962. It was ruled by the French for three times as long as Morocco was under foreign control. Here, external rule took on another dimension: Algeria was not just a French colony; it was in theory fully integrated into France's administrative structures, to be initially administered as three *départements* of the colonising country.[6] This means that 'French Algeria' was also part of the European Union's predecessor organisations until its independence in 1962. There was also a much larger population of European origin that had migrated to and settled in Algeria – the so-called *pieds-noirs* – accounting for about 10 per cent of the population, a dynamic that Tunisia did not experience to the same extent. Tunisia was also spared a lengthy war of independence, unlike Algeria, which experienced a protracted and extremely violent conflict lasting eight years from 1954 to 1962.

Although there was domestic opposition to French colonisation in Tunisia, some of the literature claims that parts of Tunisian society were not actually opposed to the establishment of the protectorate.[7] French rule during the protectorate period in Tunisia fostered the emergence of different sectors, such as an agricultural or industrial workforce (Chouikha and Gobe 2015, 11). It also "served to aid further the development of a significant urban, reform-minded middle class that had already begun to emerge during the Ottoman period" (Willis 2014, 21). Those urban Tunisians saw French rule as facilitating a welcome influx of 'modernist' ideas. They also profited from access to education in France, since Tunisians made up three-quarters of North African students admitted to French universities in the early 1930s despite the country having a much smaller population than Morocco and Algeria. As a result, French education significantly shaped the leaders of the future Tunisian state, and it continues to be a factor shaping Tunisian society today.[8] Although Arabic is the official language, French is still widely spoken in the country sixty years after independence from colonial rule. French is particularly important as a business language and among much of the urban elite.

Fight for independence

At least to some degree stimulated by the development of an educated, urban class, Tunisia was the first of these three future Maghreb states to see the formation of a nationalist party. Created in 1920, the Destour party demanded a constitution (*destour* is Arabic for constitution) and an elected parliament, as well as legal equality between the protectorate's Tunisian and French inhabitants (Willis 2014, 24). Although in the vanguard in demanding greater rights for Tunisians, Destour's leaders did not initially seek independence from France and had little interest in mobilising Tunisians from other geographical and social backgrounds than themselves, that is, those who were not part of the old Tunis-based elite. Consequently, they would eventually be challenged by "younger more radical voices" (Willis 2014, 25), well-educated personalities drawn from the coastal Sahel towns, many of whom had studied in France.[9] In 1934, a group of these individuals broke from Destour and founded the Neo-Destour, developing it into the main force opposing colonial rule (Willis 2014, 25) and initiating armed struggle against the French in the early 1950s.

A leading personality among the Neo-Destour was Habib Bourguiba from Monastir, who became the new party's first secretary-general. Bourguiba, however, was not the undisputed leader of the nationalist movement. Outside of his own party, other actors such as the religious elite in the Zitouna;[10] the Tunisian General Labour Union (Union Générale Tunisienne du Travail; UGTT), which was founded in 1946; the Communist Party; and the 'old' Destour were also active in the fight for independence. Bourguiba also faced challenges to his leadership from within the Neo-Destour, most notably from Salah Ben Youssef, another key leader of the Tunisian national movement who was secretary-general of the Neo-Destour party from 1948 (Chouikha and Gobe 2015, 12–13). Ben Youssef was highly critical of Bourguiba's gradualist approach to gaining autonomy from the French. His followers, the 'Youssefists,' "wanted to adopt a more militant strategy as part of the broader pan-Arab effort to expel European colonial power" (Alexander 2010, 31). While Ben Youssef is often portrayed as having adopted an approach that lent more towards traditional Islamic culture – as opposed to Bourguiba's 'modernism' – and close relations with traditional religious and commercial elites (Alexander 2010, 31), "[t]he Youssefi Movement had a pronounced internationalist agenda, reflecting the emerging Afro-Asia solidarity associated with [the] Bandung [conference]" (Jdey 2012, 72). Thus it would be incorrect to view the Youssefist movement as solely grounded in 'tradition,' since they also shared a forward-looking, "affirmative vision of Third World Revolutionaries."[11]

Due to his role as a leader in the armed struggle against the French, in 1952 Bourguiba was imprisoned for two years before being released for negotiations in Paris. During this period, France faced increasing geopolitical pressure from several directions: violent struggle in Morocco, Algeria, and Indochina, as well as Cold War dynamics in which the United States was willing to support Tunisian independence given Bourguiba's commitment to a pro-Western foreign policy. As a result, holding on to Tunisia seemed increasingly less attractive to France (Alexander 2010, 32–3). However, the Neo-Destour under Bourguiba's leadership initially negotiated autonomy rather than independence. The negotiations that started in Tunis in September 1954 produced a total of six conventions that were signed in Paris in June 1955 (Masri 2017, 186). The agreements stipulated that France, while granting Tunisia autonomy, would retain control over the country's army and foreign policy. Yet when Bourguiba returned to Tunis, he faced opposition from those inside his own party who were not satisfied with the autonomy agreement and were pushing for full independence. Bourguiba came out on top in this internal conflict and managed to retain his position of power within Neo-Destour. Ben Youssef was excluded from the party and went into exile (Chouikha and Gobe 2015, 14). However, challenges from within the party, and public opposition to autonomy with continuing French influence, put pressure on Bourguiba to change his gradualist approach, ultimately leading him to negotiate full independence from France.[12]

This final period of the fight for independence is relevant to the present study insofar as Tunisia's current transitional justice law covers a time-frame that stretches back to 1 July 1955 – a date more than eight months before independence. Thus, rights violations that took place during this immediate pre-independence period fall within the remit of the transitional justice institutions as long as they were committed by "the State's appa-ratuses or by groups or individuals who acted in State's name or under its protection" or unspecified "organized groups."[13] Thus, it would not only be possible to hold to account those who took up positions and may have carried out abuses in the emerging independent state, but also, for example, members of the Neo-Destour party who were active before independence.

Bourguiba's rule

Tunisia was under authoritarian rule from its earliest days as an independent state in 1956. While Lamine Bey, the last king of Tunisia, was the first head of state after the country's independence, the leaders of the independence movement soon came to oppose the monarchy. The *Bey* was deposed in 1957, opening the way for Bourguiba, who was one of the leaders in the fight for independence and had initially been appointed prime minister, to become Tunisia's first president. His style of rule was authoritarian, strongly focused on the institutionalisation of personal power, and he maintained a tight grip over the civil and political liberties allowed to citizens. Larbi Chouikha and Eric Gobe (2015, 20) draw on Philippe Schmitter's notion of 'authoritarian corporatism' to describe the system linking society and state under Bourguiba. A single-party system was established, basically eradicating all official opposition. Bourguiba ruled by co-opting civil society, playing different organisations or streams within them against each other (Alexander 1997) and implanting party representatives within the leadership structures of the major civil society organisations (Chouikha and Gobe 2015, 20–30). Fearing a coup d'état, Bourguiba formally banned the military from politics. Members of the military were prohibited from joining political parties and were not even allowed to vote (Grewal 2016). This prohibition was only lifted by parliament in 2017 (Grewal 2017). Bourguiba pursued a foreign policy that sought to maintain the country's close relations with France and other Western states that he believed would defend the country in case of emergency (Willis 2014, 86f.).

Given the strong personalisation of power that Bourguiba's rule was based on, he was able to dominate the single party and "cast himself in the roles of patriarch, teacher and disciplinarian, making it clear that he, the founding father of modern Tunisia, knew better than anyone else what its people, his children, required" (Perkins 2014, 135f.).[14] In 1975, parliament declared Bourguiba president for life. Yet despite his authoritarian tendencies, Bourguiba continues to have the reputation of having been an 'honest' ruler, someone who was not interested in personal enrichment and had a genuine interest in leading the country on a path to 'modernity' (Willis 2014, 52).[15] Along with this striving for 'modernity' and the suppression of religious power – the powers of the religious judicial institutions were transferred to ordinary courts and the Zitouna dissolved (Chouikha and Gobe 2015, 18–19) – Bourguiba placed a strong emphasis on access to education, gender equality, and secularism and retained good relations with France, including economic and cultural links, "making Tunisia one of the most socially progressive countries in the Middle East and North Africa" (Fraihat 2016, 58) – at least on paper. In practice, though the regime (and later Ben Ali's as well) was successful in creating this progressive appearance for an external audience, 'on the ground' the situation looked different, as any liberal political policies were soon abandoned (Chouikha and Gobe 2015, 26).

Bourguiba held on to his position during and after the struggle for independence, yet he was clearly concerned by Ben Youssef's potential to challenge his leadership. Ben Youssef was ultimately assassinated in Frankfurt in 1961, officially under unclear circumstances but allegedly through a plot carried out by Bourguiba loyalists (Chouikha and Gobe 2015, 14). Bourguiba subsequently purged Youssefists from positions in the ruling Neo-Destour party, and "in the years that followed, his supporters were arrested, tortured, and executed in Tunis" (Fraihat 2016, 118). Over the coming years and decades, the social strata making up Ben Youssef's supporters was undermined both politically and economically. The western and inland southern regions, where most of the Youssefists came from, were deliberately marginalised (Anderson 2014; Fraihat 2016; Wolf 2017).

This strategy is crucial for understanding today's cleavages and conflictual dynamics, because the tactic of depriving regions that could become opposition strongholds of their potential challengers was also used by Ben Ali (Fraihat 2016, 118). Hence Bourguiba's neglect of the Youssefist regions' economic development may have laid the ground for the regional economic marginalisation that still prevails in the country today. Unemployment rates are much higher in the interior regions, which have also been deprived of investment in public infrastructure, education, and health. This regional inequality is often seen as one of the main triggers for unrest, including the uprisings of late 2010/early 2011 that led to Ben Ali's ouster, as will be explained later.

In addition, when the conflict with the Youssefists first broke out, Beji Caid Essebi, who went on to serve as Tunisia's president from 2014 until his death in 2019, led the Ministry of the Interior, which was central to the 'deep state' and the institution responsible for political imprisonments and torture. Hence, as Ibrahim Fraihat points out, this conflict originating in the era of decolonisation remains a delicate issue even today, sixty years after independence. This is reflected in the text of the transitional justice law,[16] which identifies the marginalised and systematically excluded regions as a whole as potentially having the status of victims while leaving the resolution of the 'Youssefist issue' to a later date (Fraihat 2016).[17]

Members of the extreme left were also highly affected by political imprisonments under Bourguiba, with many still being students when they were detained (Chouikha 2010). Here, the rationale seemed different than for detaining the Youssefists and was more related to exerting control. Chouikha describes how Bourguiba made 'generous' use of his presidential pardon or granted "conditional liberty" (Chouikha 2010; own translation), meaning young leftists were released from detention but kept under surveillance. Cases of political detainees from the far left were also examined by the transitional justice institutions. They are exemplified by Tunisian writer Gilbert Naccache, who gave testimony during the truth commission's first public hearing.[18] Moreover, in 1978 the UGTT called for a general strike, and workers, supported by students, took to the streets. These country-wide protests were brutally crushed: according to Anne Wolf (2017, 44), between fifty and two hundred people died and over 1,000 were wounded.

Another prominent cluster of human rights violations covered by the transitional justice process took place in connection with the unrest known as the 'Bread Riots' in late 1983 and early 1984. In 1983, the government, under pressure from the IMF and World Bank (Perkins 2014), cut subsidies on key food items, most importantly bread and semolina (the basic ingredient of couscous). This led to steep price rises and was met with outbreaks of violence, notably in the interior regions but also in the capital and the better-off areas in the coastal Sahel region. The army was deployed to restore order, and the security forces ruthlessly fired at protesters. Around one hundred people died and about 1,000 were wounded (Chouikha and Gobe 2015, 37).[19]

In summary, several groups of potential victims can be identified solely from the period of Bourguiba's rule: political opponents, such as the Youssefists and the far left; inhabitants of the geographical areas that were systematically marginalised economically and politically; and those who died or were injured in the bloody crackdowns on protests. Sometimes there was an overlap, with individuals falling into more than one of these groups.

Yet a purely negative assessment of Bourguiba's historical role would not go uncontested, as many Tunisians praise his role in the fight for independence and leading the nation on a path to 'modernity.' According to Fraihat:

> No national consensus exists over his role in Tunisia's contemporary history. Some Tunisians view him as a reformer who made education his first priority, built a modern state, and even advanced women's rights. [...] Others, however, consider him an absolute dictator who monopolized authority, established a one-party system [...] and fiercely cracked down on political dissidents. (Fraihat 2016, 117)

This ambivalent perception of the country's first president inevitably affects how the past is dealt with. As Bourguiba still evokes positive associations for many Tunisians, the inclusion of his period of rule in the transitional justice project has caused friction between those who respect his legacy and those who suffered under his rule. This has fostered conflict over the reach and scope of the transitional justice project.[20]

Violence and nepotism: systems of power under Ben Ali's rule

Ben Ali took over the presidency in November 1987 through a non-violent coup. After obtaining a medical certificate signed by seven doctors stating that Bourguiba was not fit to continue in office, Ben Ali used a radio message to announce that he had assumed power. He stayed in power until he fled to exile in Saudi Arabia on 14 January 2011, where he remained until his death in September 2019.

This section will show that Ben Ali's rule shared several characteristics with Bourguiba's in that the regime often made use of the same repressive repertoire and exerted power in a similar logic. However, their ruling styles differed with regard to nepotism and the degree to which members of the President's extended family were allowed to personally enrich themselves – an issue that fostered rage against the Ben Ali regime.

The 'net of fear': violence and repression

In the initial years following his seizure of power, Ben Ali pursued a course of a slight political opening by, for example, releasing political prisoners – including Rachid Ghannouchi, the leader of the moderate Islamist Ennahda party – allowing exiles to return, abolishing the life presidency, and granting legal recognition to civil society organisations, such as the Tunisian branch of Amnesty International as well as the Islamist-leaning student organisation Union Générale Tunisienne des Etudiants (Chouikha and Gobe 2015, 45–6).

After this short period, Ben Ali kept a firm grip on the country, as can be verified through the reports of various NGOs working on freedoms and human rights (see e.g. Middle East Watch and International Human Rights Law Group 1992; Alexander 1997).[21] His rule was marked by massive human rights violations and significant limitations of civil and personal liberties. The repressive repertoire of the Ben Ali regime ranged from "arbitrary economic barriers to jailing, disappearances and torture" (Chomiak 2011, 72). Looking at the example of press freedom, in 2010, the year before Ben Ali's fall, Freedom House listed Tunisia as "not free" (Freedom House 2010) and Reporters Without Borders placed Tunisia as 164 out of 178 listed countries of its World Press Freedom Index (Reporters Without Borders 2010). Béatrice Hibou talks about a "total absence of freedom of the press and of assembly" (Hibou 1999, 48; own translation).

The political police played an important role in securing Ben Ali's hold on power. Not only did "violence and police control [make] all political life impossible" (Hibou 2011), but the omnipresence of the police also wove a "net of fear" (Hibou 2011). The recruitment of informers from among the wider public fostered distrust within society (Gray and Coonan 2013, 349). Political imprisonment was commonplace, and forced disappearances were a "tactic used on active regime opponents as well as the remains of executed prisoners" (Fraihat 2016, 119). Political imprisonment was accompanied by the harassment of relatives or former prisoners after release. For example, the duty to report to the police station up to five times a day, referred to as *pointage* (Wolf 2017, 85), made any reintegration into working life impossible, and women under *pointage* reported that police officers would come to their homes unannounced at any time (Gray and Coonan 2013). Punishment of those engaged in opposition activities or suspected of such activities extended to those around the affected individuals.[22]

In general, "the political space and influence afforded to the ordinary populations […] was minimal" (Willis 2014, 38), minimising opportunities for democratic participation in a republic that only existed on paper. Yet, like Bourguiba before him, Ben Ali strove to project an image of a progressive leader. He continued to pursue the secularist course taken by Bourguiba, drawing heavily on the reformed legal status of women and retaining the ban on wearing the veil in public schools, universities, and government buildings. This made Tunisia an often-cited model of an Arab country that was 'progressive' on women's issues (see e.g. Charrad and Zarrugh 2014, 230–1; Willis 2014, 4). However, it should be noted here that despite both presidents' superficially progressive stance towards women, very few women obtained positions of power.

With the secularist opposition weakened by the end of the 1980s, the Islamist movement's appeal increased despite the regime's attempt to keep it out of politics. Consequently, there was growing political polarisation between the Islamists and the ruling party. Repression of the Islamist movement became even stronger, and non-Islamist human rights actors were also subject to further control (Chouikha and Gobe 2015, 49–52).

Human rights violations committed by the Ben Ali regime, such as torture and forced disappearances, as well as the restriction of freedom of movement and house arrest, are therefore included in the transitional justice project. These issues concern several societal groups: members of the Islamist movement, of course, but also other oppositional actors, such as human rights activists. The specified human rights violations to be covered in the process also include the infringement of freedom of expression, including media and publishing freedoms.

Nepotism and the 'market of power'

To understand the grievances and conflicts that emerged during Ben Ali's time in power, it is necessary to look at the means of societal control beyond violence and political repression. The Ben Ali regime controlled the associational and political space through more or less formal state structures, while the President and his wider family, the so-called Trabelsi-clan (mainly consisting of relatives of his second wife Leila Trabelsi[23]), eventually gained control of large parts of the country's economy. So not only did Ben Ali continue to pursue Bourguiba's regional marginalisation strategy, but the corruption and embezzlement promoted by his clan added to the exclusionary practices. Chouikha and Gobe claim that Ben Ali and the Trabelsi clan were responsible for seizing assets corresponding to more than a fourth of Tunisia's GDP following the uprisings in 2011, comprising "550 properties, 48 boats and yachts, 40 stock portfolios, 367 bank accounts and 400 companies in Tunisia and abroad" (Chouikha and Gobe 2015, 57). This includes numerous key companies that allowed the clan to control crucial sectors such as building (Carthage Cement) and communications (Orange Tunisie and Tunisiana) (Chouikha and Gobe 2015, 57). Hence, in addition to 'simple' economic deprivation of certain regions in the country, a predatory quasi 'mafia-state' developed (Ayeb 2011; Cavatorta and Haugbølle 2012).

The legal system was also deeply affected by the system of favouritism and the sometimes competing striving of clan figures for control. Members of the extended Ben Ali–Trabelsi family would interfere in judicial proceedings, with competing members sometimes intervening simultaneously on either side of a case. This would be done as a demonstration of power. In a "market of power,"[24] these contacts and abilities to interfere was the capital of individuals who acted as power brokers. 'Favours,' for example, kept the judges safe from being transferred to unpopular places or were used to reward them with a mission or training abroad.[25] According to estimates by an anti-corruption official, "not more than 1 per cent or 2 per cent [of the judges] resisted that system."[26] The overarching system of favouritism (not only in the judicial sector), combined with the powerful secret police mentioned above, led to pre-emptive obedience to the system of control and denigration, thus eroding civic and societal trust in the state as well as fellow citizens.

These activities are related to transitional justice on several levels. On the one hand, examination of past corruption and embezzlement formed part of the TDC's mandate, and there was a special arbitration mechanism in place that could be applied to financial crimes (although not in the area of human rights violations). On the other hand, the implication of the judiciary in the 'market of power' as described above, and the system of corruption and cronyism, led to a lack of trust in the judicial system. This is why special judicial mechanisms were put in place to ensure that transitional justice was not left to a compromised judicial system. But whether and how transitional justice measures can eventually contribute to the goal specified in the transitional justice law of restoring public confidence in state institutions[27] remains to be seen.

The fall of the regime: trajectories and possible explanations

The Ben Ali regime was deemed one of the most stable of the Arab states, and its fall took many by surprise – in the literature, the possibility of the country experiencing such an upheaval had not featured before the 2011 uprisings (Cavatorta and Haugbølle 2012; Willis 2014). The scarcity of dissonant voices was often equated with "consent, or lack of opinion, or the political views of the 'silent majority'" (Allal 2013, 192). Yet the regime quickly collapsed in January 2011, only weeks after the uprisings had started at the end of 2010, which clearly suggests that "[t]hose who don't say a word do not necessarily consent" (Allal 2012, 828; own translation).

Possible precursors to the fall of the regime

What, then, brought about the fall of the regime? Favouritism and cronyism prevailed, and large parts of the population were deprived of prosperity and economic development. Development mainly took place in the country's northern and coastal areas while the southern and central parts remained marginalised – though the country's natural resources are mainly situated in these areas. The resource-wealthy south and centre, with deposits of phosphate and mining sites, are among the most deprived in the country. Hence, the value added to the economy has mostly been detached from the sites of resources.[28]

Meanwhile, Ben Ali introduced reforms that artificially drove up the numbers of students taking the *baccalauréat*.[29] This in turn meant that ever more students were entering university and ever more graduates were entering the employment market, often seeking government jobs. However, this growth in the numbers of students aspiring to continue to higher education was accompanied by a decline in educational quality, since the requirements for obtaining degrees had been lowered. There was a widening gap between the skills of the graduates seeking employment and the skills looked for by the employers.[30]

By continuing Bourguiba's marginalisation policy while simultaneously producing ever-growing numbers of graduates, the Ben Ali regime created a "socio-territorial and generational double cleavage" (Allal 2012, 824; own translation) cutting through Tunisian society. Those who were young, well educated, and from the interior regions were generally the worst off in this set-up.

On the surface, Tunisia experienced an 'economic miracle' of constant growth from the mid-1990s (Hibou 1999; Allal 2012; Cavatorta and Haugbølle 2012), which may at least partly have been due to neoliberal economic reforms under the auspices of international financial institutions. Economic growth rates between 2005 and 2010 were reported as around 5 per cent annually (Lust 2011), suggesting a steady increase in wealth and living conditions. There was even growth of more than 3 per cent annually through the peak of the global financial crisis in 2009 and 2010 (Cavatorta and Haugbølle 2012).

But growth has not been distributed evenly within the country; nor has everyone profited equally. Economic reforms implemented according to international financial institutions' guidelines, as mentioned above, were partly credited with contributing to the favourable economic situation. However, as part of the reforms the government reduced the number of public-sector jobs rather than increasing them, leaving many of the rising number of university graduates unemployed. In Gafsa, for example, the state-owned Gafsa Phosphate Company (Compagnie des Phosphates de Gafsa), one of the biggest phosphate producers in the world, was reformed "following neoliberal standards, mainly thanks to World Bank credits" (Allal 2012, 824; own translation). This led to a substantial decline in employment in the region, since the company basically stopped hiring and cut about two-thirds of its workforce (Allal 2012). The system thus failed to deliver for an ever larger, better educated young workforce. These new entrants to the labour market were disappointed in their expectations of doing well or better than their parents' generation (Lust 2011). They faced mass unemployment in an economic system that no longer guaranteed state jobs for university graduates, leading to a "crisis in employment for graduates in higher education" (Mabrouk 2011, 628) from the mid-1990s. Huge potential for unrest emerged.

Besides being repressive, the regime also aimed at an "a-politicisation" of society (Hibou 1999, 50) through a fiscal and economic policy that encouraged "Western-style consumerism" (Perkins 2014, 211). The regime allowed overconsumption by the middle class, turning a blind eye to parallel markets such as the border economy,[31] as well as excessive borrowing and interest rates. However, the 'pacification' strategy of allowing overconsumption did not last: the middle class in the urban centres did not profit sufficiently from the favourable economic situation and was no longer willing to accept the perceived drift of the country into mafia-like structures initiated by the 'uncultured' ruling clique (Allal 2012, 822). Amin Allal describes how even long-standing supporters of Ben Ali and the ruling party, and beneficiaries of the system, became alienated by the excesses of the clan's behaviour. He states that his interview partner picked up "the craziest rumours" (Allal 2012, 830; own translation) about the Trabelsis. In my own research, I observed this diffusion of rumours or urban legends about the Trabelsis as contributing to a feeling that 'enough is enough.' On two occasions, for example, I heard the rumour that the Trabelsis had kept white tigers in their palace, leading a taxi driver to conclude: "They were really going too far."[32]

Accordingly, explanations for the regime's collapse in Tunisia usually focus on the economic situation in the country, the repression exerted by the regime, or a combination of those two factors (Cavatorta and Haugbølle 2012). Francesco Cavatorta and Rikke Hostrup Haugbølle identify three self-propagated myths about the Tunisian regime that led to its image of stability, namely "its economic miracle, its democratic gradualism and its laicité" (Cavatorta and Haugbølle 2012, 182). As long as it lasted, the regime managed to "mask [...] inequitable growth and [a] high unemployment rate" (Ayadi and Matoussi 2014, 2) as well as the high level of repression that lay behind its progressive façade.

Foreshadowing the revolution?

Certain events can retrospectively be seen as concrete precursors to the 2010/11 uprisings, above all the uprising in the central mining town of

Gafsa and its surroundings in 2008, which lasted over six months. These events followed the announcement of the lists of individuals who had been successful in a hiring round at the state-owned public phosphate company, which was perceived as following wrongful and nepotistic practices (Allal 2012, 824). This flaring of unrest, however, remained confined to the central regions (Chouikha and Gobe 2015, 75). Another example is the protests in the border town of Ben Guerdane after the closure of the border with Libya brought border economic activities to a halt. While it is important not to look at the so-called Arab Spring in Tunisia as an isolated series of events, but rather to view it as the manifestation of a potential for unrest and mobilisation that existed before the end of 2010 (Mabrouk 2011; Cavatorta and Haugbølle 2012; Mabon 2020), criticism has been voiced of the teleological perspective that sees the 2008 unrest as the beginning of the revolution with the ouster of Ben Ali as the inevitable ending (Allal 2012). Nevertheless, one can identify, and distinguish between, structural factors that led to general dissatisfaction and unleashed mobilising potential, and 'momentum factors' that led to the spill over of protests across the country and across socio-political groups and, eventually, to the ouster of the President.

While Cavatorta and Haugbølle point out that *causal* mechanisms for the success of Tunisia's 2011 uprisings are hard to identify (Cavatorta and Haugbølle 2012, 191), one can certainly identify structural and momentum factors. Starting with structural factors, Ellen Lust, looking at the seeming stability of Arab authoritarian regimes in general, asks "Why Now?" (Lust 2011): Why did the uprisings gain momentum in 2010/11? One of her arguments is the general momentum associated with the "inevitable life-cycles of long-standing dictators" (Lust 2011) who had become old, and "[a]ge raises the specter of succession, making palpable a vision of the regime without its leader" (Lust 2011). Lust's main point, however, suggests that we should not think of the uprisings in the Arab world as the sudden events they appeared to be, but rather as products of gradual changes in different spheres that paved the way for such a revolutionary moment (Lust 2011).[33]

While the implications of the more general precursors such as marginalisation and repression were tackled above, this section also takes into consideration those who were wounded (and in some cases died) in 2008 in the mining basin unrest in its review of who may be subject to the transitional justice process.

Dynamics of the revolution

The self-immolation of street vendor Mohamed Bouazizi on 17 December 2010 in Ben Arous triggered a wave of protests across the country, starting in his hometown Sidi Bouzid in central Tunisia, that eventually led to the ouster of President Ben Ali. Habib Ayeb ascribes a particular importance to the context of Bouazizi's action, since many people in the interior regions were, and still are, in a similar situation to "this young unemployed graduate seeking dignity, recognition and social and economic 'security'" (Ayeb 2011, 471) and thus could identify with him.

The uprisings started in small towns in the south and centre and only reached the capital a few days before the fall of the regime (Schwedler 2013b, 231f.). The protests were initially confined to the interior regions, but from early January 2011, supported by the UGTT, they spread to the greater Tunis area. The brutality with which the security forces cracked down on the protesters may have startled many and provided further reason for those who had not initially been part of the protests to mobilise (see example in Allal 2012). Unable to secure the army's support (Allal 2012, 823), Ben Ali and his family fled into exile in Saudi Arabia on 14 January 2011. Allal thus describes the "revolutionary moment" (Allal 2012, 823; own translation) as an interplay of various factors, from the disassociation of the army and the solidarity shown by the labour unions to the fact that people from very different social strata and ideological backgrounds made their way on to the streets, calling for dignity and social justice (see also Berman 2019, 146) and occupying a political space that had until then been off-limits. Therefore, "insurrectional timing" (Chouikha and Gobe 2015, 75; own translation) can only be understood when the dynamic interplay of spontaneous moves is combined with the phenomenon of organised protests.

In this revolution, at least 132 people died and 1,452 were wounded. These crimes have been the subject of several investigations and have been followed by several measures ostensibly aimed at achieving justice for the victims. The so-called 'martyrs and wounded of the revolution' cases were initially tried in military courts before being referred to the transitional justice institutions.

Post-revolutionary reconfigurations

After Ben Ali's ouster, an interim government took over. Fouad Mebazaa, former speaker of parliament, became interim president, and Mohammed Ghannouchi, who had been Tunisia's prime minister since 1999, continued in power for about six weeks. Ghannouchi removed all Democratic Constitutional Rally (Rassemblement Constitutionnel Démocratique; RCD)[34] members except for himself from the government but eventually had to step down following protests at the end of February 2011.[35] Beji Caid Essebsi replaced him as prime minister and led an interim government up to the elections of the NCA in October 2011 before handing over to his successor in December of that year.

The elections are usually seen as the first free elections in the country since it gained independence (Freedom House 2012). In these first 'post-revolutionary' elections, members of the former ruling party, the RCD, were not allowed to run for office. Thus, the NCA was vetted to ensure that none of its members had been complicit in the old regime. The moderate Islamist Ennahda party received the largest number of votes and formed a coalition with two secular parties: the Congress for the Republic (Congrès pour la République; CPR) and Ettakatol (Democratic Forum for Labour and Liberties), the so-called 'Troika' government. Moncef Marzouki from the CPR became Tunisian president, Ennahda assigned Hamadi Jebali to succeed Essebsi as prime minister, and Ettakatol's Mustapha Ben Jafar was nominated president of the NCA.

As well as being assigned the task of drafting a constitution, initially foreseen as a process that would take just one year, the NCA also functioned as the country's legislative body in the period before the process had completed. This was a cumbersome process, and it was not always clear that it would be successful. One of the main cleavages was the question of proposed references to Islam and sharia law in the new constitution. Ennahda initially proposed articles that provoked public opposition only to back down in negotiations with other parties once a compromise on the points at issue had been arrived at internally, through negotiations among its own members (Ben Hafaiedh and Zartman 2015, 65).

Political polarisation and rapprochement

Protest and violence have been continuous features of the Tunisian political landscape since the 2011 revolution: "Between 2011 and 2013, street politics, which occasionally turned violent, competed with – and eventually dominated – the formal institutional process" (Boubekeur 2015, 1). Protest has been smouldering since the upheavals and never really stopped.[36] As Chantal Berman claims, "citizens became increasingly polarized in their expectations for the post-revolutionary state" (Berman 2019, 138), mainly along questions of Islam's role in the post-revolutionary state.[37] In a particularly intense period of conflictive action, protest events peaked in August 2013, and though it is hard to assess how likely such a development would have been, many authors and interview partners have stated that Tunisia was on the verge of civil war in the summer of 2013 (Boubekeur 2015; M'rad 2015).

The protests were accompanied by waves of Islamist/Salafist violence, to which Ennahda was perceived as showing too much leniency (ACLED 2015; Ben Hafaiedh and Zartman 2015). Ennahda was also accused of involvement in the assassination of two opposition politicians, Chokri Belaid and Mohamed Brahmi, in February and July respectively. After the Belaid assassination, Jebali offered to form a technocratic government but the offer was rejected by his own party, and Ali Laarayedh (also from Ennahda) took over as prime minister (Pickard 2015, 24). By July 2013, the country was in a political deadlock, and the NCA was no longer functioning as a forum for hammering out differences. The process of drafting a new constitution came to a halt, and the 'Troika' government was under pressure as its political opponents organised sizeable rallies demanding that it step down while also calling for the dissolution of the NCA. The governing parties vehemently refused to consider dissolving the assembly, drawing on their electoral legitimacy. These dynamics were exacerbated by the events in Egypt, where President Mohamed Morsi of the Muslim Brotherhood was toppled in a military coup. On the one hand, the coup emboldened the opposition who hoped to similarly topple the 'Troika' (Marks 2015, 8). On the other hand, the imprisonment of the Islamist leaders after the military took power in Egypt may have stirred fear that Ennahda would face the same fate if they lost power in the conflict. This may have served as a factor preventing Ennahda from seeking further confrontation and agreeing to the National Dialogue.

The 'National Dialogue' was initiated by a group of civil society organisations who acted as "insider mediators" (Frazer 2014):[38] the UGTT, the Tunisian Confederation of Industry, Trade, and Handicrafts (Union Tunisienne de l'Industrie, du Commerce et de l'Artisanat; UTICA), the Tunisian Human Rights League (Ligue Tunisienne des Droits de l'Homme; LTDH), and the Tunisian Order of Lawyers (equivalent to a Bar Association). This National Dialogue managed to balance the competing claims of electoral legitimacy – claimed by those who won the elections – and popular legitimacy – claimed by the opposition associating with protesters[39] – by only allowing parties that had assembly members to participate in the talks, but each one with only one representative and *not* with a number of participants corresponding to their electoral strength. The road map developed within the Dialogue, and to which Ennahda reluctantly agreed (Hartshorn 2017, 414), foresaw the 'Troika' government stepping down and a technocratic government taking over to bring the constitution-writing process to a successful conclusion. Members also worked hard to find compromises within the NCA. Maria Glenna (2016) describes how several delegates to the Dialogue recount how they changed their perceptions of 'the other side' over the course of the talks. However, it was also recognised that it would not be possible to resolve all of the issues within the plenary of the assembly or within the Dialogue. So a 'consensus committee' was formed within the NCA to negotiate on certain points before they were discussed and voted on in the plenary of the NCA.[40] In a feat of strength, the constitutional project was brought to a successful end at the beginning of 2014, paving the way for parliamentary elections later that year.

Although Ben Ali and his close family fled to Saudi Arabia, the major part of the old regime stayed in Tunisia. While some were imprisoned, others initially kept a low profile. The RCD, the single party in Ben Ali's system, was dissolved in March 2011. However, in 2014, a provision in the electoral law governing subsequent elections to the ARP that would have excluded RCD members from running for parliament was not passed by the NCA. Dropping the envisaged ban on former RCD members who had held positions of responsibility – proposed Article 167 of the electoral law – was an important, albeit controversial, contribution from Ennahda in reaching a compromise as part of the transition.[41] Thus, in the 2014 elections, which were also rated as free and fair (Freedom House 2015), many former RCD members ran and won seats in the ARP, many of them on the ticket of Nidaa Tounes, the party of President Essebsi.

Social and political unrest have not disappeared since the 'revolution.' The economy has not been "in good shape" (Diwan 2019, 2). Many people, especially in the interior regions, believe that nothing has changed, and there are frequent protests.[42] The economic situation has been undermined by two major terrorist attacks that deliberately targeted tourists in the spring and summer of 2015. This unstable security situation has not helped to foster a climate attractive to foreign investment, and the instability in neighbouring Libya has led to further security concerns because of weapon smuggling, the presence of Islamic State, and the radicalisation of young Tunisians. It has also hit the Tunisian economy, particularly in the more southern regions, since oil-rich Libya used to be an important trading partner for those areas with regard to legal business, but also through smuggling activities and informal trade (Allal 2012; Meddeb 2015). The security situation, furthermore, offers opportunities to justify restrictions on political freedoms.

Political polarisation and a subsequent period of rapprochement were important for the transitional justice project insofar as polarisation probably only made the project possible in the first place. However, the efforts to reduce political tensions and foster compromise may have played a role in the decision to abandon, at least in part, the transitional justice process as originally envisaged – a tendency that began to loom more clearly once the Nidaa Tounes-led government took over in early 2015. Moreover, given the very different political and parliamentary set-up in the ARP, with many old-regime figures back as elected MPs, as well as Ennahda's participation in so-called 'national unity governments,' support for the transitional justice project as it had been passed by the NCA has faded. This became clear when the assembly passed legislation in September 2017 that was in effect an amnesty for officials who had previously engaged in corruption, which was a presidential initiative. In early 2018, the truth commission decided that its mandate needed to be extended by another year. Parliament voted against any extension in a controversial vote at the end of March 2018, but two months later the Ministry of Relations with Constitutional Bodies, Civil Society, and Human Rights nevertheless decided to extend the mandate of the TDC until the end of 2018.[43] After the end of its mandate, the TDC delivered its final report to the President of the republic, the Prime Minister, and the President of the ARP and published a version on its website in March 2019. As was to be expected, during the remaining term of the so-called national unity government, transitional justice was shelved. In September and October 2019, then, Tunisia voted for a new president and parliament, which led once again to a reconfiguration of the political landscape, changing power constellations, alliances, and adversaries. It proved difficult to form a stable government: a first attempt after the 2019 elections failed, and Prime Minister Elyes Fakhfakh, who led a government based on a broad coalition of different parties from across the political spectrum, was in office for less than five months before he resigned following accusations of corruption and a dispute with Ennahda. Newly elected President Kais Saied, as well as Prime Minister Hicham Mchichi, however, have been more interested in bringing the transitional justice process forward, and the TDC's final report was eventually published in the country's official journal in June 2020.

Given the political turmoil, the unclear power constellations in parliament, and other, more pressing issues, such as the coronavirus pandemic, it is probably not surprising that at the time of writing at the end of 2020 it was still unclear who would prevail in the political struggle over transitional justice and whether and how any of the recommendations emerging from the truth commission's work would be implemented.

Conclusion

To understand the past being covered by Tunisia's transitional justice process, it is important to note that the cleavages and problems in the context of the repressive regimes of post-independence Tunisia are not straightforward. Nor do they only run between the 'state' and 'society,' as is often proclaimed in research on authoritarianism, or represent *one* conflict *between* different societal groups as being the only relevant 'problem' of the past. Cleavages are cross-cutting and interlinked. It is therefore necessary to look at several conflicting 'streams' that may have drawn their momentum from much earlier in history. But since the past is not another country, past conflicts and frictions have after-effects in current discussions about dealing with the past. These streams partly run in parallel, partly cross each other at some point, and partly do not have traction points. Broadly speaking, one can identify several victim groups that have been repressed during different periods because of their political or religious convictions and activities and which are to be considered within the transitional justice process: for example, 'Islamists,' 'Youssefists,' 'leftists,' or the 'martyrs and wounded of the revolution.'

As a result of the economic and political marginalisation of areas that were opposition strongholds, or regions where there was little support for the authoritarian leaders, socio-economic victims were produced almost indiscriminately among the general population. Similarly, the system of control and repression through a powerful secret police apparatus, which makes almost everyone at least indirectly complicit and the perpetrator elusive, evokes dynamics of indiscriminate victimhood. And although the process is also perpetrator-focused, at least for economic crimes, the elusive perpetrator, even if a real one is known, is 'the system' (Fraihat 2016). As a consequence, one could infer that "[t]here is no enemy to reconcile with."[44]

Notes

1 This chapter title is borrowed and adapted from Tony Judt's (1992) essay "The Past Is Another Country."
2 I do not aim to provide a comprehensive political history of Tunisia here. For an account in English, see Willis (2014). For a historical account in French that covers the period from Tunisia's independence until 2014, see Chouikha and Gobe (2015).
3 Al-Saghir al-Salihi traces these dynamics back to the Hafsid dynasty (Al Riahi 2016, 5). He describes the economic, political, and social relations that stem from historical developments as "internal colonization" (Al-Salihi 2017).
4 See Chomiak (2017) for a discussion of how Tunisia's colonial legacy can be linked to transitional justice.
5 In Morocco, France was not the only colonial power, since parts of the country were under Spanish rule.
6 *Départements* are administrative divisions of France, the middle level of three levels below the central government. There were three *départements* in Algeria until 1955. In 1955, a fourth one was created by a previous *département* being

split into two, and in 1956 eight new ones were created, followed by three new ones in 1958.

7 Please note that I strongly believe that colonialism cannot be justified.

8 In the academic year 2016–17, for example, more than 12,000 Tunisian students studied in France (Campus France 2018).

9 In Tunisia, the Sahel refers to the region along the country's eastern coast, with its Mediterranean port towns.

10 The Zitouna university mosque in Tunis's old city is the oldest and most important mosque in the capital.

11 Video interview with activist/relative of victim, November 2020.

12 France initially kept a military presence in Tunisia. While most of the French forces withdrew in 1958, they retained an airbase in Bizerte until after the Algerian War in 1963 (Masri 2017, 198–9).

13 Organic Law on Establishing and Organising Transitional Justice, Article 3.

14 This tradition of the personalisation of power lingers today. To give an example, various political commissions in Tunisia are commonly referred to not by their official names, but by the names of their respective leaders (e.g. 'the Amor Commission' for the National Investigation Commission on Corruption and Embezzlement). When I talked about this issue with the former minister of human rights and transitional justice, he claimed that as children they would refer to the President of France not as 'President,' but as "Bourguiba of France" (personal interview, Tunis, October 2015).

15 The idea that Bourguiba was not corrupt was also mentioned in conversation with the head of INLUCC, Tunis, October 2015.

16 Organic Law on Establishing and Organising Transitional Justice, Article 10.

17 The Youssefist issue is one of eighteen topics on which the TDC produced a mapping (a table dispatch, as well as a narrative report drawn from publicly available sources). Personal observation and conversation with two staff members of the truth commission's 'mapping department' responsible for mapping the Youssefist issue, Tunis, September 2016.

18 Personal observation, Sidi Dhrif, November 2016. Naccache is best known for his writings about his time in prison.

19 The reported number of deaths varies.

20 For example, one politician (from the Afek Tounes party) described the inclusion of the Bourguiba period as 'going too far.' Video interview, March 2016.

21 Various reports on torture, incommunicado detention, and other human rights violations have been published by Amnesty International since 1990. As an example, see Amnesty International (1991).

22 Fraihat (2016, 129) quotes Oula Ben Nejma (a member of the technical committee and later of the Tunisian TDC) as stating that reintegration for political prisoners under Bourguiba was easier, because he had "believed in giving them a second chance." This perpetuates the narrative of Bourguiba having been a fatherly, honest ruler who had intended only the best for his country.

23 The 'stealing' of the Trabelsi family triggers even more outrage than 'normal' corruption, since they are not deemed 'worthy' of the position they secured

due to Leila's marriage. This also applies to Leila, who was often reported to have worked as a hairdresser before she rose to become 'First Lady' of Tunisia (several personal conversations in Tunis, 2014/15). Allal (2012) also refers to the contemptuous way Leila Trabelsi was described as 'the hairdresser' (*la coiffeuse*).

24 Personal interview with anti-corruption official, Tunis, October 2015.

25 Ibid.

26 Ibid.

27 Organic Law on Establishing and Organising Transitional Justice, Article 15.

28 This was also mentioned by an NCA member from Kebili in relation to agricultural products. Personal interview, Tunis, April 2014. Dates, for example, grow in Kebili, but as they are processed on the Cape Bon, the value added does not reach the marginalised regions.

29 French for a high-school exam that acts as a qualifying stage for entering university or other higher education institutions.

30 Several personal interviews and conversations; see also Mabrouk (2011).

31 For an account on social injustice and the border economy, see Meddeb (2015). For a study with a focus on smuggling, see Gallien (2020).

32 Personal conversation, Tunis, spring of 2014.

33 She uses the term "earth-shattering events" and explains why the term 'revolution' may be inappropriate (Lust 2011, 8, footnote 2). However, I find the term 'revolutionary moment' to be helpful here for three reasons: (1) it captures the "earth-shattering" nature of the events Lust describes; (2) it pays homage to the term used in the countries concerned, and in this case Tunisia, by the citizens themselves, who usually speak of 'revolution'; (3) it still acknowledges the open nature of the eventual outcome of these events.

34 The former ruling party of the Ben Ali regime.

35 These two rounds of mobilisation are commonly referred to as Kasbah I and Kasbah II, named after the prime minister's constituency.

36 The number of protest events remained relatively steady throughout the years after 2011 and even rose after 2015 (Vatthauer 2015; Vatthauer and Weipert-Fenner 2017). However, the intensity of conflict has varied in transitional Tunisia.

37 She finds that polarisation did not occur so much along lines of social class.

38 'Insider mediators' since they were coming from inside the country. Ian Hartshorn describes them as 'outside,' since they were outside the formal constitutional process in the NCA (Hartshorn 2017, 414).

39 This was sometimes also called 'consensus legitimacy' since they wanted to negotiate consensus instead of relying on formalised, majority-based decision-making procedures.

40 On visit to the NCA in April 2014, I was told by an MP that NCA parliamentarians had to develop these parliamentary practices from scratch, including how to work on and negotiate issues, because previously the parliament was only supposed to vote and not to actually function as an independent legislature. There was no proper office infrastructure and insufficient meeting rooms in the parliamentary building.

41 To which a majority of Ennahda's parliamentarians did not subscribe.
42 According to ACLED (2020), "Tunisia has consistently registered some of the highest demonstration levels in Africa." After an initial decline in 2020 due to the coronavirus pandemic, numbers of protest events have again increased since April 2020.
43 For discussions of this issue, see the following reports: Huffpost Maghreb (2018); Blaise (2018); Middle East Monitor (2018b). In several prior conversations, interview partners voiced scepticism about the ARP's willingness to extend the mandate, or even the strong assumption that it would not do so. Personal interviews, Tunis, August 2016.
44 Personal interview with NGO leader, Tunis, May 2014.

2

Transitional justice in process: developments and dynamics

Transitional justice is an interdisciplinary field with blurred boundaries, which accounts for its "energy and vibrancy but also the immense disagreements inherent in the field" (Clark and Palmer 2012, 1). These disagreements start with attempts to identify the origins of transitional justice. A major difference in the various accounts is whether the authors set the starting point of their analysis at when transitional justice – in the author's opinion – *started to be done*, or when what was done *started to be called* transitional justice. The former set of authors sometimes go back as far as the ancient Greeks (see e.g. Elster 2004). For this book, however, when what was done started to be called transitional justice is of more relevance, as it discusses the emergence of a field of scholarship and practice (Arthur 2009), questions of labelling (Bell 2009), knowledge production, and the transmission of ideas to and their adoption in other contexts (Ben-Josef Hirsch 2006; Rowen 2017; Jones 2020).

Categorising transitional justice

Phases or generations of transitional justice

One prominent way of categorising phases of transitional justice is Ruti Teitel's genealogy.[1] Teitel's differentiation of phases as presented in her genealogy is widely echoed in the literature, and various efforts to trace the development of transitional justice have built on her work. Teitel situates the pursuit of justice in times of change within an *intellectual history* and traces the origins back to World War I. She then defines three phases of transitional justice, structured along "critical cycles" (Teitel 2003): post-World War II, as the Nuremberg Trials laid the foundation for modern human rights law and international criminal justice; the post-Cold War period, with "accelerated democratization" (Teitel 2003, 71) in Central and Eastern Europe and Latin America and the proliferation of domestic accountability measures; and a "steady-state phase" at the end of the twentieth century (Teitel 2003, 71), with the continuation of transitional justice, including in post-conflict situations. In a later identified 'global phase,' she finds that transitional justice has become more complex and extensive, both in terms of the actors involved in the respective processes and the expectations of what transitional justice should achieve (Teitel 2008). Building on Teitel's genealogy, Dustin Sharp (2013, 157) lays out his understanding of a "fourth generation" of transitional justice, which is mainly characterised by attention being paid to issues and debates that were previously neglected, such as socio-economic concerns, local voices, and traditions. These have not replaced the prominent issues of earlier phases but complement them. Transitional justice in Tunisia can be situated both within the 'global phase' and the 'fourth generation': a range of international and domestic actors has been involved and a variety of issues addressed, including those that had previously been neglected. Socio-economic concerns have played a particularly important role in the process.

Becoming a 'field'?

Whether transitional justice has emerged as an "entire field of inquiry, analysis, and practice" (Teitel 2008, 1) or simply as "a label or cloak that aims to rationalize a set of diverse bargains in relation to the past as an integrated endeavour" (Bell 2009, 6) is contested. Notwithstanding this discussion, transitional justice has become a ubiquitous concept in scholarship and practice, exemplified by the launch of specialist transitional justice journals,[2] the establishment of research institutions and other organisations dedicated to the topic,[3] interest groups engaged in lobbying, and a vast number of conferences and websites.

Paige Arthur (2009) outlines the emergence of the term, with an intellectual framework – a common knowledge base – as well as a community of scholars and practitioners taking the concept forward. She identifies the field as being rooted within the human rights community and as having emerged due to the changes in the practical conditions that political rights activists faced in the late 1980s. Human rights scholars, practitioners, and activists, mainly concerned with the changing political situation in Latin America, met at conferences to discuss the duties, merits, and repercussions of punishing state atrocities and developed a new intellectual framework, as the previous approach of 'shaming' governments for their *current* atrocities no longer seemed appropriate. "Human rights work," as Arthur quotes Juan Méndez,[4] "almost seamlessly turned [...] from an adversarial to a supportive position" (Arthur 2009, 335). Activists were now supporting new governments in dealing with the *past*, with the repressive legacies of their predecessors. Research and practice have thus intermingled from the very beginning of the concept's development and have determined what is important in transitional justice. A figuration has formed of individuals from different backgrounds – professions, countries, vantage points, etc. – representing an emerging order of how to deal with past abuses during times of transition.

The 'transition paradigm' and teleological assumptions of transitional justice

The initial idea of transitional justice emerged as part of the development of the 'transition paradigm' (Arthur 2009, 337). There was a shift in the dominant understanding of a 'transition' away from that mainly prevalent in socialist thinking, whereby a transition meant transition to socialism. 'Transition' in this new interpretation meant a transition to democracy, a notion that is still dominant today, at least in the framework of transitional justice. This was accompanied by the assumption that countries in transition strive for economic growth (Boraine 2006, 18). In transitional justice, the desired end-point of the transition in question "typically resemble[s] a Western liberal market democracy" (Sharp 2013, 149). This leads to the "teleological assumption that all societies should be encouraged toward similar forms of democracy" (Clark and Palmer 2012, 8), notwithstanding their diverse political, historical, and cultural backgrounds. This interpretation of transition to a fixed end-point – liberal democracy, or rather, peace and later liberal democracy – also entails the assumption that there has been a clear break between present and past, a lacuna that has to be filled in a fixed period of time in order to lead to a better future (Nagy 2008, 280).[5] According to Arthur (2009, 358), this normative goal of transition to democracy is a distinct feature of the field of transitional justice, which also sets it apart from the human rights movement, from which it at least partly emerged.[6] Rosemary Nagy (2008, 281) posits that this linkage of transitional justice with a 'transition to democracy' implies that transitional justice is in a sense not universal, not 'for everyone,' because those states that are generally seen as having already reached a state of consolidated democracy were not usually expected to pursue transitional justice efforts. However, transitional justice measures have since been introduced in consolidated democracies, such as the Truth and Reconciliation Commission of Canada, and there have also been numerous calls for transitional justice in the United States (see e.g. Murphy and Zvobgo 2020). Thus, transitional justice is slowly being decoupled from the 'transition to democracy' paradigm and towards broader understandings of transition.

Measures, practices, and preferences

Next to particular legitimate justice claims, a set of transitional justice measures and practices emerged that shaped the early development of the field: Arthur (2009, 331) compiles a "neat list" consisting of commissions of inquiry (including truth commissions), prosecutions, lustration or purges, and restitution or reparations programmes. Among these measures, the literature often identifies a privileging of civil and political rights and their violations, as well as legal responses, in law and practice (Arbour 2007, 4, 9; Nagy 2008, 276). As such, the paradigmatic liberal transition and the preferred legal justice measures run the risk of leading to a reductionist "one-size-fits-all" (Sharp 2015, 152) logic in transitional justice. However, next to the expansion of critical scholarship problematising these approaches,[7] there is also increasing reflection among practitioners (see e.g. Ladisch and Yakinthou 2020).

There has nevertheless been plenty of discussion about what kinds of atrocities and abuses transitional justice measures can and should be directed at. The field has developed significantly since the 1980s and the early 'conscious'[8] conceptual roots of transitional justice. What is considered necessary and appropriate for transitional justice to do, and how this is supposed to be done, has changed over time: the toolbox and its scope have expanded, as have the corresponding instructions for use. Transitional justice's increasingly global character has played a vital role in this, as has the mainstreaming and standardising of transitional justice ideas and measures and their vernacularisation. These features characterise the transitional justice efforts initiated in Tunisia after the uprisings, as they have been shaped by ideas of international transitional justice processes and the experiences of other countries, but also by the ideas of domestic actors from different spheres, such as politics and civil society.

Goal-orientation and 'process gap'

As outlined above, transitional justice promulgates certain initiatives that have often been criticised for focusing on and preferring legalistic measures and a particular form of a desired transition. At least initially, political change in transitional justice has predominantly been understood as transition to democracy in a liberal, market-oriented sense (Arthur 2009). The concept has a strong goal-orientation that has echoes both in practice and scholarship. Processes of transitional justice, which are often introduced after periods of conflict or violent rule, usually have explicit or implied teleological ends, such as societal reconciliation, peace, and democracy (Andrieu 2010, 540–3; Jones 2020, 5) – categories that are themselves rather blurry and have to be filled with meaning – or the guarantee of the non-recurrence of past violence and rights violations.[9] Institutionalised transitional justice is promoted as a planned, societal effort, that is, a mainstreamed transnational professional project. Although interlinked, it is possible to analytically distinguish these planned efforts, or *projects*, from transitional justice as something that happens in societies, or *processes*.[10] The goal-oriented perspective falls short of acknowledging the contested nature of such efforts, as well as their *processual* and contingent dimension. Thus, "the unplanned and the unexpected have no place in the performance of success" (Jones 2020, 6), foreclosing other interpretations of success and failure (see also Mosse 2005; see also Chapter 5).

Let me briefly recall what has already been outlined in the introduction to this book: one prominent strand of transitional scholarship deals with questions of what transitional justice should do and achieve and therefore focuses on the normative goals, outcomes, and effects of transitional justice measures, for example peace, human rights, democracy, or political institutions – both from quantitative and qualitative perspectives (see e.g. Crocker 1999; Olsen, Payne, and Reiter 2010a, 2010b; Wiebelhaus-Brahm 2010; De Greiff 2012; Salehi and Williams 2016; Kochanski 2020a; 2020b). Another strand focuses more on the role of domestic and international political dynamics and the transition part of transitional justice (see e.g. McGrattan 2009; Subotić 2009; Jones and Bernath 2017; McAuliffe 2017b; Cronin-Furman 2020). This book contributes to the second strand. In order to challenge an "understanding that society [develops] more or less 'automatically' towards a better social order" (Elias 1978, 151) when transitional justice measures are introduced, it is important to put processual dynamics at the centre of social scientific enquiry (Elias 2006b) in transitional justice. Exploring how transitional justice relates to processes of political and social change and putting the justice and the transition part in conversation with each other can help us to understand the questions of *how* and *why* (Elias 1977, 138) transitional justice processes develop, certain goals become prominent, and effects come about. This book aims to contribute to such a research agenda by analysing transitional justice through a process lens.

Broadening the scope: the normative ideal of a 'holistic approach'

Like any other political process related to the proliferation of international norms and ideas, the Tunisian transition and the corresponding transitional justice efforts are situated in a particular "world time-context" (Finnemore and Sikkink 1998, 909) in history and global politics. As Michal Ben-Josef Hirsch (2006, 187) notes, there is "an ideational environment in which what is a 'good' or 'desirable' policy choice is clearly defined." Thus, it is useful to sketch the state of transitional justice scholarship and practice during the time that the Tunisian transitional justice process was being set up to identify the dominant thinking that guides the design of planned, institutionalised transitional justice processes, including the Tunisian one.

While the question of what transitional justice *should* achieve has frequently been discussed, less attention has been directed at what transitional justice *can* achieve. Nagy (2008, 276) notes the selectivity in determining the *problems* that transitional justice should tackle which results from a narrow understanding of the concept. Thus, when (transitional) justice is being discussed, its opposite, injustice, has often been absent (see Nader 2010, 322). This may lead to the perception of transitional justice as flawed or incomplete. Perceived omissions can relate either to measures that are not taken, or to topics that are not tackled by any particular transitional justice process. One normative response to these perceived flaws is the idea of a 'holistic' or 'integrated' approach to transitional justice (see e.g. Sharp 2019). This approach is now a mainstream normative ideal (McAuliffe 2017a, 250), especially in transitional justice policymaking. This holistic/integrated approach has also shaped transitional justice in Tunisia (see also Salehi 2021).

Holism to the rescue?

None of the different measures introduced in transitional justice processes are free of criticism. There is "a tendency toward binary debates: peace versus justice, punishment versus reconciliation, retributive versus restorative justice, law versus politics, local versus international, individual versus collective" (Clark and Palmer 2012, 3), success versus failure. Which of the supposedly clashing options should be chosen represents a core question in transitional justice debates (Friedman and Jillions 2015, 142). In response, there has been a growing tendency towards conceptual holism, especially in the practitioners' realm.[11] In 2004, the UN Secretary-General's report on "the rule of law and transitional justice in conflict and post-conflict societies," one of the main documents guiding policymaking in the area of transitional justice, contends that "[w]here transitional justice is required, strategies must be holistic" (UN Security Council 2004, 9). The dominant assumption among the proponents of a holistic approach is that the various transitional justice measures applied in isolation have limited reach and would have greater potency in interaction. Measures that are perceived to be weak when they stand on their own may develop more force when combined with others and based on concerted efforts (De Greiff 2012, 35–9).[12] A holistic approach should also broaden the spectrum of claims for justice that are deemed legitimate and thereby rectify a greater array of injustices. This fits well with the Tunisian context, in which there was systematic socio-economic marginalisation under dictatorship, and thus it only seems logical to also address socio-economic grievances in a transitional justice project. The preference of some international transitional justice professionals for a holistic approach consequently fell on fertile ground in Tunisia.

However, problems in conceiving transitional justice holistically may occur when, for example, the actors involved in the process assume that different measures can be traded off against each other. Thus, a complementarity of means does not necessarily mean that there is institutional cooperation, since transitional justice is based on "messy, contentious politics" (Friedman and Jillions 2015, 147). Inclusiveness, therefore, may be both a strength and a challenge of a holistic approach (Clark and Palmer 2012, 1). A holistic approach also demands more from transitional societies than single measures of transitional justice in terms of political will, effort, and the employment of resources, which may equally lead to challenges, as we can see in the Tunisian case (see Chapter 5; see also Salehi 2021). Transitional justice, therefore, seems to tack between the goal of providing all-encompassing guidance for achieving justice in transition on the one hand and tailor-made solutions that pay attention to the local context and conditions on the other – two approaches that are not always easy to reconcile.

Professionalised transitional justice

With the emergence of the field of transitional justice – a community of scholars and practitioners as well as an intellectual framework and a common knowledge base – transitional justice has increasingly become professionalised. Often, transitional justice efforts are not introduced spontaneously but are carefully planned and institutionalised and "guided by various best practice formats" (Yakinthou 2018, 177). The Tunisian case is temporally and conceptually situated within these developments: after the initial deployment of relatively spontaneous justice measures, a carefully planned, institutionalised process accompanied by international transitional justice professionals was set in motion.[13]

The 'justice industry'

As a global enterprise, transitional justice is brought to different parts of the world by a "nonlocalized quasigroup, consisting of pockets of social interaction and shared meaning through which individuals [and with them ideas] circulate" (Levitt and Merry 2011, 83). These form the so-called "justice industry" (Subotić 2012, 117), an 'epistemic community' that contributes to the field's internationalisation and institutionalisation (Ben-Josef Hirsch 2006, 197). The 'justice industry' comprises professionals with different types of expertise who are sometimes called "justice entrepreneurs" (Madlingozi 2010) (or "post-conflict justice junkies" (Baylis 2008)). They are often seen as having been 'parachuted' into countries without much prior knowledge of the context and particular situation they find themselves in and which they have been hired to tackle. While being 'mobile' is an important feature of being an expert (Jones 2020, 6), due to their frequent displacements, they would not have the time (and sometimes not the interest) to gain detailed knowledge of the sites in which they work (see also Levitt and Merry 2011, 83). They rely on "technical institutional responses" and "ready-made models," on "'toolkits', 'toolboxes', 'menus' [or] 'templates'"[14] (Clark and Palmer 2012, 6), which can enforce a technocratic (self-)imagination.[15] The 'justice industry' also draws heavily on the legitimacy, attention, resources, and leverage available through the assemblage of the UN, NGOs, and activist movements (see also Finnemore and Sikkink 1998, 900).

However, it is worth mentioning here that those involved in this 'industry' do not comprise a homogenous group and that there are also differing viewpoints among transitional justice professionals themselves. Thus the focus on technical, institutionalised responses has not only been criticised by academics (see e.g. Jones 2020), as it has also been lamented from the practitioners' side. To generalise, those who come from a more activist human rights tradition perceive the field as being overtaken by technocratic jurists who perceive transitional justice work as a professional endeavour rather than a 'matter of the heart.' And those who favour a more pragmatic approach to transitional justice, and are willing to make political concessions to achieve what they regard as a better outcome, criticise the 'textbook mentality' of those who want to stick as strictly as possible to the existing frameworks.[16] In Tunisia, transitional justice professionals – mainly through the ICTJ, UNDP, and OHCHR – were heavily involved in setting up the planned transitional justice project (see Chapters 3 and 4) and offering expertise and access to financial resources. Thus, international transitional justice professionals were part of the Tunisian transitional justice figuration that shaped the processual developments (see also Elias [1981] 2006a, 48–9, [1986] 2006, 100–2).

The 'apolitical illusion' of technocratic logics

The transitional justice toolbox, with its various possible measures to hand, is often criticised for encouraging a box-ticking approach based on a technocratic logic: which measures are introduced, in what timeframe, and with what kinds of (quantifiable) activities? This can foster the introduction of a variety of measures in institutionalised transitional justice processes in order to tick the respective boxes of the holistic approach. On the other hand, it can also lead to a focus on measures that are easy to assess. An example of this would be a focus on prosecutions that can be assessed by counting the numbers of suspects "arrested, transferred, and prosecuted" (Subotić 2015, 366). Similarly, truth commissions can adapt to a bureaucratic accounting logic. In the Tunisian case, the number of dossiers that people have submitted to have their cases reviewed and to declare themselves as victims, as well as the count of hearings held by the TDC, was regularly updated on the commission's homepage and on social and conventional media.[17] This is intended to lend quantitative legitimacy to the body by showing that people are making use of it as planned – although its otherwise meagre outreach and information activities are often criticised.[18] Quantifiable measures fit much better with technocratic logics than messy concepts like 'truth,' which can be invoked by various sides, or 'reconciliation,' which is hard to define (Subotić 2015, 366).

Moreover, transitional justice initiatives sometimes appear to follow a logic of action that is more concerned with 'the project' of transitional justice in itself[19] and less with the surrounding political developments or the 'transition' – which it should in fact be facilitating and making more just. In these cases, transitional justice risks becoming self-referential, despite the fact that "[b]y itself it cannot resolve anything" (Bleeker 2010, vii; see also Kerr 2017, 131). In the same vein, if a transitional justice process fails to produce the envisaged outcome, this can be attributed to "'minor' technical implementation problems" (Millar, van der Lijn, and Verkoren 2013) of the 'good' transitional justice project, without paying attention to the underlying reasons for the failure and the political dynamics at play.

Looking at the issue from a different angle, it may seem necessary to convey such an 'apolitical illusion'[20] if transitional justice is to gain traction in a context in which 'politics' has negative connotations, as in the Tunisian case. Here – and this probably also holds true for many repressive and conflict-ridden contexts – the political space was monopolised by the ruling party/elite. 'Doing politics' meant being part of the oppressive system and being deeply linked with favouritism and structures of corruption (see also Kappler 2013, 355).[21] There is also an expectation in Tunisia that leading figures in civil society should not be politicians at the same time and vice versa.[22] Therefore, acknowledging that transitional justice is a matter of politics could discursively exclude civil society from the project. Hence transitional justice efforts often convey an apolitical illusion by reformulating political issues in apolitical terms (Leebaw 2008, 106). Processes of social and political change can therefore be "rendered technical" (Li 2011), a process which can in turn serve deeply political functions.

The politics of transitional justice

Despite conveying an 'apolitical illusion,' transitional justice is inherently political: transitional justice processes deal with political rights violations and co-determine who is able to participate in a country's transitional politics. They have direct consequences for political reconfigurations, be it on an institutional level within the political system or on a discursive level, shaping politics as well as political and social relationships (Buckley-Zistel 2014, 144). In contexts of transition, in which a new political architecture is being developed and power structures are in flux, like in Tunisia after the uprisings, transitional justice can both challenge and sustain privilege and power. Those previously in powerful and privileged positions "will fight hard to maintain them" (Goodhart 2013, 34), while others would benefit from challenging and ultimately altering the power dynamics, making transitional justice a site of contention, as conflict and friction are likely to increase when power differentials decrease in favour of previously weaker actors (Elias 1977, 139). Moreover, international norms, practices, and institutions of transitional justice can be (mis-)used by domestic elites for their own political ends (Subotić 2009). International actors may likewise pursue a political agenda with the "political enterprise" (Ottendörfer 2016, 21; my translation) that transitional justice represents.

The political nature of the process and the technocratic logic outlined above might seem to be at odds with one another, and it is often assumed that the political nature of the process is forgotten or purposefully ignored by deploying technocratic approaches (see e.g. Leebaw 2008; Rubli 2012). But this is not necessarily the case. Expert authority, which is often derived from technocratic approaches as well as from the involvement of international actors (see e.g. Jones 2015, 2020; Nesiah 2016; Menzel 2020), can indeed be invoked to achieve certain political goals or, to use a stronger term, it can be instrumentalised for political purposes. Moreover, the very set-up of technocratic transitional justice structures – such as a transitional justice ministry, as in Tunisia (Lamont, Quinn, and Wiebelhaus-Brahm 2019) – may serve the political interests of some actors over those of others. As such, there is no either/or of technocracy and politics or of international and local agendas. By examining the Tunisian case, this book aims to contribute to a strand of literature in transitional justice that examines settings in which technocracy and politics intersect and international and local actors pursue their goals with the help of both realms.

Transitional justice gaining ground

Over time, the idea and the practice of transitional justice has spread to different geographical areas and political contexts around the globe. Idea and practice are mutually constitutive, leading to the normative ideal of a holistic approach to transitional justice.[23] At the same time, transitional justice has become professionalised, a process directly related to the discourse surrounding what transitional justice can and should achieve (Rowen 2017, 153). This professionalisation influences ways of knowing about ideas and practices, but also a bundling of competence. This does not deprive transitional justice of its political or contested nature but determines the dominant dogma and socio-technological offering – or 'supply mechanism,' which is influenced by international agents (Ben-Josef Hirsch 2006, 185) – for planned, institutionalised processes of change. To prepare the ground for the empirical analysis of how transitional justice was initiated, designed, and performed in Tunisia, the remainder of this chapter explores the dynamics of the transitional justice norm, how ideas and practices were able to spread and take root in different contexts, how they were appropriated and contested, and the importance of knowledge in their dissemination and vernacularisation.

Transitional justice as a dynamic norm?

Transitional justice is not only inherently political; it also necessarily requires grappling with normative perspectives (Ottendörfer 2016, 16). In International Relations scholarship, norms are defined as "a standard of appropriate behavior for actors with a given identity" (Finnemore and Sikkink 1998, 891). They include both ideas and practices. Norm-breaking behaviour is recognised because it is disapproved of. Consequently, norms and norm-conforming behaviour are by definition 'good,' at least from the perspective of those who are promoting them (Finnemore and Sikkink 1998). Hence, norms are always relational; their very existence depends on context and actors. Martha Finnemore and Kathryn Sikkink (1998, 895) define normative change as part of a 'life-cycle': the norm emerges, gains ground, and manifests itself. The process of 'gaining ground' or achieving broad international acceptance is termed a "norm cascade."[24]

Transitional justice has become a "norm or standard practice for state behavior after conflict" or violent rule (Subotić 2012, 106). Pursuing accountability and the idea of transitional justice has now become commonplace and is codified in laws and institutions domestically and internationally. There has thus been broad acceptance of the accountability norm, or a "justice cascade" (Sikkink 2011) has taken place. Initially, in the body of literature analysing international norm cascades, normative change was predominantly understood as an evolutionary process of convergence (Finnemore and Sikkink 1998, 905). However, by now "the interface between global ideas and those of local groups" (Merry 2006, 222) has gained more attention in the analysis of global norms (see e.g. Zimmermann 2017). Given the problem of purposive assumptions outlined above, this book relies on conceptions of normative change that allow for non-linearity, that are equipped to accommodate complexity, and pay due attention to the influence of "domestic political structures and agents" (Acharya 2004, 240) on processes of change. This section therefore introduces further options for looking at normative change, adoption, and the appropriation of 'global ideas.'

A circulating value package?

Norm dynamics may have dimensions other than convergence. The adoption of norms may be a contested process, facing resistance and/or setbacks. Adoption could also happen on the surface without penetrating the core of a society and its consciousness. Or adoption could accompany appropriation. One would therefore need to examine these more nuanced aspects of normative change and the appropriation and translation of norms (Merry 2006). Activism may not be the sole factor needed for a normative idea to gain momentum, since the broader historical and political context is also of crucial importance. This can include certain events as well as the question of what other ideas are prominent at a certain place and point in time (Levitt and Merry 2011; Atalay 2016). Peggy Levitt and Sally Merry introduce the idea of 'values packages' that are important for a certain idea or norm to spread (Levitt and Merry 2009). A transitional justice value package would be based on human rights and embrace the idea that those who carried out the repression and violence should be held to account. Those who have suffered from repression and atrocities should be able to know who the perpetrators were as well as the systemic logics behind periods of violent rule, and they should also be compensated for their suffering.

Values packages circulate transnationally, with porous boundaries between the global, national, and regional "layers of social experience" (Levitt and Merry 2011, 90). For the 'career' of the values package, it is crucial who carries the ideas, as well as the knowledge, that make up the package: "The organizational channels and networks through which values packages circulate strongly influence where they are appropriated and by whom" (Levitt and Merry 2011, 90). In order to establish the basis for looking at the appropriation and customisation of transitional justice ideas, the following section takes a closer look at the question of knowledge circulation, as well as its initial production, to determine how and by whom the ideas of a value package, of transitional justice in particular, are spread.

Knowledge circulation

Global diffusion processes, like that of transitional justice, also happen through knowledge and expertise (Ben-Josef Hirsch 2006; Bonacker 2012; Rowen 2017; Jones 2020; Menzel 2020; Zvobgo 2020).[25] For transitional justice, with its universality claims, it is necessary to identify movable and activating knowledge that travels across places and cultures (Tsing 2005, 7). This lens offers several entry points at different levels. Some authors have warned that there is the potential in transitional justice to enable a certain sort of neo-imperialism that produces specific forms of knowledge like "human rights discourses, liberal ideals, new histories" (Hinton 2010, 7; see also Jones 2020). The predominance of these specific forms of knowledge, then, may be facilitated by an unequal distribution of power.

Another possibility for looking at this is the field's common knowledge base, which developed from human rights advocacy and within the framework of several conferences, bringing scholars, practitioners, and activists together (Arthur 2009). Since the field came into being in the 1990s, several knowledge 'hubs'[26] have emerged where transitional justice expertise is pooled. "Knowledgeable individuals" (Levitt and Merry 2009, 444) from among these hubs and the wider academic, activist, and practitioner communities play a part in particular transitional justice figurations and may also shape the flow of information and knowledge. A crucial knowledge hub in transitional justice, especially with regard to truth commissions, is the ICTJ (Rowen 2017), an NGO based in New York City with several field offices around the globe. It has developed what can be regarded as something like an authoritative narrative on what transitional justice *is* and *should do*. Knowledgeable individuals based at transitional justice hubs have played a crucial role in designing and implementing the institutionalised transitional justice project in Tunisia.

Discursive resources

An obvious, and very hands-on, possibility for knowledge dissemination in transitional justice processes is the provision of workshops and training. These training opportunities are mostly offered by justice entrepreneurs working for a knowledge hub organisation. Training may be offered to members of a newly established truth commission, for example, or to a broader audience. In Tunisia, those participating in the national consultations on transitional justice – the so-called 'National Dialogue on Transitional

Justice' – received training in transitional justice. This equipped participants with knowledge of the concept and the discursive resources to participate in debates as well as to frame their causes within the lexis of transitional justice and situate their cases within the discourse.[27] They could therefore communicate within the transitional justice figuration (Elias [1981] 2006a, 100).

Following Nancy Fraser, to oppose injustice there is a need for discursive resources and interpretative schemes to be available (Fraser 2012, 51). These can be provided by the circulation of knowledge through the aforementioned knowledge hubs and justice entrepreneurs. This is not to assume that domestic actors represent a "blank slate in terms of existing knowledge and experience" (Orford 2003, 139). However, 'new' knowledge can offer thought-provoking impulses that help to enlarge actors' repertoires of ideas and their options for expressing them (Levitt and Merry 2009, 447). In order to be persuasive, claims need to be phrased in a language that is convincing to those who are to be addressed. Transitional justice represents a distinct field or figuration with its own technical language and practices, which individuals need to be familiar with to be able to act effectively within it. Being equipped with discursive resources and knowing these 'technologies' may also open the door for domestic actors to successfully acquire material resources, such as funding (Levitt and Merry 2009, 443).

Limiting options, reducing complexity?

Knowledge transmission, for example through training, can also limit discursive options and distribute discursive resources unequally. Hence it can sideline certain actors[28] or determine trajectories, foreclosing other options (Tsing 2005, 14). Finnemore and Sikkink go even further: "[Professional training] actively socializes people to value certain things above others" (1998, 905). Thus, transitional justice as an arena of knowledge production that has created an image of how the world ought to be (Nagy 2014, 217)[29] may reduce "sociocultural complexity [...] into more manageable (and, often, controllable) categories" (Hinton 2010, 7). Global knowledge may as a result be subject to standardisation, supressing those voices that are incompatible with standards that do not allow for much diversity (Tsing 2005, 13). The field has come to be characterised by particular 'politics of knowledge' and "power relations between different epistemic actors" (Jones 2020, 2). In Tunisia, as Corinna Mullin and Ian Patel point out, some actors may not be prepared to institutionalise their demands for justice due to their past experiences of institutional repression. This in turn runs the risk of them "being branded as 'hardliners' or 'spoilers'" in the planned transitional justice project (Mullin and Patel 2016, 107).

This standardisation of global knowledge and corresponding discursive resources has practical implications for who is heard in transitional justice processes: should it be everyone who was affected, or only those who are equipped with the discursive resources, have a good command of English or French, and use the correct terms? Should the process solely hear from mainstream opinions or deviant[30] voices as well? It furthermore influences how funding is distributed, as only those who use the right terms in their grant application are likely to be successful. Moreover, the standardisation of acceptable knowledge and the use of jargon produces homogenous narratives – which can lead to the impression of an absence of friction among the respective actors (Kappler 2013, 356). Turning to the concrete work of transitional justice measures and institutions, the practices of truth commissions are connected to "powerful transnational forms of knowledge" (Shaw 2007, 197; see also Ben-Josef Hirsch 2006), enabled by the global political economy of transitional justice expertise (see e.g. Rowen 2017, 153; Jones 2020; Menzel 2020). Hence the intellectual knowledge base of transitional justice, as well as the corresponding epistemic community, is an issue with regard to discursive resources and in determining how knowledge production is *practised* in the societies concerned. It influences who can be an expert, who can give input, who is heard, whose knowledge is valid (Jones 2020, 2), and "who knows well enough to do to the work" (Seabrooke 2014, 50). For example, although 'local' knowledge may play a vital role for transitional justice professionals in designing policies (Jones 2020, 7), a Tunisian transitional justice expert complained to me that the knowledge of Tunisian experts was marginalised in the process: "All the experts come from New York. We can't be experts here. [...] But it's us who know best the country and the context. [...] The frameworks are too rigid."[31] It has also influenced how and what kind of knowledge has been produced by the Tunisian TDC, for example through the questions that have been asked in closed hearings or through the victims that have been selected to give testimony in public hearings.

The turn to 'the local'? Appropriating transitional justice

There has not always been a 'universal' idea of transitional justice. What is now understood as such – and the common knowledge base – emerged over time and not in a way that was unidirectional and top-down from the global to the local/domestic but rather as a multi-directional process.[32] Transitional justice has looked different in different places, and different ideas and manifestations that "derive from a concrete locality" (Buckley-Zistel 2018, 154) have fed into what is now considered a global norm. Although the 'labelling' or conceptual emergence of transitional justice, as well as its transmission, was indeed a process pushed forward on an inter- and transnational level, this was fed by domestic efforts to deal with the past that had emerged before any global paradigm or universal transitional justice norm was in existence.

Shifting focus

Transitional justice as a "normal, institutionalized and mainstreamed" (McEvoy 2007, 412) practice following a period of conflict or violent rule was often perceived to neglect local contexts,[33] conditions, and communities (Lundy and McGovern 2008). Following a (socio-)technological logic, institutionalised transitional justice processes would not engage deeply enough with "the messiness of global and transnational involvements and the local, on-the-ground realities with which they intersect" (Hinton 2010, 1).[34] In more recent years, however, scholarship and practice have paid more attention to 'the local' in transitional justice (Sharp 2014, 72; Kochanski 2020a, 2020b). A common theme in the literature is the exploration of whether global norms fit with local understandings of justice (Buckley-Zistel 2018). This opens the way for several conclusions. The simplest ones are either that what is taking place is a neo-imperial imposition of norms and practices by and through international justice entrepreneurs at the one extreme, or that there is an outright rejection of global norms by local actors at the other extreme. A common debate around the Tunisian case is whether transitional justice norms are compatible with Islamists' values (Khatib 2014).[35]

However, there are various shades between these two extremes in how global norms/international efforts are perceived by local actors, what they make of it, and how different understandings interact. Several authors have accordingly sought to render visible a normative divergence (Bell 2009; Subotić 2015), 'localisation' (Hinton 2010; Shaw and Waldorf 2010), or a 'local turn' (Kochanski 2020b) in transitional justice. Different "local meanings" (Bell 2009, 15) may be assigned to seemingly similar institutional provisions for dealing with the past, a "disconnection between international legal norms and local priorities and practices" (Shaw and Waldorf 2010, 3), different expectations in transitional justice measures (Shaw 2007), "tensions between the global and the local" (Sharp 2014, 73) about transitional justice interventions, or there may be a diverging normative *outcome* from normative *intent* (Subotić 2015). However, in Tunisia these localised perceptions and understandings are not linear and are subject to change (see Chapter 4). Stepping outside of the transitional justice logic (Jones and Bernath 2017) can help us understand such unfolding processes and their functions and not only see unplanned dynamics as unintended consequences, but as integral parts of processual developments.

While the increasing focus on the local generally has a positive appeal (see e.g. Sharp 2013), there are also implicit risks in 'localising' transitional justice. One would be an uncritical approach towards 'the local,' bearing with it the danger of romanticisation and neglecting power dynamics (Kochanski 2020b, 27). Another risk lies in creating a narrative that localises transitional justice and thereby also localises the origins and dynamics of conflict. Hence the larger context in which conflict emerged can be ignored or neglected (Hinton 2010, 10). Localisation could therefore reinforce the tendencies outlined above, giving rise to a tendency to look for responsibility for past violence only with the transitional societies, ignoring global dynamics and omitting the responsibility of Western democracies for atrocities.[36]

Reconfiguring transitional justice in different contexts

Whether universal models of transitional justice can be modified without losing their normative appeal is contested in transitional justice research (see e.g. Shaw and Waldorf 2010, 4f.; Subotić 2015, 365). However, rather than examining the question of normative erosion, this section looks at the reconfiguration of global ideas in different contexts. One approach that offers a conceptual starting point for examining the adoption and appropriation of global ideas is vernacularisation, that is, the translation of "globally produced ideas into myriad specific social settings in ways that are often indirect, fragmented, and diffuse" (Levitt and Merry 2011, 88). This approach goes beyond the mere translation of concepts into local cultural and linguistic terms. While the term originally meant translation into native or everyday language, its conceptual use in the social sciences – mainly anthropology – goes beyond the linguistic understanding to include an appropriation in meaning to make an idea suitable for a certain context.

The reconfigurations described in this book are part of an "interactive process" (Björkdahl and Gusic 2015, 270; see also Zimmermann 2017, 5–6), an encounter between different international as well as local normative legal and moral visions. This encounter is essentially constitutive: it entails the production of new but necessarily contingent accounts that bear traces of multiple, cross-cutting, and often disparate discursive influences. These influences are interconnected and dynamic. A discursive hybrid is therefore produced that may be both greater than, and different from, its parts (Goodale 2013, 6–7). This process involves new theories and practices: new ways of thinking about certain ideas and new ways of doing certain things. Most importantly, it makes ideas more acceptable (Levitt and Merry 2011) to a particular audience. This, of course, brings about the possibility that ideas become *less* acceptable to *another* audience. Hence processes of exclusion and inclusion may be at play when global ideas are vernacularised locally (Kappler 2013, 352). While transitional justice in Tunisia has been vernacularised in a literal manner linguistically, the notion's appropriation in meaning and reinterpretation over time has been a contested process (see also Salehi 2019).

Resonance and points of reference

Like liberal peacebuilding, transitional justice relies on the assumption that there is a normative void that needs to be filled through the involvement of international actors in transitional societies (for a critical view, see Björkdahl and Höglund 2013, 291), and that these "societies provided an almost clean slate into which could be injected the institutions of democracy and liberal economics" (Millar, van der Lijn, and Verkoren 2013, 137).[37] Policies, then, are built on the assumption of convergence and (in policy-analysis language) a 'race-to-the-top' in which local actors gradually come closer to what is understood as the universal norm, despite acknowledged differences (Kappler 2013, 351). However, as we could already see in Chapter 2 for the Tunisian case, a perspective that also allows us to think in continuities, not only in clear ruptures, is more helpful for the context of this book, since this approach is actually inherent in the idea that there is a past that needs dealing with.

Transnational normativities usually gain traction when and where they resonate with existing ideas of justice (Acharya 2004, 243).[38] By combining existing ideas with aspects of the 'travelling global concept' of transitional justice, vernacularisers can create meaning, (re)frame issues, and use these ideas as discursive, moral, and political resources (Levitt and Merry 2011) to advance their own agenda. Local actors "add [ideas] to their 'political vernacular' by taking ownership and claiming authority" (Atalay 2016, 396). As we can see in the Tunisian case, vernacularisers may also 'prune' (Atalay 2016) or enrich (Salehi 2019) global norms such as transitional justice. These processes involve negotiation between transnational actors, mediators, and local actors – between these groups as well as across them. They are frictional, since the meaning and form of transitional justice may be mediated, appropriated, translated, modified, misunderstood, ignored, or rejected (Merry 2006). However, appropriation and the emancipatory 'politics of contestation' may be the very reason that gives legitimacy to normative ideas and practices, and hence to a transitional justice process (Goodhart 2013). Similarly, Briony Jones and Julie Bernath (2017) would argue that resistance, in different shapes and understandings, is necessary and constitutive to transitional justice processes.

Points of resonance and communication strategies differ among various actors and can potentially lead to friction. Friction does not necessarily hinder the process, as it can catalyse change (Björkdahl and Höglund 2013, 290). These points of resonance may be manifold. They include long-standing traditions and historical normative concepts, as well as those that have been introduced into the socio-cultural context more recently. This assemblage resulting from a combination and (re-)configuration of 'new' and 'old' ideas is (co-)determining for power structures, for who has influence in vernacularisation processes, and who may speak for 'the local'/'the people'/'civil society,' and so forth. As indicated above, it is a frictional process – a notion that I will explain further in the following section.

Frictional encounters in internationalised processes of change

Friction can be an additional way to understand internationalised processes of change, such as transitional justice. The concept helps to explain how ideas are "charged and changed by their encounters with [...] realities" (Björkdahl and Höglund 2013, 292). Originating in physics, where it describes resistance in encounters between substances, leading to energy production and transformative effects (Kappler 2013, 351), the concept was initially harnessed for use in the social sciences by Anna Lowenhaupt Tsing (2005), who used it to describe 'global connections' in capitalism, nature, and social justice. The notion gained traction in peace and conflict studies, for example in peacebuilding (e.g. Björkdahl and Höglund 2013), and has also been applied to transitional justice, offering varying degrees of conceptual explanation (Shaw 2007; Hinton 2010; Shaw and Waldorf 2010; Sharp 2014; Buckley-Zistel 2016; Yakinthou 2018).

Notions of ambiguity

Connections that come about through friction are not straightforward, nor do they imply conformity. Rather, in Tsing's understanding friction is a form of interaction that connects across difference in an "awkward, unequal, unstable, and creative" (Tsing 2005, 4) manner. Friction, then, has an ambiguous character: its transformative power can be both productive and disruptive. On the one hand, it can lend strength to global connections – on the other, it can be an obstacle to the functioning of global power structures (Tsing 2005, 6). In transitional justice, some authors concentrate more on the conflictive aspect of friction, describing where 'global' and 'local' are at odds (e.g. Shaw 2007), while others look more closely at the notion of productiveness (e.g. Buckley-Zistel 2016). Christalla Yakinthou (2018, 208) sees particular analytical value in observing friction in both its productive and unproductive manifestations. Annika Björkdahl and Kristine Höglund (2013) find that frictional encounters, although conflictive, do not necessarily have negative consequences for societies in transition. Friction should be understood in a processual sense, not as an outcome. This process, then, can drive change (as an outcome) (Elias 1977, 1978, [1986] 2006). Moreover, with respect to their outcome – for example, the creation of transitional justice institutions that are not accepted by all actors – frictional encounters can lead to new realities and trigger feedback loops, which again produce frictional encounters (Björkdahl and Höglund 2013, 296). Because of this processual notion, friction is particularly useful for studying phenomena related to political change, such as transitional justice in Tunisia and elsewhere, through a process lens.

Stefanie Kappler (2013, 364) contends that there is a general tendency among the actors involved in internationalised processes of change to aim at eliminating friction rather than understanding its nature and function. While I do not want to anticipate the empirical analysis at this point, it is worth mentioning that eliminating friction is a common tendency in Tunisian politics, where political conflict or tensions are not seen as productive. Processes are geared towards reaching consensus, fulfilling the expectations of a much-praised Tunisian 'compromise culture' and eliminating visible friction in representative settings, such as parliament.[39]

Cross-cutting frictions

In internationalised, planned processes of change such as transitional justice, friction is "a process of local just as much as global connectedness, in the light of the energy that is produced through local–global encounters" (Kappler 2013, 353). There is the possibility of friction becoming 'compounded' (Millar 2013) when different international actors and their respective fields of action or intervention are grouped together in the perception of local actors or vice versa, although they may actually embrace different paradigms and ideas. Moreover, when the 'international community' perceives itself as internally coherent, the compounding logic may result in policies built on false premises: a *coherent* international community needs to deal with conflictual relations among domestic actors that, according to this view, need to be eliminated (Kappler 2013, 353–4). However, the grouping is often arbitrary, as international and local actors do not represent compounds or homogenous blocs. Different arenas and actors operating within them are inevitably linked, and the boundaries between them are blurred and constantly subject to change. This also means that parts of the 'local' are sometimes closer to the 'global' than others. Thus, one can observe frictional dynamics within and across these pre-defined groups. Although Kappler (2013) draws a distinction here between vertical and horizontal friction, for the purpose of this book the cross-cutting dynamics may better be described in terms of non-linearity and multi-directionality. Cross-cutting frictions are linked, can only be understood in connection to each other, and may eventually influence and shift existing power structures (Björkdahl and Höglund 2013, 298; Kappler 2013, 352; Björkdahl and Gusic 2015, 266; Arnould 2016, 334). As relationships are not fixed, friction and its transformative potential may lead to changing 'alliances' among different actors and groups of actors in processes of change, such as transitional justice. Given that large parts of the population were excluded from the political sphere during the period of authoritarian rule, the emergence of 'vertical' communication channels and power structures opened new possibilities for those previously marginalised to gain a voice and influence.[40]

Conclusion: the international and domestic politics of transitional justice and the 'process gap'

By outlining the conceptual origins and the development of transitional justice, this chapter has identified the dominant approach in the design of internationalised transitional justice. Many of the dynamics that can be observed in the Tunisian transitional justice process are specific to this particular phase in the conceptual development of transitional justice, which has become a standard practice for states following periods of conflict or violent rule and led to the prompt engagement of the 'justice industry' after the fall of the Ben Ali regime (see Chapter 3); it can also be seen in the international support and professionalised manner in which the planned transitional justice project was set in motion (see Chapter 4) and the conceptual holism on which the design of transitional justice in Tunisia has been built (see Chapter 4). The chapter went on to challenge the assumption that holistic approaches are necessarily better at delivering a sense of justice in transitional justice processes. The chapter also discussed the transitional justice professionals who take an active part in transitional justice and how their professionalisation may contribute to an 'apolitical illusion' of the issue, with the chapter instead arguing that transitional justice is always political, notwithstanding – or precisely because of – technocratic tendencies. The international politics of transitional justice also play a decisive role in how the notion gains ground in different contexts. This is shaped by the transmission of dominant knowledge, power relations, and inclusion and exclusion processes. How these global ideas are adopted and appropriated in different contexts, then, is an inherently political process, too. The chapter identified friction as a driver in internationalised processes of change – encounters that are ambiguous and can have either productive or disruptive effects. Friction, then, can occur between different actors and across different actor groups. It may change power structures, lead to new, contingent processes, and from there open new pathways in transitional justice.

The chapter has provided the conceptual background for analysing transitional justice in Tunisia as a process in which a planned, internationalised set of activities that is expected to bring about change interacts with political and social dynamics in a context in flux. The goal-orientation and teleological appeal of transitional justice practice and the accompanying focus on goals, outcomes, and effects in the scholarship has been garnering more attention and critique, with other scholars also pointing to the importance of analysing transitional justice as a political process (see e.g. Jones and Bernath 2017, 1). However, the 'process' in and of itself has rarely been the focus of enquiry. Thus, in order to contribute to closing this 'process gap,' the book looks at transitional justice through a processual lens and introduces a processual heuristic.

The chapter has shown that processual developments in transitional justice are heavily influenced by dynamics of international connectedness (see also Elias [1981] 2006a). However, the norms and standard practices that are brought to different contexts are rarely implemented as planned but instead interact with processes of contestation and appropriation (see also Elias 1977, [1986] 2006). These processes are driven and defined by frictional encounters and conflictive dynamics (see also Elias 1977, 1978, [1986] 2006). In the next three chapters, the processual heuristic for analysing transitional justice in process is used to structure the analysis of these dynamics.

Notes

1 Without offering further explanation, Teitel refers to Michel Foucault's essay "Nietzsche, Genealogy, History," in which Foucault outlines his understanding of genealogy. Hence, one can assume that Teitel follows Foucault's understanding of the term, distancing genealogy from the uncovering of linear developments and the search for "origins" (Foucault 1977, 76f.). However, a Foucauldian genealogical analysis would instead aim "to show that a given system of thought [...] was the result of contingent turns of history, not the outcome of rationally inevitable trends" (Gutting 2014).

2 For example, the *International Journal for Transitional Justice* or *Transitional Justice Review*.

3 For example, the ICTJ, No Peace Without Justice, Impunity Watch, and Oxford Transitional Justice Research, to name just a few.

4 Juan Méndez is a lawyer and human rights activist of Argentinian origin who became known for representing political prisoners. Until 2016, he was the UN Special Rapporteur on Torture.

5 Alexander Hinton (2018, 6) terms the teleological perspective that assumes that transitional justice leads to a 'better,' liberal-democratic future the "transitional justice imaginary" and its concrete manifestations as a "justice facade" that masks the complexities and lived experiences of transitional justice. In the meantime, there are examples where transitional justice measures (which are also widely recognised as such) were introduced past this obvious 'lacuna period,' for example the Extraordinary Chambers in the Courts of Cambodia.

6 Human rights usually do not convey democracy as a goal; rather, democracy is often perceived as a "means to realize human rights" (Erman 2013, 72).

7 Jones (2020, 5) explains that critical scholarship only emerged later, while the initial epistemic community – and corresponding ideas and concepts – was dominated by a "bricolage of activism and practice."

8 Christine Bell dates the development of a 'self-conscious' field to 2000 and after (Bell 2009, 8).

9 For a concrete example, see e.g. the Tunisian transitional justice law, Article 1.

10 In practice, the terminological distinction is not as easy to make, since actors often refer to the ongoing project as a 'transitional justice process.' Moreover, as will be explained in the course of this chapter, processes are not necessarily unplanned but can be both planned and unplanned, or a result of the interplay between the two.

11 Or rather at the nexus between the two realms, since boundaries are often not clear between academia and practice, as has been outlined above and will also be referred to below.

12 It should be remarked that since Pablo de Greiff was UN Special Rapporteur for Truth, Justice, Reconciliation, and the Guarantee of Non-Recurrence, the 'holistic approach' evidently has advocates in the highest ranks of international policymaking.

13 See Chapters 3 and 4.

14 Like Sandra Rubli (2012), some authors use 'toolbox' and 'template' interchangeably. I differentiate between the two, since a 'toolbox' is more flexible than a 'template' (it is possible to pick and choose from a toolbox, whereas a template offers one single design), but use 'toolkit' and 'menu' interchangeably with 'toolbox.'

15 See Chapter 5 on approaches to technical support and advocacy.

16 Personal conversations with staff members of a large international transitional justice NGO; New York, April 2015.

17 The TDC website is available here (in French): www.ivd.tn/?lang=fr (accessed 27 May 2018).

18 Several personal interviews, conversations, and observations, Tunisia, 2014–16. Implying that the meagre outreach was a deliberate decision, a communications consultant told me in an informal conversation: "I was a communications consultant with the TDC. They did not want to communicate, so I quit." La Marsa, September 2016.

19 Though I can only offer anecdotal evidence from field research here, I have observed people discussing whether something would be 'good for transitional justice' without mentioning the value of the respective idea or action for 'the transition' or 'society' at large. See also Krause (2014) on 'good projects.'

20 I use the term here in my own translation, but it is borrowed from Laurent Bonnefoy (2008) who used the French 'l'illusion apolitique' in a different context.

21 In the case of Bosnia, Kappler (2013, 7f.) describes a withdrawal of 'ordinary' citizens from the political sphere and a turn to family and neighbourhood networks, resulting in a strengthening of horizontal communities and frictions between the political class and the local population. She also found that organised civil society (or the NGO sphere) became detached from the population, as NGOs are often seen as a foreign instrument. While I describe the Tunisian perception of the political sphere above, I have not observed the latter tendency in Tunisia.

22 Personal interview with ARP member, formerly active in the leadership of a civil society organisation, who gave up her positions within the latter when she was elected to parliament; Tunis, March 2015. An exception to this unofficial rule is activism within the UGTT. The UGTT is an actor outside of official politics but with strong influence inside the political system. Though the relationship between the UGTT leadership and the Ben Ali regime varied, the UGTT was never fully co-opted, and people who wanted to be politically active during that period, and were not within the authoritarian system, often chose to join the union to exert their activism from there, even if workers' rights were not the true focus of their interests. The UGTT functioned as a 'refuge' for them (Yousfi 2015); personal interview with UGTT and human rights activist, Tunis, October 2015. More recently, the increasing dissatisfaction with the political class has led to the political success of outsiders/newcomers, as the presidential elections 2019 have shown, in which both of the candidates who made it to the run-off vote were new to politics.

23 This refers to the dominant approach at the time of writing in late 2020, which may of course be subject to change.

24 Please note that questions of norms, their emergence, and development are not at the centre of this book. The notion of norms is used in conjunction with standard practice or ideas. Thus, the discussion of this literature remains necessarily shallow.

25 Thorsten Bonacker (2012, 8) separates norms and knowledge as two different forms of diffusion processes. I do not strictly follow this separation here, because I am working on the assumption that norms and ideas can travel, and gain validity, through knowledge production and circulation.

26 I use the term here for internationally operating organisations. However, Alex Jeffrey and Michaelina Jakala (2015, 48), for example, have remarked on the creation of local hubs, consisting of NGOs and victims' associations, for networking and knowledge exchange between courts and communities.

27 Several personal interviews, Tunisia, 2014–16.

28 Suzanne Katzenstein (2003, 256) describes how East Timorese actors were sidelined by UN staff, who did not consult them on institutional design and

just took over tasks themselves instead of mentoring the domestic actors. The East Timorese then became "sick of internationals coming in and conducting 'workshops'" (quoted in Nagy 2008, 282). Another aspect is the sidelining of certain domestic actors who are not able to participate in these workshops and hence are excluded from being equipped with the dominant knowledge base and technical vocabulary.

29 Contrary to Nagy's perspective, Michael Goodhart (2013) argues that ideas may be appealing exactly because they convey an understanding of how the world ought to be and therefore have emancipatory potential.

30 For a problematisation of the notion of 'deviants,' see Jones and Bernath (2017). They posit that labelling behaviour or voices as deviant perpetuates the focus on the teleological logic and predefined goals that are seen as benchmarks in transitional justice.

31 Personal interview, Tunis, August 2016. I would like to note here that many interview partners also explicitly welcomed international engagement and the sharing of expertise. To give one example, a civil society representative stated "we had international supporters, like the ICTJ. They made sure to inform us. We learned more about the process and how to work exactly" (phone interview, September 2020). Thus, tension may evolve particularly around the question of who can be recognised as an expert.

32 Bronwyn Leebaw (2008) would challenge the idea of universality in general, since she finds that goals or aspirations of transitional justice may not necessarily be coherent and can actually be conflicting.

33 There are different understandings of what the 'local' exactly means in this regard. On the questioning of binary categories such as 'global' and 'local,' see Buckley-Zistel (2018) or Sharp (2014). While I agree with criticism of the oversimplified binary categorisation, within this book it is maintained to a certain extent for pragmatic reasons.

34 The ICTJ has published an edited volume on the role of context (Duthie and Seils 2017). Thus, the topic has also gained more attention in the practitioners' realm.

35 She discusses in particular Ennahda. For an introduction to the party, see Chapter 1. For a general discussion of the role of faith-based civil society organisations in transitional justice, see Boesenecker and Vinjamuri (2011).

36 In Tunisia, there has indeed been some effort, at least from the truth commission, to offer a broader narrative of conflict and repression that includes their colonial roots (see also the conclusion).

37 This perspective does not fit with prominent perspectives on norms in international relations: "[N]ew norms *never enter a normative vacuum* but instead emerge in a highly contested normative space where they must compete with other norms and perceptions of interest" (Finnemore and Sikkink 1998, 897; my emphasis).

38 Amitav Acharya (2004, 243), referring to Checkel (1998), notes that norm diffusion would happen more rapidly when there is resonance with domestic norms, therefore acknowledging the importance of resonance but also implying that diffusion would be possible, if slower, without it. Acharya criticises the

statist character of this notion, assuming that there is a match, rather than the necessity of matchmaking.

39 Personal observations, Tunisian NCA (Bardo Palace), Tunis, spring of 2014. Following Laura Nader (1997), it is possible to see this 'coercive compromise' as a controlling process, a power manifestation producing order of a repressive sort because it delegitimises any kind of friction.

40 According to an interview in Gafsa with a Tunisian representative of an international NGO, internationalised initiatives sometimes have a stronger presence in the marginalised regions than the central government does. Personal interview, Gafsa, October 2015.

3

Initiating transitional justice

Scholars researching transitional justice processes often deem it remarkable that transitional justice measures, and especially a planned process, were initiated so quickly in Tunisia after the fall of the regime in 2011, while the country was in the midst of a political transition.[1] Prompt and robust engagement with the past, particularly through criminal trials, has been the exception rather than the norm in other cases (Fletcher, Weinstein, and Rowen 2009, 204).[2] Early engagement in Tunisia was in part a result of the global state of transitional justice, in which dealing with the past after conflict or authoritarian rule has become a norm. There is now a machinery in place that allows the 'justice industry' to react quickly to political transitions. Measures are introduced in a timely manner in the form of planned, professionalised projects with the support of international organisations and NGOs. However, the early initiatives also fit the Tunisian context well and have been an important feature of the political reconfigurations taking place in the country since the uprisings. Still, the carefully planned initiatives for dealing with the past were only the second step of the process.

It was possible to launch a transitional justice process in Tunisia thanks to a window of opportunity and the "revolutionary spirit"[3] that came along with the 2010/11 uprisings and the ouster of the former authoritarian leader, Ben Ali. The initial measures to deal with Tunisia's repressive and violent past were introduced before the end of 2011, in a very timely manner after the fall of the regime. These ad hoc measures[4] comprised a diverse set of trials – making them an exception to the norm, according to Laurel Fletcher and colleagues (2009) – compensation measures, as well as investigative commissions and provisions for vetting and lustration. Since these initial steps towards accountability and justice were introduced so soon after the ouster of Ben Ali, when a new legal and political order was not yet in place, they were mainly introduced on the basis of 'old-regime' legislation and institutions. This chapter begins with an overview of early transitional justice activities after the revolution. It then shows how transitional justice evolved in relation to the political transition, structured by the processual characteristics identified in the analytical framework.

Early transitional justice measures

Trials and other legal measures

In this stage, legal accountability measures were established within the structures of the 'general' or 'normal' judicial framework[5] and according to legal provisions that had been in place under dictatorship. Two different kinds of courts held trials to address the crimes of the Ben Ali regime and his 'clan' (see Chapter 1). On the one hand, military tribunals heard cases concerning 'the martyrs and wounded of the revolution,' which examined the deaths and injuries of protesters during the disturbances between 17 December 2010 and 14 January 2011. During this period, 132 protesters had been killed by the regime's security forces and many more were injured across the country.[6] According to NGOs such as Amnesty International and Human Rights Watch,[7] "[m]any of the deaths and injuries, [...] resulted from the security forces' excessive use of force" (Human Rights Watch 2015; see also Amnesty International 2011). These crimes were investigated by a fact-finding commission established by the interim government.[8] Subsequently, the civil judicial authorities launched criminal investigations and issued indictments against alleged perpetrators. By May 2011, they had determined that the cases should be transferred to military courts because the accused were members of the security forces. Proceedings took place in the permanent first instance military courts in Tunis, Le Kef, and Sfax. These three military tribunals examined crimes committed in different parts of the country through group trials in Tunis and Le Kef and trials of individuals in Sfax. More than fifty former government officials and members of the state security forces were brought to trial before military tribunals in late 2011 (Human Rights Watch 2015). Ben Ali was sentenced to life in prison, while the others received shorter prison sentences of around twenty years. In October 2012, the trials went to the military court of appeal. The appeal court delivered its judgments on 12 April 2014, significantly reducing the sentences for most defendants, though not for Ben Ali.[9]

The civil courts tried Ben Ali, his wife, and members of the clan for corruption and embezzlement of public funds. In June 2011, Ben Ali and Leila Trabelsi were convicted by a civil criminal court for embezzlement and misuse of public funds and sentenced to thirty-five years in prison (see e.g. Aboueldahab 2017, 60). Since the uprisings, the Tunisian authorities have also tried to 'unfreeze' funds embezzled by the Ben Ali/Trabelsi clan and stored in Swiss bank accounts. The Swiss authorities froze several million euros in the wake of the uprisings, which was money "suspected of being 'laundered' or gained via 'participation in a criminal organisation'" (Keller 2015).

In both types of trial, Ben Ali, and his family in the civil trials, were convicted in absentia, since they had been in exile in Saudi Arabia since January 2011. Although the interim government of Mohamed Ghannouchi officially issued an international arrest warrant for the former president, mainly in connection with alleged economic crimes, securing his extradition from Saudi Arabia was not a political priority (Human Rights Watch 2015).[10] Less relevant but still worthy of mention here is that Tunisia joined the International Criminal Court (ICC) during the early transition phase in February 2011, showing a commitment to international criminal justice (Preysing 2016, 106).[11] However, this step does not have any retrospective effect on the prosecution of crimes committed under the old regime.

Political measures

Like the courts, the commissions of inquiry and reform were technically remnants of the old regime, since Ben Ali had announced their establishment in the last days of his rule "as a late attempt to appease public outrage" (Lamont and Boujneh 2012, 39). The three commissions established in 2011 covered three different areas: corruption, human rights abuses during the revolution and the initial transition period, and political reform.[12] Vetting or lustration – that is, the exclusion of certain actors from political or bureaucratic functions – also took place in the early stage of the transition. First, the RCD and the dreaded secret police were dissolved. Probably the most important initiative was the barring of Ben Ali-era officials from running for office in the elections to the NCA in October 2011. A new electoral law, which regulated these elections, included an article (Article 15) which determined the groups of individuals that would be prohibited from standing as candidates, including "individuals who held ministerial office under Ben Ali, individuals with senior positions of responsibility within the RCD, and individuals who publicly called for Ben Ali to seek an additional term in office in August 2010" (Lamont and Boujneh 2012, 41).

Reparation or compensation measures introduced in the early stages of the transition were mainly intended to benefit two groups of people: first, those injured and the families of those killed by security forces during the period between 17 December 2010 and 14 January 2011, commonly referred to as the 'martyrs and wounded of the revolution'; and second, former political prisoners. The 'martyrs and wounded of the revolution' received financial redress, as well as "aid and privileges to victims or their families in the form of a monthly salary and free transport and medical treatment."[13] Symbolic forms of rehabilitation included the formal recognition of the 'martyrs';[14] communal initiatives, such as streets being renamed after the martyrs, were also encouraged.[15] These measures relate to both "major families of justice claims" (Fraser 2005, 69): socio-economic redistribution and legal or cultural recognition.

A 'general amnesty' granted by Mohamed Ghannouchi's short-lived interim government provided for the release of political prisoners and compensation for those who had been wrongly convicted. It is worth noting here that a general amnesty in this context means that the reasons for the original conviction were treated as if they had never happened, in contrast to merely lifting the punishment.[16] The government's intention of releasing political prisoners of the old regime had already been announced in January 2011, only six days after the fall of the regime, and the corresponding decree law was promulgated on 19 February 2011. Beneficiaries included former members of the political opposition as well as trade unionists and human rights activists (OFPRA 2014). Those convicted for the following reasons were also eligible to benefit from the amnesty:

> Violation of the internal security of the State; Activities relating to breach of the press code [...]; Activities relating to breach of the provisions relating to associations, political parties, public assembly and demonstrations [...]; [p]ublic order crimes or military crimes, where there is evidence that the convicted persons were targeted for trade union or political activity.[17]

Reparation measures included compensation for former prisoners, as well as the possibility of returning to their jobs or receiving favourable access to public-sector employment.[18] According to the figures provided by the UN Human Rights Council, a total of around 8,700 amnesty certificates were granted and more than five hundred political prisoners released.[19] Islamists of various ideological currents made up a large part of the beneficiaries of the general amnesty. Those who were released not only included sympathisers of the previously prohibited Ennahda party but everyone imprisoned under the 2003 anti-terrorism law, including radical Salafists, some of whom had fought abroad (International Crisis Group 2013).

Steps towards institutionalisation

This initial stage also involved steps towards an institutionalisation and bureaucratisation of transitional justice, in which a planned, newly codified process was initiated, as opposed to relying only on ad hoc measures and 'old-regime' institutions. In December 2011, a Ministry for Human Rights and Transitional Justice was established.[20] It was headed by Samir Dilou of Ennahda, who is a lawyer and former political prisoner. An institution to examine cases of corruption, the National Instance to Fight Corruption (Instance Nationale de Lutte Contre la Corruption; INLUCC), was established in November 2011. Although INLUCC 'inherited' cases dating from 1987 to 2011, its mandate is not limited to dealing with the past, as it also examines cases of corruption that have taken place since the revolution.[21]

Meanwhile, preliminary explorations were taking place regarding the potential start of the ICTJ's engagement in the country. These were initially coordinated by a Tunisian law professor, Wahid Ferchichi, who also served in the Amor Commission, in cooperation with the New York-based staff of the NGO. These initial explorations also prompted the engagement of other actors involved in transitional justice,[22] with new Tunisian NGOs being created to deal explicitly with the issue of transitional justice. Domenica Preysing mentions here the example of the Centre de Tunis pour la justice transitionnelle, founded in September 2011 (Preysing 2016, 96). Another example is the Coordination nationale pour la justice transitionnelle, which aimed at "pushing the process in the direction of a strategic and viable process,"[23] mainly by advocating for a transitional justice law. Thus, in this early stage we can already see a shift from ad hoc measures based on pre-existing/old-regime legislation and institutions to the institutionalisation and planning of transitional justice measures (see table 3.1). This planning and institutionalisation was advanced by political and civil society actors, as well as international transitional justice professionals.

Interplay of planned and unplanned processes

The fall of the Ben Ali regime – and the "fluctuating balance of power" (Elias 1978, 131) that emerged in its wake – had significant consequences for the figurations that influenced planned and unplanned processes of change. To start with, the initial approach to forming an interim government – planned process of change – included old-regime figures in the cabinet. This set-up, however, provoked further public protests – unplanned dynamics – which were answered by Prime Minister Mohamed Ghannouchi with a cabinet reshuffle and the removal of former RCD members from the government. When the protests continued, Ghannouchi was forced to step down. He was succeeded by Beji Caid Essebsi, who stayed in office until December 2011, when he was succeeded by Hamadi Jebali of Ennahda. Thus, the interim government, which led the country to the NCA elections in October 2011, was purged of Ben Ali-era political figures. However, it is necessary to keep in mind at this point that interim Prime Minister Essebsi was already a well-known figure in Tunisian politics. He had held several ministerial

Table 3.1 Table summarising measures and purpose for the stage of *initiating transitional justice*

Ad hoc accountability/justice measures	Referring to
Military trials	Violence during revolution
Civil trials	Corruption and embezzlement
Investigation commissions	Human rights violations, corruption, political reform
Vetting	Role in old regime
Reparation/compensation measures	Human rights violations
Followed by ⇩ First institutionalisation	Referring to
Ministry for Human Rights and Transitional Justice	Official transitional justice project
INLUCC	Corruption: inheriting cases of investigation commission, but also current cases
Exploration for planned project	Official transitional justice project

posts under Tunisia's first president Habib Bourguiba, including the Ministry of Interior – which is usually perceived as being at the heart of the 'deep state.'[24] Thus his leadership could have been controversial to some parts of society because of his previous political experience.

In this stage, with several different dynamics playing a role, it is not easy to decipher and distinguish what was planned and institutionalised and what was unplanned, both with respect to the general social and political dynamics and the realm of transitional justice. A "bureaucratic jungle" (Preysing 2016, 146) emerged during the early transition period that victims and their representatives (and probably not only them) found hard to navigate, as various transitional justice institutions and initiatives were working in parallel and were at times even contradictory.

Planned accountability measures and their unplanned dimensions

As mentioned above, in the early stage of the transition no officially planned transitional justice project was initiated. But planned institutionalised processes of change took place in a number of areas that touched upon, interacted with, or could be labelled transitional justice measures. Especially in the fields of vetting, institutional reform, and compensation, the lines between what could be considered transitional justice and other processes aimed at initiating political change are blurred. They can only be distinguished in an artificial sense, since Tunisian actors rarely agree on the question of what belongs to transitional justice and what does not, with many not regarding these early measures as being 'transitional justice' at all.[25] What is conventionally considered to be transitional justice is easier to distinguish in the following stage, since the process evolved from scattered ad hoc measures to a more planned and streamlined approach to transitional justice. In this context, the ad hoc accountability measures followed what was described to me as 'normal' procedures.[26] While these were institutionalised as legal procedures under the old regime, their use in a political transition was unplanned. Here, the institutionalised nature of the legal procedures themselves stems from them having been deeply embedded in the power structures of the old regime and being "nurtured" (Preysing 2016, 99) by them. This in turn interacts with their application in an unplanned situation, and the institutions therefore suffered from a lack of trust in their independence and their ability to deliver justice in the transitional context.

Measures of transitional governance and their transitional justice dimension

In the immediate aftermath of the revolution, the 'High Commission for the Fulfilment of Revolutionary Goals, Political Reform, and Democratic Transition' (referred to as the Ben Achour Commission below),[27] as an institutionalised force initiating change, was primarily geared towards organising transitional authority. The commission was initially established on 17 January 2011 as the 'Higher Political Reform Commission.' However, after Mohamed Ghannouchi's resignation the commission was merged with the Council for the Defence of the Revolution (Mandraud 2011) and granted a mandate beyond political reform, including the responsibilities of transitional governance. For example, the Ben Achour Commission suspended the 1959 Constitution and substituted it with a decree law regulating the provisional organisation of public authority.[28] The commission was broad in its representation.[29] However, the literature differs over the extent to which it was able to 'craft' the democratic transition and therefore induce a socio-technological, planned process of change: while Alfred Stepan (2012, 92) views it as a success, journalistic reports, such as that by Eileen Byrne (2011), suggest a more cumbersome process influenced by spontaneous dynamics and frictions which made it hard to reach agreements among the different actors.

In April 2011, an Independent High Authority for Elections (Instance Supérieure Indépendante pour les Élections; ISIE) was established by decree,[30] followed in May by another decree regulating elections to the NCA.[31] These decrees played a part in determining who was allowed to run in the elections to the NCA. The electoral laws consequently functioned as a means for vetting those seeking public office (Lamont 2013). The 2011 elections accordingly resulted in a 'vetted' NCA that would function as the country's legislature for the next three years, significantly altering the political figuration and power relations: the rules and election results shifted legislative power towards those who had been powerless under the old regime (cf. Elias 1978, [1986] 2006). Those previously in power were excluded from participating in transitional political institutions, and the election results benefitted actors (mainly, but not only, from Ennahda) who had previously not had any access to the political process. This vetted legislative setting, and the exclusion of certain actors from institutionalised transitional politics, paved the way for designing and establishing the official, institutionalised transitional justice project. Consequently, many provisions in both process and results would indeed prove controversial, as discussed further below.

'Myth' or rumours as unplanned dynamics

Let us now turn to what Elias calls "forces of collectives fantasies" (Elias [1986] 2006, 114; own translation). These fantasies, which subsume rumours, 'myths,' and conspiracy narratives with varying levels of substantiation, help to fill "gaps in understanding" (Elias 1978, 27) and are particularly influential because of their emotional dimension. During this initial stage, common beliefs or myths about Ennahda's "hidden radical agenda" (Boubekeur 2016, 113), as well as its 'proper' intentions in seeking power and introducing certain policy measures, played important roles in the political dynamic, as they fostered a polarisation of the political discourse (Preysing 2016, 89–91) and a political culture of "bargained competition" (Boubekeur 2016, 107). These in turn interacted with institutionalised processes of change.

Even before Ennahda won the elections to the NCA, "a group of small parties, many of them associated with the RCD, [had] been stirring public anxiety" (Byrne 2011) over the possibility of Ennahda doing well in the elections. There was a fear that Ennahda would try to overturn the civil state and establish a religious one (Thornton 2014) with restrictions on women's rights and the introduction of sharia law. After the elections, when Ennahda was heading the government, these rumours were fuelled by attempts to introduce policy measures that could be interpreted as going in this exact direction (Charrad and Zarrugh 2014; Ben Hafaiedh and Zartman 2015). However, Ennahda usually backpedalled when such attempts were met with public protest (see e.g. Charrad and Zarrugh 2014, 240). As indicated above, these dynamics were not directly related to transitional justice but had more to do with the future face of the Tunisian state. Thus, since there was no clean slate on which the new order could be built, rumours or 'collective fantasies' about a certain group's agenda had influence on the transition in general and indirectly on the transitional justice process, since they hampered trust-building – a goal that transitional justice sets out to achieve.

A factor that may also have contributed to this polarisation and lack of trust was the "net of fear" (Hibou 2011, 81) created by the old regime, which did not disappear with the official dissolution of the secret police. Fear of the Islamists had been fostered under the Ben Ali regime, and the Islamists in turn feared the return of those who had politically and economically marginalised them for decades. Since the structures of the 'deep state' did not vanish when the respective institutions were dismantled, there were persistent rumours about the hidden nexuses of power. Ben Ali's "divide-and-rule tactics" still had an impact in this respect, producing a "hangover" (Thornton 2014) that strengthened the Islamist–secularist divide. Several approaches towards institutionalised, planned processes of change therefore interplayed with structural remnants of the old order that did not come to a halt with the fall of the regime (and therefore lacked trust), or with ad hoc initiatives that lacked a comprehensive strategy. Efforts at transitional justice, even though they may not necessarily have been labelled as such, can be found both within the planned processes of change and the ad hoc initiatives interplaying with them. Planned processes interacted further with spontaneous political and social dynamics, culminating in public protest and unrest, which in turn influenced the planned approaches to change (see also Elias 1977).

Non-linearity, trends, and counter-trends

In this early stage, it quickly became clear that processes of social and political change, including transitional justice, are not linear (see also Elias 1977, [1986] 2006). Although in this initial phase there was a willingness to deal with the repressive past and pursue accountability, counter-trends to this approach also began to emerge.

No 'business as usual'? Pursuing accountability

While the initial appointment of an interim government that included figures from the former ruling party pointed more towards inclusion than accountability, this quickly changed in the weeks and months after the revolution.

The removal of former RCD members from the interim government in the wake of public protests shows a general unwillingness at that time to accept a 'business-as-usual' approach to politics on the societal level, and suggests that the political leadership was following this trend. The initial steps taken towards implementing measures of justice displayed a will to pursue accountability for both political and economic crimes. The political leadership and members of the security forces were tried for human rights violations, while the wider family of Ben Ali was convicted of economic crimes. There were investigation commissions for both types of crimes: the Bouderbala Commission was given the mandate of examining human rights violations during the uprisings, while the Amor Commission was tasked with looking into corruption and embezzlement.

According to one of my interview partners, "in 2011, the priority of priority was transitional justice,"[32] and the topic was on the agenda of all the main political parties.[33] In general, in 2011–12, transitional justice, understood in a broader sense as ad hoc justice measures introduced in transition, was also on the agenda of the interim governments. In a more institutionalised logic, the 'Troika' government and Ennahda, as well as other political and civil society actors, strongly advocated for transitional justice. Thus, it is important to pay attention to two different dynamics: on the one hand, the abovementioned ad hoc measures, which in part followed old-regime logics and procedures,[34] and on the other hand the first steps towards institutionalising transitional justice in new bodies that had not existed under the old regime, with the establishment of the Ministry for Human Rights and Transitional Justice. Both dynamics show a trend towards a general willingness to deal with the past, while the creation of the new institutions can be seen as a trend towards a more comprehensive process.

Empathy for victims and political opponents?

Returning briefly to the theoretical foundations of this analysis, Elias sees the development of empathy for groups other than one's own as a crucial process of social change. In turn, as a counter-trend, empathy towards others can also erode over time (Elias [1986] 2006, 116–17). These processes of engagement and distancing are related to what Elias calls the societal level of fear and danger (Elias [1987] 2003), a concept that can easily be applied to the present case-study: for the norm or "global values package" (Levitt and Merry 2011, 89) of transitional justice[35] to resonate in different parts of society, the development of empathy for other parts of society is crucial. However, when this empathy begins to fade, the potential for the global values package of transitional justice to be appropriated and establish roots in society declines. Thus, a counter-trend in the sense of the present case-study would mean the *reduction of reach* of the idea that violence against groups other than one's own should not remain unaccounted for, and that members of groups other than one's own who have suffered from repression and atrocities should be able to identify their perpetrators and the systemic logics behind violent rule.

During the revolution, there was a comparatively high degree of empathy for different actors among the various groups within society. The revolution spread from the southern and interior regions to the north and the coastal areas (Ayeb 2011). Amin Allal analyses how even previous supporters of the RCD, who had benefitted from the system and their membership of the ruling party, started sympathising with the revolutionaries due to the atrocities committed by the security forces (Allal 2012, 830). The 2010/11 events have been described as the "crowning moment of [...] collaborative revolutionism" (Gana 2013, 14) across different segments of society. Internal discontent within the RCD had been developing prior to the revolution because some perceived the party to have "transformed into a repressive interest group" (Wolf 2018, 250). Former RCD politicians also spoke of the "excesses" (Wolf 2018, 251; quoting from an interview) of previous policies towards the Islamists and their doubts about the previous criminalisation of Ennahda (although most of the members of the RCD's Political Bureau had neither voiced concern about these policies nor done anything to counter them).

Hence, at this stage it would appear that there was a relatively high level of empathy, as is also suggested by the initial willingness to pursue accountability for human rights violations and economic crimes. However, 'the Islamists' – who make up a large part of the victims of the old regime and of the population of the marginalised southern and interior regions –continued to face distrust. Their suffering was often not taken seriously and not deemed worthy of compensation.[36] It is hard to establish whether empathy in this regard diminished because of the impression of favouritism in transitional justice measures (especially reparations) towards one group or because of the Islamists' transitional politics more generally. The question of "who is included in, and who excluded from, the circle of those entitled to a just distribution and reciprocal recognition" (Fraser 2005, 75) is, however, crucial for the political dimension of justice. The impression that the formerly victimised group is perpetuating old-regime practices[37] of unjust distribution, nepotism, and partial recognition of suffering may well lead to a feedback loop and contribute to an erosion of empathy towards its members – to the detriment of the overall transitional justice project.

Limited vetting, no reform: staged justice?

The ambiguity and thus non-linearity of seeking accountability can also be seen in those cases where justice seems to have been delivered at first sight. Thus a counter-trend to seeking accountability emerged in the form of resistance to the pursuit of more comprehensive institutional reforms. That the 'old justice system,' and especially the military tribunals for the cases of the 'martyrs and wounded of the revolution,' was charged with holding old-regime figures accountable was particularly problematic.[38] Preysing shows that the legal proceedings against Ben Ali and his circle were mainly framed in the notion of 'theatre' in the Tunisian media, since the judiciary was viewed as incapable of delivering independent judgments, with the trials merely being intended to serve the purpose of "appeasing the Tunisian public" (Preysing 2016, 99–100). Indeed, many of my interview partners described a lack of trust in the pre-existing institutions.[39] This sentiment was accentuated by the perception that any critique from international watchdogs at this time was, according to one human rights specialist, "met with total indifference and silence from the rulers and from the lawmakers."[40] And while there was ample criticism of the fact that cases concerning the deaths and injuries of protesters were referred to military rather than civil courts – as only the accused and not the victims were members of the security forces – the civil judicial system also lacked credibility. According to a representative of the Ministry of Justice,[41] "the problem is in the whole system of justice, not only with military justice. There is no difference between military and civil tribunals" in that respect.[42] He added that in some cases the military judicial system was actually perceived as "less aggressive"[43] than the civil courts. As an example, he mentioned judgments against Islamists in the 1990s. A judicial system that colluded with the old regime is perceived as having been one of the pillars of Ben Ali's rule: "Ben Ali was a dictator because of the judiciary. [...] So, the judiciary is important. One needs to reform the judiciary."[44]

However, attempts at justice sector reform, though perceived as essential by many of my interview partners,[45] were mainly pursued in a purely symbolic manner: "They screwed some magistrates at some points, but there were no clear criteria. They had no clear idea whether they wanted to do a proper vetting."[46] This is similar for the security services with respect to the secret police. While the secret police had officially been dissolved following the revolution, the underlying structures of the 'deep state' did not suddenly vanish. No real effort was made to dismantle these structures, and Ennahda instead tried to counterbalance old-regime dominance of these institutions by appointing their own people rather than initiating a proper vetting process (International Crisis Group 2014).

In this stage, we can thus see a general trend towards seeking knowledge about, and accountability for, the crimes committed under the former regime, both in the economic and the political spheres, compensating victims, and vetting some of those involved in the political system. However, other tendencies were also visible, specifically a lack of will or ability to purge the political, bureaucratic, judicial, and security systems. These trends did not occur in a linear manner but simultaneously and sometimes even seemed to be at odds with each other. In general, accountability measures tend to target the political leadership more than the underlying structures or the system as a whole (Lamont and Pannwitz 2016, 279). Moreover, at this stage, transitional justice efforts were undertaken in an uncoordinated, piecemeal way rather than according to a comprehensive strategy (Ferchichi 2011, 244). However, initial steps were taken towards the institutionalisation of transitional justice with the establishment of the Ministry for Human Rights and Transitional Justice in December 2011 and with civil society beginning to advocate for a transitional justice law.

International interconnectedness

These early stages of the transitional justice efforts were marked by domestic Tunisian action that often relied on previously existing rules and institutions. As such, international interconnectedness does not seem to have played a crucial role in the planned initiatives or the unplanned dynamics of change. However, given that such far-reaching processes of change rarely remain confined to domestic boundaries (Elias 1978, 168–9), on closer examination it is possible to trace international influence even in this initial stage. Several international governmental and non-governmental organisations either observed and commented on the ad hoc measures of justice or became involved with them once they had been introduced. Human Rights Watch, for example, monitored several sessions of both the group trials at the courts of first instance and the appeal court and commented on them in their reports (Human Rights Watch 2015). A representative of the organisation stated in an interview that their starting point was that "in order to have a break with the legacy of the past, we need to have trials and prosecutions which are effective and fair and lead to justice for the victims and fair trials for the perpetrators."[47] That is why they felt a need to support accountability measures.

An influx of transitional justice expertise

The ICTJ and UN agencies (UNDP, OHCR) started their work in Tunisia in early 2011.[48] Habib Nassar identifies a "post-Arab Spring transitional justice landscape [characterised by] the horde of international actors that have deployed their personnel in the region to promote transitional justice and offer their expertise" (Nassar 2014, 69). Initially, the involvement of the 'justice industry' was generally welcomed by the Tunisian authorities and civil society representatives.[49] As mentioned above, initial explorations by the ICTJ went alongside the formation of domestic NGOs dedicated to the issue, which then joined forces in advocating for a planned and institutionalised transitional justice project. In addition, several international conferences took place convened by the ICTJ in partnership with the UN's OHCHR, Tunisian partners, the Arab Institute for Human Rights, as well as LTDH (Preysing 2016, 107).

Interconnectedness comes to the fore through conferences, international organisations, and NGOs setting up offices and programmes, hiring Tunisian staff as well as sending international staff to the country. But it also manifests in the transfer of norms, discourse, and knowledge of transitional justice. While most domestic actors may initially have had only a limited knowledge of the concept,[50] they nevertheless started adopting a language of transitional justice early on (Preysing 2016, 95). They also began to vernacularise the concept by using it in literal translation[51] while filling it with specific meanings (Salehi 2019). Moreover, Tunisia started "becoming 'part of the club'" (Preysing 2016, 106) of adherents to international criminal/transitional justice norms. In addition to joining the ICC and other international treaties and conventions in 2011,[52] the adoption of a language of transitional justice based on international expertise, situating Tunisia within this discourse, as well as the domestic appropriation of transitional justice concepts, also became part of this process.

General increase of international attention and donor activities

Looking beyond the narrowly defined area of transitional justice, the crucial domestic–international dynamic in this stage can be identified as broader engagement or intervention in the transitional situation: the political and financial support of foreign governments and international organisations and NGOs for the political transition and the pursuit of democratic reforms. The uprisings and Tunisia's perceived role as a vanguard of regional democracy, as well as its status as the "birthplace of the Arab Spring" (Kausch 2013), encouraged donors to increase their financial aid. Thus, transitional justice is only one field of transitional politics and policy in which international actors have provided funding and expertise. Specific to the transitional context, international involvement brought about a new figuration of actors interacting with each other, since prior to the revolution political engagement by foreign organisations had been subject to numerous restrictions that effectively blocked their involvement in Tunisia (see e.g. Bush 2015). As with transitional justice, Tunisian actors generally welcomed the international technical and financial support in designing new legal and political frameworks during the transitional period (Kausch 2013, 1–2; Bush 2015, 190). International funding and support also helped to build up civil society structures, though more in the cities than in the rural areas. Jelena Obradovic-Wochnik remarks that this unequal distribution of resources and inequality in the implementation of externally funded projects produces new "*governing agents* [who are] able to discipline and regulate other local actors' voices" (Obradovic-Wochnik 2018, 2; emphasis in the original) and therefore produces new inequalities and power asymmetries. However, despite the overall welcoming of funding and expertise, some feared that foreign funding had the potential to influence the electoral process (Ennahda, for instance, received support from the Gulf countries, while other parties were regarded as 'favourites' of Western governments). Thus Kristina Kausch (2013, 6–8) reports that civil society actors often carefully enquired about the origin of donors' money. In general, given that support both in terms of money and expertise is often linked to bureaucratic requirements,[53] those actors that were already better organised, and whose 'capacities' had already been better built, inevitably found it easier to benefit from increased international attention and donor activities.

Thus, while the ad hoc measures of transitional justice may have been purely domestic initiatives, international interconnectedness did play a role even at this early stage. International experts and donors provided both expertise and financial means for the pursuit of a democratic transition more generally as well as for the launch of a planned transitional justice project. International actors also commented on the ad hoc measures and did advocacy work for a planned, institutionalised transitional justice project. Tunisian actors mostly welcomed this international engagement, and those who were involved in the transfer of knowledge and expertise quickly adopted, but also appropriated, the concepts to hand. However, already at this stage it became clear that international influence played an important role in shaping ideas about what transitional justice and the democratic transition more generally should look like. Likewise, the steps taken at this stage also indicate the role of knowledge transfer and the provision of and access to material and immaterial resources in determining who may play a part in transitional justice and in shaping the future Tunisian state.

Conflict and friction

Conflict and friction are important drivers for processes of social and political change (Elias 1978), especially for transitional justice, which is embedded in conflict, and influence both planned processes and unplanned social and political dynamics. Both can emerge from conflict and friction, or they can be steered in a particular direction by them. In general, in this stage the conflict and friction that influenced the processes analysed here occurred at several levels and in a cross-cutting manner between different actors in the figurations. They were cross-cutting depending on which actors had frictional or conflictive encounters, and they differed in type with regard to their origins and consequences and with respect to how they became noticeable.

Transitional struggles, in institutions and on the street

This initial stage was still marked by post-revolutionary conflict, which was expressed in public unrest. As mentioned above, the protests did not stop with the ouster of Ben Ali. In the immediate aftermath of the revolution, protests were directed at overturning the interim government, which included Ben Ali-era politicians and did not represent a clear break from the repressive past. The protests were later related to the substance of transitional politics and the debates over the future of the country. Here, we can see friction between different political actors, roughly divided between the Islamists and the secularists and later between the 'Troika' government and the opposition. There was also a growing polarisation of the political debate, culminating in an 'us-or-them' logic (Preysing 2016, 90). Before the elections to the NCA, for example, these frictions came to the fore in the Ben Achour Commission. Although the commission was a particularly successful "consensus-building bod[y] in the history of 'crafted' democratic transitions" (Stepan 2012, 92), negotiations within the commission did not proceed without conflict. Political parties, in particular Ennahda, repeatedly pulled out of the meetings because they did not feel that the commission was representative. By his own account, Ben Achour "went running after" (Byrne 2011) them to reach an agreement.

During this period, and intensifying after the elections, "street politics, which occasionally turned violent, competed with [...] the formal institutional process" (Boubekeur 2015, 1). The protests were initiated both by secular and Islamist actors, and mobilisation was used as a means of doing politics. Thus, next to controversial political initiatives or actions that triggered unrest, the abovementioned mistrust between different political actors and their supporters in society was an important factor in producing friction.

Questions of inclusion and exclusion

The electoral law (specified by decrees) determined those who were not eligible to run in the 2011 elections as those who had held government positions under Ben Ali; those who had held positions within the former ruling party, the RCD, at the national or the local level; and those who had signed a petition in August 2010 calling for Ben Ali to stand as a candidate in the presidential elections scheduled for 2014 (Carter Center 2012, 18).[54] These rules excluding former members and supporters of the old regime from running in the NCA elections were met with criticism and produced friction in the transitional figuration. According to the Carter Center (2012, 18), the ISIE, which was responsible for determining which individuals would be included on the first two lists – government responsibilities under Ben Ali and responsibilities within the RCD – did not have access to the RCD's own archives and had to rely on the National Archives Office and the country's official gazette. The names included on the list, however, were not matched with national identity card numbers, leading to confusion when people had the same names. This also made it possible for former RCD officials to go unnoticed and be elected, as happened with a former RCD official in one of the constituencies for Tunisians living in France (Carter Center 2012, 18). The last category was especially controversial, since some of the people affected had not even been notified that their names had been included on the list. Others successfully managed to contest their inclusion and have their names removed. One of my interview partners criticised this criterion, stating that those who had signed the petition had been approached to give a statement of whether Ben Ali should *run* again in 2014, which is not the same as saying that he should *win* again. Despite not necessarily supporting Ben Ali's politics, they had not really been in a position to say no. My interview partner concluded that "they did nothing wrong"[55] and that their exclusion was unfair. Therefore, so his argument went, this criterion deprived Tunisia's transitional politics of many intellectuals who would have been an asset to the NCA. This exclusionary measure had a particularly conflictive potential because the signatories did not necessarily have a strong party affiliation and were drawn from various fields of social life.

Moreover, the implementation of the general amnesty went against the logic of carefully vetting public employees and establishing a carefully designed reparations scheme. It therefore led to an intensification of friction and conflict. The appointments to public-sector jobs within the framework of the general amnesty led to friction for several reasons. On the one hand, the beneficiaries were often ill-qualified for the positions to which they were appointed (Ben Hafaiedh and Zartman 2015, 65).[56] On the other hand, the Ennahda government was accused of using the general amnesty to alter the personnel structure in public institutions by bringing in the party's own followers. There was also an accusation that reparations would only benefit those with influence,[57] with the compensation measures being seen as having mainly benefitted Ennahda's supporters, and especially those with access to power. The measures consequently created an impression of favouritism, a perpetuation of old-regime practices,[58] and the creation of 'new' injustices:

> The reparations introduced by the Nahda government are a big mess. They are too complicated, even for their own victims. You needed luck to get something, especially when you were far away from Tunis, for example in Gafsa. There was no training for people taking the jobs. But they thought they needed to do something and created the myth that everybody will get tons of money. But they know that they did a mess and agreed to an evaluation.[59]

The introduction of these measures, and how they were communicated, raised several expectations that remained unfulfilled. Measures aimed at rectifying past injustices provoked new friction and feedback loops. Leftist activists often rejected the idea of reparations, believing that they were morally superior because, as they explained, justice was not about money,[60] while other victims who benefitted from the compensation measures were accused of having been bought off by the Ennahda government in exchange for supporting the Islamist party.[61] They were asked "how much for a kilo of your militancy?,"[62] implying not only that their political convictions were for sale, but also that they did not deserve the compensation they had received. Discursive connections were also made between those released within the framework of the general amnesty and terrorist activities, leading one of my interview partners to conclude that a badly executed amnesty can entail "catastrophes for the country and hence, new injustices,"[63] especially in a strongly polarised political climate (see also Kazemi 2019, 605).

Friction over institutionalisation of transitional justice

Frictions also emerged in this stage over the initial efforts to institutionalise transitional justice, particularly between civil society and political actors – both groups were seeking to pursue accountability in an institutionalised manner, but they differed over the approach to be used. The government made a start on institutionalisation by establishing a Ministry for Human Rights and Transitional Justice (Lamont, Quinn, and Wiebelhaus-Brahm 2019). Civil society organisations were also advocating for a more comprehensive, planned transitional justice project and an institutionalisation of transitional justice. They were especially pushing for the transitional justice project to be codified in a law: "So, our objective [...] was foremost to think about a transitional justice law. This was an immediate objective, and to push the process in the direction of a process that is strategic and viable and all that."[64] However, civil society representatives were not necessarily in favour of the creation of the ministry,[65] since they were concerned that "[t]he minister could instrumentalise the ministry for his political or electoral agenda."[66] As a former political prisoner and member of Ennahda, the relevant minister, Samir Dilou, had two attributes that prevented him being perceived as a 'neutral' personality in transitional justice.[67] One interview partner active in a civil society organisation dealing with transitional justice, who was critical of the ministry being created, stated: "Listen, regarding the transitional justice ministry – that was just a ministry of façade."[68]

There was also friction between different civil society groups over the first institutionalisation efforts. Tunisian civil society is not a homogenous mass but representative of different segments of society with different interests and convictions. For example, one civil society representative described to me how initial efforts to form an integrative alliance of civil society organisations, including secularist and Islamist groups, were not successful: at first, it was hard to lobby the secularist groups to accept the Islamist groups, and then the Islamist organisations left the secular-dominated alliance.[69] Thus, political allegiances and identity politics also played a role among civil society actors, adding another frictional layer to the process. At this stage, it was already clear that frictions were cross-cutting and alliances were not necessarily emerging spontaneously between actor-groups that are often grouped together, such as civil society.

Conclusion

In this first stage of *initiating transitional justice*, there was a trend towards seeking accountability that initially followed old-regime logics and was mainly targeted at high-level figures of the regime, including, in a broad sense, those politically responsible and the security forces, as well as Ben Ali's wider family. However, there was a simultaneous counter-trend that pointed towards a lack of willingness or inability to dismantle the system at a deeper level. Therefore, despite the introduction of individual accountability measures, measures to address the 'system' as a perpetrator remained elusive. There was little confidence in the level of justice and security that these measures could bring about. The attempts to pursue transitional justice were scattered, ad hoc, and mainly took place within the framework of pre-existing structures. However, there was nevertheless an initial trend towards an institutionalisation of the process. It is therefore possible to observe interdependencies between different institutionalised processes of political change and unplanned political and social dynamics. In this stage, institutionalised processes of change were mainly geared towards changes in the political system: elections and the creation of a new constitution. Planned accountability measures, such as the vetting of parliamentary candidates with the aim of excluding old-regime figures, evolved from efforts in other spheres rather than from the efforts to implement transitional justice. These ad hoc measures nevertheless had an influence on these planned processes of change in other spheres, as for example in co-determining who could participate in the political reconfigurations and who could not. In effect, the ad hoc measures helped to determine who could and could not play a role in transitional politics, if only to a limited degree. For instance, while some individuals were sent to prison, others were rehabilitated through the general amnesty. Consequently, the early transitional justice efforts also influenced transitional politics and the "new political architecture"[70] of the country. In this first stage, international actors had little direct influence on the ad hoc transitional justice efforts. However, there was a substantial increase in international attention directed at Tunisia, accompanied by increased donor activity and the provision of funds for the country during its transition. International NGOs dealing with human rights had also begun to monitor the ad hoc measures, and those dealing specifically with transitional justice had already started their work in the country, paving the way for more institutionalised engagement in the future. This stage was mainly marked by political struggles over the direction of the Tunisian transition and the country's future political architecture. Speculation about the intentions of the Islamists when in power and their potential lack of commitment to democratic values played a decisive role, as well as the question of the future role of old-regime actors. Thus, in this first stage, one can clearly see the intensification of conflict and friction, in a cross-cutting manner, among political and civil society actors. The emergence of new perceptions of injustice through the pursuit of justice and accountability measures played a significant role in this dynamic and also contributed to a stiffening of prejudices and the circulation of rumours about other social groups.

Transitional justice measures are one powerful tool in times of political transition that can be used to redefine the character of a country's political institutions and administrative apparatus. In Tunisia, in this initial stage, it can be concluded that they were partly introduced to fix a momentary status quo, a "snapshot of relations of social [and political] interaction" (Giddens 1979). This proved problematic in a political context that was in an extreme state of flux and was in the midst of ongoing processes of social and political change. However, in retrospect, both political and civil society actors from various political orientations commonly perceived transitional justice to have been 'delayed' in Tunisia.[71] Although "justice delayed is not [always] justice denied" (Fletcher, Weinstein, and Rowen 2009, 219), this statement does not necessarily agree with the perceptions expressed by my interview partners. As we will see in the following chapters, this perceived delay may indeed have been consequential; the post-revolutionary window of opportunity for significant, lasting reform was closing as time passed.

There are two further preliminary conclusions I would like to draw here that will be developed in the following stages. The first concerns the often binary debate over whether transitional justice is bureaucratic/technical *or* political. In this stage, what James Ferguson (1994) found for development efforts can also be said of transitional justice: technocratic measures, by their very nature, can be political too.[72] Thus, in Tunisia, certain transitional justice measures, such as the creation of the Ministry for Human Rights and Transitional Justice, were political exactly *because* of their technocratic nature, which served particular interests (see also Kennedy 2016, 3). Second, the performative nature of transitional justice measures came to the fore, exemplified through the perception of these measures as 'theatre,' 'façade,' or attempts at 'appeasement.' While this has the implication of transitional justice efforts not being genuine, it also demonstrates that they do not remain without effect. Yet by constituting something how it ought to be (see Butler 1990), "[p]erformative [...] acts have productive effects in the world; they configure worlds differently and bring something new or different into being" (Amicelle, Aradau, and Jeandesboz 2015, 298).

Notes

1 Several personal conversations, e.g. at academic conferences.
2 This may be different in war contexts with a clear victor, in which justice may then be labelled 'victor's justice.'
3 Interview with the former minister for human rights and transitional justice, Tunis, October 2015.
4 Other terms to describe them are "interim" (Lamont and Boujneh 2012, 37) or "revolutionary" (International Crisis Group 2016, 2) measures of justice.
5 Terms used by my interview partners (representatives of a civil society organisation and of an international organisation) in personal interviews; Tunis, April and May 2014.
6 The number of deaths identified by the Commission for the Investigation of Abuses Registered during the Period from 17 December 2010 until the Fulfilment of Its Objective, commonly referred to as the 'Bouderbala Commission,' is much higher at 338 because it also includes prisoners, police officers, and members of the military (Bouderbala Commission 2012). Thanks to Eileen Byrne for pointing out the large number of those who died in prison riots and not on the street (see also International Committee of the Red Cross 2011).
7 This depiction of the judicial proceedings is mainly based on the quoted Human Rights Watch report, since it offers an excellent overview of events. The report was previously available in a shorter version and updated in 2015.

8 The Bouderbala Commission (see below for further explanation).

9 The implications of this will be discussed in the next chapter.

10 There is no formal extradition accord between Tunisia and Saudi Arabia (Preysing 2016, 100). According to my interviews, it was also not a priority of civil society actors, as I will discuss further below.

11 In her study of the prosecution of political leaders after the uprisings in the Arab region in 2010/11, Noha Aboueldahab (2017, 75) points out how little importance her interview partners assigned to Tunisia joining the ICC.

12 All three commissions are commonly referred to using the names of their respective leaders: the Amor Commission (after Abdelfattah Amor; full name: Commission for the Investigation of Corruption and Embezzlement Affairs), the Bouderbala Commission (after Taoufik Bouderbala; full name: Commission for the Investigation of Abuses Registered during the Period from 17 December 2010 until the Fulfilment of Its Objective), and the Ben Achour Commission (after Yadh Ben Achour; full name: High Commission for the Fulfilment of Revolutionary Goals, Political Reform, and Democratic Transition).

13 UN Human Rights Council and Working Group on the Universal Periodic Review (2012); A/HRC/WG.6/13/TUN/1.

14 The final list of those recognised as 'martyrs and wounded of the revolution' was only published in Tunisia's official gazette in March 2021. The families of those affected have raised this issue in public hearings of the Tunisian TDC. Personal observation, Tunis, November 2016. For a critical discussion of the social construction of the category 'martyr,' see Lachenal (2019).

15 I would concur, however, that redistribution does not necessarily have to be socio-economic but could also relate to the redistribution of power, for example.

16 UN Human Rights Council and Working Group on the Universal Periodic Review (2012); A/HRC/WG.6/13/TUN/1.

17 Ibid.

18 The latter was established in the law of 22 June on recruitment in the public sector. According to International Crisis Group (2014, 9), about 10,000 Islamists profited from these provisions.

19 UN Human Rights Council and Working Group on the Universal Periodic Review (2012); A/HRC/WG.6/13/TUN/1.

20 Though the literature discusses this measure as a novelty in the field of transitional justice (see e.g. Andrieu 2016, 281), there has previously been a Ministry of National Unity, Reconciliation, and Peace in the Solomon Islands, established in 2002, which ICTJ explicitly lists as a transitional justice measure (ICTJ 2011; see also Lamont, Quinn, and Wiebelhaus-Brahm 2019).

21 According to its former director, the INLUCC inherited about 90,000 files from the Amor Commission. Personal interview, Tunis, October 2015.

22 Personal interview with the mentioned Tunisian law professor, later member of the Technical Committee, Tunis, October 2015.

23 Ibid.

24 A 'deep state' is "[a] body of people, typically influential members of government agencies or the military, believed to be involved in the secret manipulation or

control of government policy" (available at https://en.oxforddictionaries.com/ definition/deep_state (accessed 10 June 2016)). Initially coined for the Turkish context, in Tunisia the term is often used to describe the abovementioned power of the secret police and the Ministry of Interior. In several personal interviews and informal conversations in Tunisia with both Tunisians and international observers of Tunisian politics, the Ministry of Interior has been described to me as an opaque agency that has a life of its own and as being responsible, among other things, for systematic torture and political imprisonment. This role of the Ministry of Interior was also brought to the fore at the first public hearings of the Tunisian TDC (17 November 2016, personal observation).

25 Several personal interviews with representatives of civil society organisations, NCA members of various parties, Tunis, April/May 2014.

26 Cf. footnote 5.

27 Duncan Pickard describes Yadh Ben Achour as "a well-respected scholar of law and Islam" (2011, 638).

28 "Décret-loi n° 2011–14 du 23 mars 2011, portant organisation provisoire des pouvoirs publics"; available at www.wipo.int/edocs/lexdocs/laws/fr/tn/tn052fr.pdf (accessed 10 June 2018).

29 The commission had over 150 members, including members of political parties, scholars, former government officials, and representatives of the labour union (Pickard 2011).

30 "Décret-loi n° 2011–27 du 18 avril 2011 portant création d'une instance supérieure indépendante pour les élections"; available at https://legislation-securite.tn/sites/ default/files/lois/Décret-loi%20n°%202011-27%20du%2018%20Avril%20 2011%20%28Fr%29.pdf (accessed 3 August 2021).

31 "Décret-loi n° 2011–35 du 10 mai 2011, relatif à l'élection d'une assemblée nationale constituante"; available at https://constitutionnet.org/sites/default/files/ decret-loi_ndeg_2011-35_du_10_mai_2011_fr_0.pdf (accessed 3 August 2021).

32 Personal interview with head of Tunisian branch of international human rights NGO, Tunis, March 2015.

33 Ibid.; however, as he went on to mention, in 2014, the year of the next elections, the topic fell into oblivion, as will be discussed further in the third stage.

34 How far these measures were introduced according to old-regime logics varied. Trials followed old-regime procedures, the investigation commissions had been announced by Ben Ali but were established under the first interim government, the vetting criteria were determined by one of the commissions, and reparation measures introduced independently by the 'Troika.'

35 This was previously defined as based on human rights and the idea that repression and violence should not remain unaccounted for, and that those who have suffered from said repression should be aware of the perpetrators and systemic logics behind the period of violent rule.

36 Personal interview with truth commissioner, Tunis, March 2015, and personal interview with NCA member, Tunis, April 2014. See also the part on questions of exclusion and inclusion.

37 Personal interview with NCA member, Tunis, April 2014.

38 Personal interview with representatives of international NGO and the government, Tunis, 2014–15.

39 Personal interviews with representatives of civil society, international organisations, NGOs, and the government, Tunis, April/May 2014.

40 Personal interview with representative of international NGO, Tunis, May 2014.

41 At the time of the interview, the Ministry for Human Rights and Transitional Justice had been dissolved and its portfolios taken over by the Ministry of Justice.

42 Personal interview with representative of the Ministry of Justice responsible for transitional justice, Tunis, April 2014.

43 Ibid.

44 Personal interview with civil society representative of NGO of former political prisoners; Tunis, April 2014.

45 Personal interviews with civil society representatives, politicians, representatives of international organisations, and NGOs, Tunis, 2014–15.

46 Personal interview with UNDP official, Tunis, May 2014.

47 Personal interview with Tunisian representative of international human rights NGO, Tunis, May 2014.

48 Personal interview with Tunisian law professor who worked for ICTJ at that time, Tunis, October 2015. The UN OHCHR office opened in Tunisia in July 2011 (Preysing 2016, 107).

49 Several personal interviews with government and civil society representatives, Tunisia, April 2014–October 2015.

50 In 2011, Ferchichi (2011, 241) wrote about a "lack of clarity regarding the concept of transitional justice and a lack of awareness" of the relevant techniques and methods. In 2016, an interview partner who had been engaged in transitional justice in several capacities early on stated that "we asked for transitional justice without knowing what it is." Personal interview with civil society representative, member of the technical committee, Tunis, August 2016.

51 'Justice transitionnelle' in French or 'Al-adala al-intiqalia' in very simply transliterated Arabic.

52 In February 2011, Tunisia joined the ICC (formal accession in June), as well as a convention on enforced disappearances and optional protocols to the civil covenant and the torture convention (Ferchichi 2011, 243–4).

53 See Kausch (2013, 17); this was also confirmed in several personal interviews and observations in Tunis, Gafsa, and Kasserine between April 2014 and August 2016.

54 Those individuals were named 'munachidine,' meaning "those who implored" (Carter Center 2012, 18). A list of the original signatories and reaction to the petition can be found in the French weekly *L'Express*, which published an article on the issues shortly after Ben Ali's ouster in late January 2011 (Gouëset 2011).

55 Personal interview with a lawyer and frequent critic of the truth commission, Tunis, August 2016.

56 According to one of my interview partners, this measure was also transferable from the original beneficiaries to their children, which makes the measure even

more controversial. Personal interview with Ennahda politician, Tunis, May 2014.

57 The latter aspect was even mentioned by a young Ennahda politician in Tunis in the spring of 2014, who was not an MP at that point of time. Personal interview, Tunis, May 2014.

58 Personal interview with opposition NCA member, Tunis, April 2014.

59 Personal interview with UNDP official, Tunis, May 2014.

60 Personal interview with a historian who was a member of the technical committee, Tunis, May 2014, and leftist NCA member, Tunis, April 2014.

61 Observation in TDC workshop with women victims' representatives, Tunis, March 2015, field notes taken on the basis of ad hoc translation from TDC staff member.

62 Personal interview with truth commissioner, Tunis, March 2015.

63 Personal interview with history professor and politician, Tunis, March 2015.

64 Personal interview with civil society representative and member of the technical committee, Tunis, October 2015.

65 Personal interview with law professor, former secretary-general of the National Coordination for Transitional Justice, Tunis, October 2015.

66 Personal interview (in group) with civil society representative, Tunis, May 2014.

67 For a discussion of the 'apolitical illusion' (Bonnefoy 2008) in Tunisian transitional justice discourse, see Chapter 2.

68 Personal interview with civil society representative, Tunis, October 2015.

69 My interview partner said that it was the Islamist organisations who did not want to be part of that alliance and that they had left to join "networks involving only Islamist organisations" (personal interview (in group) with civil society representative, Tunis, May 2014). However, since he is a representative of the secularist spectrum, I cannot exclude potential bias in his statement.

70 Term used in personal interview with ministerial staff member, Tunis, March 2015.

71 Personal interviews with NCA members, civil society representatives, (former) government/state institution representatives, academics.

72 In a similar vein, when describing the changing nature of war through civilisation according to Eliasian sociology, Andrew Linklater (2011) emphasises the importance of harnessing bureaucratic power for the Nazis to reach their political goals.

4

Designing transitional justice

The second stage in Tunisia's transitional justice process was marked by a shift in the focus of transitional justice activities from ad hoc measures to *designing transitional justice* and the introduction of a planned transitional justice project that went beyond the first steps towards institutionalisation discussed in the previous chapter. This shift is crucial for understanding the development of transitional justice in Tunisia and how the process interacted with the volatile political context, as the planned project became the determining influence. Temporally defined, this stage encompasses the period between 2012 and 2014 and comprises the processes from the launch of the National Dialogue on Transitional Justice to the nomination of truth commissioners.

Old and new forms of transitional justice

Remnants of the ad hoc measures

Even though the focus shifted to institutionalised transitional justice efforts, some of the ad hoc measures launched in the previous stage continued in this stage, albeit often with changing dynamics. There was, for example, the military court of appeal, which delivered its judgments in the appeal cases of the 'martyrs and wounded of the revolution' in mid-2014 towards the end of this stage.[1] The judges confirmed the life sentence given to Ben Ali and upheld his conviction for complicity in murder. For other high-level defendants who had likewise been sentenced to long prison sentences, such as former interior minister Rafiq Haj Kacem,[2] the crimes were requalified and their sentences reduced from a maximum of twenty years to three. Since the ruling on their appeals specified that the time they had already served would be deducted, most of Ben Ali's security chiefs went free almost immediately (Andrieu 2016, 275). The former chief of the presidential guard, Ali Seriati,[3] for example, was released from prison in May 2014 (Huffpost

Maghreb, 2014). Subsequently, the cases were referred to the court of cassation, which meant they returned to the civil justice system.

Some of the bodies that were created in the earlier stage continued to operate in this later stage. Thus, at a point when all of the investigation commissions had ended their work, INLUCC – as the successor of the Amor Commission – continued its work on cases of current and past corruption. The work of the Bouderbala Commission, meanwhile, remained incomplete at this stage insofar as the definitive list of martyrs and wounded was only published by the Tunisian government much later. This had important consequences for compensation claims by the injured or the families of those killed.[4] This commission was not the only body tasked with producing a 'martyrs list,' as there was also a parliamentary committee within the NCA (later in the ARP), as well as the Ministry for Human Rights and Transitional Justice. These two institutions were carrying out the same task in parallel (Andrieu 2016, 288). Furthermore, other ad hoc compensation measures, such as the (re-)appointments into public-sector jobs in the wake of the general amnesty, continued to have after-effects in this stage. Those profiting from these provisions had to be integrated into their posts, despite often being ill-qualified or lacking professional experience, due in some cases to decades of exclusion or imprisonment. The uncoordinated and delayed execution of the compensation provisions related to the general amnesty led to protests by beneficiaries – as well as by would-be beneficiaries who believed they might be overlooked – and subsequently to a new decree law (El Gantri 2015, 10).

As mentioned in the previous chapter, a Ministry for Human Rights and Transitional Justice was established under the 'Troika' government at the end of 2011. However, in early 2014, under the interim technocratic government that was in power after the 'Troika' stepped down (as agreed in the National Dialogue),[5] the transitional justice portfolio was integrated into the Ministry of Justice. Here, a *chargé de mission* (Mohsen Sahbani of Ennahda), who had already been in charge of the same post in the Ministry of Human Rights and Transitional Justice, remained responsible for transitional justice.[6]

The National Dialogue on Transitional Justice

In April 2012, a broad, nationwide consultation process, the National Dialogue on Transitional Justice (hereafter 'transitional justice dialogue' to avoid confusion with the 'National Dialogue') was launched, setting in motion the official, planned transitional justice project. In Tunisia, the launch of this official transitional justice project was highly professionalised.

International experts from governmental and non-governmental organisations (in particular ICTJ and two UN agencies, the UNDP and the OHCHR) were involved with the transitional justice dialogue. A technical committee was charged with overseeing the dialogue and drafting a transitional justice law. This committee was composed of six permanent members and six deputies (both sets were made up of five members from among different networks of civil society organisations, and one representing the Ministry for Human Rights and Transitional Justice). While the ministry should have played more of an organising and mediating role in a fragmented process, it would eventually play a significant role in the national consultations leading to the drafting of the transitional justice law (Andrieu 2016, 281). Civil society representatives came from diverse backgrounds and represented several different groups and agendas,[7] including the secular as well as the Islamist part of the political spectrum. The participants included some who had had previous experience, or at least contact, with the theme of transitional justice or related issue areas. Others were victims' representatives, while some of them had taken up civic engagement within the realm of transitional justice after the uprisings. On the regional level, consultations with victims and stakeholders took place in all twenty-four governorates. In total, more than 2,000 participants took part in the regional dialogue sessions (Ministry for Human Rights and Transitional Justice 2013, 18). At the end of each consultation session, they received questionnaires about their understanding and expectations of transitional justice, twelve hundred of which were eventually filled in (Andrieu 2016, 282). Among the participants in the transitional justice dialogue, one hundred candidates were selected to be debate moderators and would receive specific "training on transitional justice, on debate moderation, on writing reports,"[8] and so on, harmonising their level of knowledge and equipping them with discursive resources.

The transitional justice law

The transitional justice law, then, was drafted by the technical committee, taking into account the questionnaires together with consultations with representatives of political parties, civil society organisations, trade unions, and the National Archives, as well as international personalities.[9] This participatory and unusually transparent law-making procedure (for Tunisian legislation, but also in comparison to other transitional justice laws) was described as challenging[10] but evoked pride among Tunisian officials: "For the first time in Tunisia, we found ourselves with a law project that was not developed behind closed doors."[11] In early November 2012, the draft law was handed over to the Minister for Human Rights and Transitional Justice who submitted it to the President and the Prime Minister. There were several rounds of comments from the legal community as well as the executive, and a ministerial council decided on the final wording before passing the law on to the NCA for approval in January 2013.[12] It was a turbulent political year, however, and the NCA took almost a year before considering the issue and putting the law on its legislative agenda.[13] The Organic Law on Establishing and Organising Transitional Justice was eventually adopted by the NCA in December 2013. The law defines violations relevant to the transitional justice process, establishes who can be a victim under the law, and provides for the establishment of a TDC (as a financially and administratively independent legal entity), as well as specialised chambers within the Tunisian court system. It also defines (more or less explicitly) who can serve on these bodies. A particularity of the law is the provision that not only individuals, but also marginalised regions can be regarded as victims (Article 10). Covering both political and economic crimes and acknowledging individual and collective suffering, the law relates to claims for socio-economic redistribution and claims for legal or cultural recognition, the two major families of justice claims (Fraser 2005, 69).[14] It also determines reparation and compensation measures (Part 4) and provides for the establishment of a 'Fund for the Dignity and Rehabilitation for Victims of Tyranny' (Article 41).

Thus, while the ad hoc measures in Tunisia already dealt with quite a broad range of rights violations and introduced various corresponding measures of justice, the official, planned transitional justice project goes even further in striving for inclusivity and a 'holistic approach' to transitional justice. It includes a carefully designed procedural and institutional structure for performing transitional justice in Tunisia that covers a long timeframe (1955–2013) and political as well as socio-economic crimes. It also relies on a broad definition of victimhood, acknowledges various root causes of grievances, and provides for a broad repertoire of retributive or restorative justice measures, such as the TDC, specialised chambers, and a reparations fund.

The TDC

Among the most important provisions in the transitional justice law is the establishment of the TDC, since it was the central institution that would start to perform transitional justice in Tunisia. One of the most significant changes in the final version of the law, in comparison with the draft which had been developed by the technical committee and then passed on to the NCA for approval, concerned the selection of truth commissioners. The parliamentarians retained the prerogative of choosing the fifteen truth commissioners and determined that they would be nominated by a selection committee within the NCA – much to the opposition of civil society actors. These changes marginalised those who had previously been deeply involved in the participatory process of designing the transitional justice project and had played a decisive role in drafting the law.[15]

Candidates to become truth commissioners could hand in their applications to the parliamentary selection committee. In general, each gender needed to be represented by at least one-third of the members of the TDC (Article 19). Two members should come from among the victims and two from human rights organisations, while the remaining members should include a "civil court judge, an administrative judge, a lawyer, a specialist in religious sciences, and a specialist in financial affairs" (Article 20). Truth commissioners needed to be Tunisian citizens; thirty years and older; and be competent, independent, neutral, and persons of integrity (without further specification). They should not have a criminal record for deliberate crime involving moral turpitude, nor any previously declared fraudulent bankruptcy, and should not have been dismissed for honour-related causes (Article 21).[16] The law also stipulated that the following individuals should be excluded from being truth commissioners: all NCA members and party officials; those who had served in parliament or government since 1 July 1955; those who had held executive positions in public institutions (such as governors or mayors) since 20 March 1956; former RCD officials; those who had supported Ben Ali running for another term as president in 2014;[17] and judges who had participated in "trials of political character" (Article 22).[18] Towards the end of this stage, fifteen truth commissioners were nominated by the parliamentary selection committee. There was a one-week time window in which citizens could object to the nominees. Objections were handed in against seven of the fifteen nominees.[19] These candidates had to go through an additional hearing, conducted by the same parliamentary selection committee that had nominated them in the first place. Eventually, all fifteen nominees were confirmed and subsequently appointed by the Prime Minister.

During the next half year, the commission did preparatory work. It elected its leaders internally, gave itself a structure and internal regulations/bylaws, secured office space, and hired administrative and other staff before it started inviting victims to submit their cases at its head office in Tunis in December 2014. The internal structures provide for the establishment of sub-commissions for victims, research, reparations, women/gender, arbitrage, and conciliation, as well as institutional reform. Each sub-commission is composed of a certain number of truth commissioners and has a president and a vice-president. Thus, truth commissioners usually sit on more than

Table 4.1 Table summarising measures and purpose for the stage of *designing transitional justice*

Institutionalised/designed transitional justice measures	Function
Ministry for Human Rights and Transitional Justice	Co-coordinating policymaking
Technical committee	Coordinating transitional justice dialogue, drafting law
Transitional justice dialogue	Allowing broad participation and input
Transitional justice law	Establishing rules for transitional justice project
Truth commission	'Doing transitional justice'

one sub-commission. Although the transitional justice law specifies certain groups with specific expertise from among which members should be chosen (Article 20, see above), the sub-commissions were not necessarily staffed with, or by, the corresponding experts.[20]

Overview

As should be clear from the table above, transitional justice activities in this stage mainly focused on the institutionalisation of transitional justice, while the previously initiated ad hoc measures proceeded in parallel, with little linkages to the institutionalisation efforts[21] and sometimes with changing dynamics compared with the previous stage. The shift in the focus of activities from ad hoc to institutionalised measures led to a change in the perception of what transitional justice actually *is*. Transitional justice was only just starting to vernacularise in Tunisia during that stage, and the concept had been used by only a small number of actors before the uprisings.[22] Consequently, most of the actors involved only started dealing with the issue of transitional justice at this stage, including the acquisition of a discursive repertoire of transitional justice language, for example through training. Therefore, the shift in focus may correspond to a shift in labelling of what constitutes transitional justice, since new developments concerning the ad hoc measures, such as the delivery of the judgments by the military appeals court, still attracted attention but were often not considered to be part of the institutionalised transitional justice process but rather as developments independent of it.

Interplay of planned and unplanned processes

In this stage, a clearer understanding of a planned, internationalised process of change with regard to transitional justice emerged with the launch of the transitional justice dialogue and the drafting of the law. However, this planned process of change interplayed with unplanned, spontaneous political dynamics (Elias 1977, 138–9) both inside and outside the concrete area of transitional justice.

The perils of constitution-writing

Let us start the analysis in this stage by looking at dynamics outside the concrete area of transitional justice. To a large extent, political developments in this stage were marked by the constitution-writing process. This is another area in which the interplay between planned and unplanned political and social processes became visible and was particularly crucial. In turn, these dynamics also interacted with transitional justice, since the processual developments in constitution-writing brought about new political logics.

The institutionalised constitution-writing process within the NCA was heavily influenced by spontaneous processes of change related to public protest, unrest, and violence as well as what Amel Boubekeur calls "bargained competition" (Boubekeur 2016, 107). Initially, the envisaged drafting period for the constitution had been set at one year by decree. This limited drafting period was further outlined in a written agreement among the country's leading political parties (Pickard 2011, 639). And while this timeframe was highly ambitious to start with, it later allowed the opposition to challenge the NCA's legitimacy after the drafting process exceeded the mandated period. This led to a competition of legitimacy between the government forces, which claimed legitimacy through elections, and the opposition within and outside of parliament, which claimed 'popular legitimacy' through 'the street' (Boubekeur 2015, 2). Thus, the institutionalised constitution-writing process could not proceed as planned due to a combination of politically motivated violence and opposition protests, as well as the suspension of the NCA's work. Over a fourth of the parliamentarians boycotted the assembly and staged a sit-in (called 'Errahil,' meaning 'departure') in front of parliament, demanding the dissolution of the NCA. In the summer of 2013, Tunisia was reportedly on the brink of civil war and the constitution-writing process in a deadlock. This was accompanied by a power shift in the transitional figuration, as neither of the political camps could enforce its own agenda with the political repertoire available to them. The adversarial factions were in a 'balance of weakness,'[23] since there was an "inaptitude to wage war" and an "impotence to organise peace" (Krichen 2016, 264; own translation). Therefore, a spontaneous crisis-solving process – the National Dialogue – was launched in an ultimately successful attempt to prevent further escalation and keep the institutionalised process of political transformation on track.

A quartet of civil society organisations[24] initiated the National Dialogue. This would serve as a crucial conflict-resolution forum between October 2013 and January 2014[25] and was composed of representatives of those political parties represented in the NCA, but with the same number of delegates for each party and not according to electoral strength. Parties that were only represented in the NCA through defections and not by election could also participate, which allowed Nidaa Tounes to send representatives. The National Dialogue allowed political adversaries to get to know each other better and therefore served as a trust-building mechanism (see also Chapter 1).[26] While this facilitated political compromises that brought the constitution-writing process to a successful conclusion, it also paved the way for more 'back-room' political bargaining and deal-making between the different factions. From the perspective of constitution-writing, compromise and deal-making as logics of political decision-making were essential for the political process to continue, which also influenced transitional justice insofar as preventing any further escalation of tensions and violence became a political priority. This led the assembly's focus to shift away from the transitional justice law[27] while also giving an impulse to political deal-making, which often allowed former members of the regime to return to politics and thus meant that the pursuit of justice and accountability was no longer the main political priority. These processes also revealed a power shift in the transitional figuration, since those newly in power who had been excluded from political processes under the old regime ceased to view vetting (and thus a fixation on post-revolutionary power structures) as a core priority.

The planned transitional justice project and its interaction with political dynamics

The changing figurations and power relations after the uprisings had a significant influence on the design of the official transitional justice process and the surrounding discourse. There are several reasons for this, the first of which is that the exclusion of old-regime elites from transitional politics opened a window of opportunity for a far-reaching transitional justice process, as was decided on in the consultative process and then codified in the transitional justice law. Second, the changing power relations manifested in the vetted NCA, which also functioned as legislative body, and its political composition determined the selection of truth commissioners. To recap, the NCA decided on a parliamentary selection committee to choose the members of the TDC that reflected the majority situation in parliament,[28] thus ensuring that the composition of the TDC remained under the control of the vetted, elected body. Since the selection committee was staffed proportionately according to strength in parliament, Ennahda was the strongest party in terms of representation on the committee. This led to an impression of a partisan bias in the selection process and, eventually, partisan commissioners: "But unfortunately, the commission was established proportionately. As a consequence, decisions will be taken based on partisanship."[29] Moreover, the transitional justice law was competing for attention with various other legislative initiatives, not least the constitution. While one policymaker reflected that "normally, the transitional justice law project should have been the first law project adopted by the NCA,"[30] it was not on the top of the assembly's agenda. The NCA had to balance its constitutional mandate – which was initially limited to only one year prior to elections – with its legislative tasks, comprising pressing issues such as approving the state's annual budget (Carter Center 2014). Given the contested nature of the issue, it comes as no surprise that the transitional justice law was pushed back.

Another unplanned, spontaneous dynamic that may have influenced the course of the institutionalised transitional justice project and the eventual adoption of the law was the publication of "Livre Noir: le système de propagande sous Ben Ali" by the communications department of the presidency under President Moncef Marzouki. This *livre noir* (black book) "named and shamed" (Preysing 2016, 115) those suspected of collaborating with the former regime, many of whom were alleged to have been paid to help the regime manipulate its image at home and abroad.[31] The publication of these names served as an "electric shock" (Preysing 2016, 115) for transitional justice, as it became even more apparent that a legal framework for dealing with the past was still missing. This may have eventually catalysed the long drawn-out adoption of the transitional justice law by the NCA.

Rumours and conspiracy narratives

The unplanned dynamics stemming from rumours and conspiracy narratives may be grounded in experiences, reports, and cues. But their fluid nature makes them influential, adding an emotional and personal layer to the processual dynamics that can also influence planned processes of change. The nomination of the truth commissioners was a frictional process that engendered and influenced rumours and conspiracy narratives. While political struggles over the nomination of the commissioners were confirmed from within the parliamentary selection committee,[32] there were also rumours about "Ennahda think[ing] that it has its hand on" the TDC[33] and about how many and which members were Ennahda sympathisers, respectively elected to the commission on a 'Nahdaoui ticket.'[34] Thus, the commission's composition was described as a "limping compromise"[35] that led the impartiality of the TDC to be questioned from the very beginning and with it the commission's legitimacy and ability to deliver justice to the various categories of victims in Tunisia. Looking at individual commissioners, most of the rumours revolved around the president of the truth commission, Sihem Ben Sedrine. She was said, variously, to be complicit with Ennahda, the Ministry of Interior, or the 'thugs' of the Leagues for the Protection of the Revolution in seeking to divert the whole project in her preferred direction.[36] Some also questioned Ben Sedrine's integrity. For example, some of my interview partners claimed that Ben Sedrine had not paid the journalists who worked for her radio station 'Radio Kalima,' even though it received funding from foreign donors.[37] These rumours influenced the standing and trustworthiness of the TDC as a whole, which in turn affected the commission's ability to deliver on its mandate and hence interacted with the institutionalised process.

In addition, there was a lack of transparency in the way deals were reached between the different political camps. A human rights activist and journalist described the processes as "tacit" and "not really clear to us."[38] This in turn fuelled rumours about the substance of the agreements reached between the previously opposing camps, especially with regard to a repressive agenda. Progressive civil society actors feared counter-revolutionary tendencies and complicity between those previously repressed and those now in power – Ennahda – might facilitate a return of 'the system.' Although at this stage most of my interlocutors believed that it was still unlikely that old-regime figures would return to the forefront of politics (Salehi 2014),[39] there were widespread rumours about Ben Ali returning to Tunisia in accordance with a supposed agreement between the leaders of Ennahda and Nidaa Tounes.[40]

The pursuit of accountability on the one hand and the opaque deal-making process on the other did not necessarily proceed in direct, institutionalised relation to each other. But nevertheless, there was an interplay between these different planned and unplanned dynamics. "Figurations [...] characterized by power balances of many sorts" (Elias 1978) constantly changed during this time of transition – and continue to do so. At this stage, it became clear that it would not be possible to permanently shift power away from those in influential positions before the revolution to those who had previously been marginalised. The political configuration easily slipped back into a state of flux, which changed the dominant logics of political decision-making.

Non-linearity, trends, and counter-trends

This stage was marked by the "play and counter-play of [...] dominant trends and counter-trends" (Elias 1977, 139; my translation). Generally, the trend of dealing with the past, seeking accountability, and compensating victims continued through this second stage. However, there were some important differences from the previous stage: counter-trends to the pursuit of transitional justice/accountability at various levels became more visible than in the first stage; and although the ad hoc measures continued to proceed (not necessarily in favour of accountability), there was also a growing institutionalisation (and 'projectification') of transitional justice that changed how the process was understood.

The military appeal judgments: two steps back?

Indicating a counter-trend to the pursuit of accountability, the military court of appeal dealing with cases concerning the 'martyrs and wounded of the revolution' revised several convictions for deliberate killings to 'manslaughter,' opening the door for several well-known figures of the old-regime to be released from prison and return to public and potentially political life. However, as Ben Ali was judged to have been primarily responsible for the regime's crimes, his sentence was not reduced. His trial was described to me as a "trash-can trial"[41] in which the judges were able to 'dump' responsibility on to Ben Ali, so that the other accused could be relieved of the more serious charges. The appeal judgments therefore confirmed the assessment of several interview partners who did not view Ben Ali as the most pressing problem, first because he had been in exile in Saudi Arabia since the revolution,[42] and second because Ben Ali was perceived as only the tip of the iceberg, with the structures of 'the system' having not been properly dismantled after the revolution:

> Well, people are worried because they have experienced the Ben Ali system. That's very diffuse, the Ben Ali system, that's many responsible people, [...] that's a clientelist network.[43]
> The head of power quit the country, but the others stayed and they've stayed until now.[44]

Hence those released and actually present in Tunisia were of greater concern than the exiled former head of state, since for them old-regime structures could easily be reactivated. In this sense, the appeal judgments were perceived as countering previous transitional justice measures. They invoked the impression that high-ranking figures were not properly being held accountable for human rights violations, which again changed the transitional figuration and power structures, leading to a trend of letting old-regime figures 'back in.'

Diverted attention and elite compromise

Transitional justice, or the trend of seeking accountability, also interacted with political crisis-solving measures like the National Dialogue. As mentioned above, during the greater part of this stage Tunisia was experiencing a severe political crisis that peaked in the summer of 2013 after the assassination of two opposition politicians. The government was under pressure from protests on 'the street,' and the NCA's work was suspended by a unilateral decision of its president Ben Jafar, who hoped to defuse the situation. He was reacting to nightly opposition rallies and a sit-in in front of parliament staged by more than a quarter of the institution's MPs. Since those in positions of power were preoccupied with averting further escalation on the streets as well as in the NCA, transitional justice was not high on their list of priorities. This not only applies to parliamentarians and the domestic mediators; the attention of those parts of the international community that did *not* directly work on transitional justice was similarly directed at other issues through the summer and autumn of 2013:

> And when the National Dialogue started, the quartet, the four organisations that initiated the National Dialogue,[45] did not prioritise transitional justice [...] and all deputies we met said 'not now.' Even the international community, even embassies, because we tried to sensitise embassies and we tried to sensitise other organisations. It was only us at ICTJ, UNDP, and OHCHR trying to push for this with national, with local civil society organisations.[46]

Conflict-resolution functioned as a counter-trend to the pursuit of accountability because it fostered elite compromises and deal-making between the major political forces in the country, including those close to the old regime:[47]

> [T]here is a lack of will to really seek accountability in these regards. There's a kind of deal. Maybe a tacit deal which is not really clear for us. We do not have enough proof to say that it is a deal. [...] But there is a feeling that there is a kind of deal between the old guard of the Ben Ali regime or the old establishment which is still rooted in the administration, ministries, in the government, business sphere, security partners, ministers, etc. who still have kind of power or hands or infiltration within the system [...].[48]

At the end of this stage, moreover, a proposed article in the draft electoral law (Article 167) that would have continued to ban those who had held positions of responsibility within the RCD from holding public office failed to pass parliament, falling one vote short of approval. Rejecting this article, and therefore ending the ban, was by then the policy of Ennahda's leadership, but despite Ennahda's usually strong party discipline, many of its MPs wanted to prolong the ban and voted in favour of the article (Marks 2015, 10). Thus, it is possible to identify a counter-trend to the original policy of the vetting and lustration of figures from the previous regime, as old-regime figures were allowed to return to politics, which indicates a rapprochement between the elites of the major political factions and therefore a shift in the transitional figuration's power structures. This also became evident in the power the opposition was able to exert vis-à-vis the government through 'street politics.'

Codification, shift in understanding, and decoupling 'transitional justice' from seeking accountability

Simultaneous to the counter-trend of letting old-regime figures return to politics, the NCA eventually passed the transitional justice law, strengthening the trend for justice and accountability. Somewhat contradicting the turning away from vetting in practice, the law included a mandate to draft recommendations for vetting state institutions (Article 43), as well as for institutional reform with the goal of establishing a "State of Law" (Article 14). The law commits the state to hold lower-tier officials and those involved in the regime's criminal activities – 'the old guard' mentioned in the quote above – to account, but no immediate, tangible action was undertaken.[49] On the one hand, this confirms the trend away from ad hoc activities to more planned and institutionalised transitional justice measures. On the other hand, it is also possible to identify a decoupling of current politics, which are shaped by logics of pragmatic conflict resolution, from abstract political goals codified in law. First, transitional justice (the postponement of discussing, amending, and voting on the law) and the task of vetting certain institutions – the promise to drop Article 167 but include vetting in the law – were postponed to a later point in time, and responsibility was delegated to different actors. In behaviouralist terms, this reveals a 'present bias,' which means that less weight is given to the consequences of decisions in the future than their consequences in the present.

There was also a change in how transitional justice was understood. While in the initial stage the broad approach of ad hoc measures made up the transitional justice portfolio, at the beginning of the second stage and of a planned and institutionalised project, the understanding shifted towards activities related to this project. At the end of this stage, however, the trend was for an even narrower understanding of transitional justice. As mentioned above, several interview partners believed that transitional justice had been 'delayed,' revealing a very specific definition of transitional justice. A common understanding was that transitional justice "ha[d] not really started yet"[50] and that the previous justice measures were not transitional justice:

> What has happened, that was outside the transitional justice law.
>
> [...] Author: "So, you think that doesn't count as transitional justice?"
>
> No, I don't think so. I don't think so.[51]

These measures were viewed as "ordinary justice"[52] or "[j]ustice in a general manner"[53] and therefore distinct from transitional justice. Transitional justice would only start when the TDC took up its work.[54] The narrowing down of transitional justice to what is done within a specific institutionalised framework is even clearer in the following quote: "These were initiatives that *could* enter the framework of transitional justice, but it's not transitional justice."[55] Therefore, the ad hoc measures were excluded from the common understanding of what constitutes transitional justice. Moreover, the whole participatory consultation process preceding the drafting of the transitional justice law, and thus the design and establishment of transitional justice institutions, in particular the TDC, was similarly excluded. This development may at least partly be due to a sentiment that the ad hoc measures had not been able to deliver justice. Taking the 'martyrs and wounded of the revolution' cases as examples, the widespread perception was that they were failing to deliver justice and that "the justice is not fair."[56] Thus, neither seeking accountability, nor the understanding of what constituted transitional justice, proceeded in a linear manner; nor were they necessarily working towards the concept's teleological ends.

This stage showed that the common understanding of transitional justice was non-linear and subject to change. A decoupling took place between the task of pursuing justice and accountability in transition through trials, compensation, and so on and what was perceived to be transitional justice. While practised measures of justice, such as trials, were denied the status of transitional justice when they were not perceived to have delivered justice, the label was granted to a carefully designed project laden with hopes and expectations whose institutions were not yet operational.

Struggle over victimhood

Temporal distance from the revolution, the development of an official transitional justice project, as well as the broadening of the scope of transitional justice and the potential population of victims, brought about a 'victims' competition' (see also Andrieu 2016, 287) and a shift in the perception of those recognised as victims in the immediate aftermath of the revolution. For example, the grievances of the 'martyrs and wounded of the revolution' as well as their contribution to the revolution were initially recognised in a very timely manner through trials seeking justice for any violence they had suffered as well as compensation measures and symbolic forms of recognition. However, with the broadening of the scope of transitional justice, and other parts of the population acquiring or wanting to acquire victim status, it became clear that there was no linear understanding of who was a legitimate victim and who was not. Thus, at this stage one could observe an erosion of empathy towards the 'martyrs and wounded of the revolution' and towards the young people who were at the forefront of the revolution more generally (see also Elias [1986] 2006, 117).[57] While the revolution was initially perceived as "the revolution of the young,"[58] this later changed, since the participation of 'young people'[59] in transitional justice and other processes of transitional politics was regulated by "quotas and limitations."[60] Denying the 'martyrs and wounded of the revolution' their status as victims, a group of interview partners stated that going on the street and protesting against the regime makes someone a 'political militant,' which bears certain risks, and that such individuals should not be considered a victim. Moreover, the argument continued, not all those killed during the protests could count as martyrs or heroes, as some had merely sought to use the turmoil to enrich themselves. Victims, on the contrary, were those who "hadn't done anything" but who had nevertheless been subject to violence.[61] There was also a partial return of old-regime practices towards individuals that those in power viewed as a threat. This can be illustrated by the example of Aziz Amami, a blogger who was active in the revolution. In May 2014, he was imprisoned for marijuana possession, a crime that at the time was penalised in Tunisia with a minimum of one year in prison with no probation. This was a well-known tactic often deployed under the old regime to silence critical voices. In addition, at his trial there was a strong presence of state security forces in the courthouse, which also signalled a return to performative practices of intimidation.[62]

In a different vein, due to increased political polarisation during this period, positions hardened between political camps. This was related to the impression that the different actors were failing to contain – and may even have encouraged – violence and unrest: Ennahda being too lenient towards Islamist/Salafist violence (Gobe and Chouikha 2013; Hachemaoui 2013; ACLED 2015) and the UGTT/secularist camp using strikes as a means of political opposition to put pressure on the government (Boubekeur 2015; Berman 2019). Given that many Salafists, some of them regarded as violent extremists, went free thanks to the general amnesty, empathy for Islamist victims began to fade. Some expressed the opinion that victims of Islamist violence were not receiving a similar amount of attention to the Islamist victims of state repression.[63]

Thus, during this stage, there was an ongoing trend for pursuing account-ability in tandem with a trend towards an institutionalisation of efforts to do so. However, it is also possible to identify a counter-trend to these developments, since the vetting of political institutions, especially parliament, was no longer being pursued. Therefore, the trend of seeking accountability was countered with a trend towards elite political deal-making as an acute problem-solving mechanism. These trends of advancing the institutionalisation of transitional justice on the one hand and countering previous efforts on the other occurred simultaneously, displaying non-linearity and a 'present bias' in political decision-making. The understanding of who constituted a victim in transitional Tunisia also proved to be non-linear and contentious. While there was now less empathy towards those who were at the forefront of the revolution, there was also a widening of the spectrum of those considered to be victims, and who was therefore able to claim victimhood.

International interconnectedness

In analysing this stage, it is clear that there was increased international influence in the *design of transitional justice*. Looking specifically at the planned transitional justice project, interdependencies and interaction between domestic and international actors became more pronounced than in the previous stage, which had mainly been characterised by domestic efforts.[64] As mentioned above, the planned transitional justice process, including the consultative transitional justice dialogue and the law-drafting process, was closely informed by international organisations and NGOs from the very beginning. And those international actors most prominently involved in the issue – ICTJ, UNDP, and OHCHR – were the ones advocating for the transitional justice project to proceed at a time when it was being neglected politically because the priority was to solve the 2013 political crisis.[65]

Knowledge transfer

The strong international support for the process of *designing transitional justice* – the workshops and training sessions Tunisians received – equipped Tunisian actors with interpretive schemes and discursive resources that allowed them to orientate themselves and communicate in the transitional justice figuration (Elias 2006, 100). As a member of the technical committee reported, those citizens involved in the participatory part of the transitional justice dialogue and chosen as moderators and multiplicators all received the same training provided by international transitional justice professionals: "[A]nd they all went through the same training on transitional justice, on debate moderation, on writing reports, on all of this."[66] This led to a harmonisation of rhetoric on transitional justice, albeit not necessarily on the question of what transitional justice should mean and entail. For example, on the surface transitional justice was vernacularised in a rather technical manner, with literal translations of the term,[67] and a dominant technical vocabulary emerged. Transitional justice was now defined as being composed of four pillars or axes: truth, justice, reparations, and the guarantee of non-recurrence.[68] Here, a frequent reference was to Pablo de Greiff, whose job title was often cited: the UN Special Rapporteur for Truth, Justice, Reparations, and the Guarantee of Non-Recurrence (see also Salehi 2019). Nevertheless, understandings of what transitional justice and these pillars should mean and entail, as well as the prioritisation of the pillars, continued to differ among domestic actors, despite the knowledge transfer from the international sphere. Interestingly, however, although international actors would usually include the ad hoc measures in their assessments of transitional justice in Tunisia in this stage,[69] among the Tunisian actors, a narrower understanding of transitional justice, confined to the institutionalised project, emerged with the further transfer of knowledge and expertise.

In addition to the on-site influence of international organisations and NGOs, Tunisian actors active in transitional justice visited several other countries to become better informed about different transitional justice processes and experiences. Here, Morocco,[70] which had a truth commission in 2004/5, was often cited as a regional neighbour and fellow Arab state that could serve as a source of inspiration. The experiences of more distant countries, such as Poland or South Africa, were also cited as examples from which Tunisians could draw knowledge.[71]

Support or interference?

Although a member of the technical committee stated that initially, "[w]e asked for transitional justice without knowing what it is,"[72] the general impression from my research is that Tunisian actors perceived international involvement as supporting domestic processes rather than interfering in them – the former was welcomed and even requested, while the latter would be rejected: "I think it's important that at this stage, there's no interference."[73] This perspective was mirrored by my international interview partners. They saw a challenge in 'just offering advice' and 'doing advocacy,' but not prescribing a certain solution or being perceived as taking a particular side.[74] This contrasts to some extent with transitional justice scholarship that assumes that prescribing a set of solutions that work towards a particular type of change is the principal aim of the 'justice industry.' Several of my interview partners described how they worked well with international actors, for example in organising workshops or drafting the transitional justice law.[75] For the latter process, international actors were merely described as 'observers' who offered expertise,[76] with truth commissioners and government officials usually referring to UN agencies and NGOs (especially ICTJ) as 'partners.'[77]

However, the role of international actors and their handling of the support for the Tunisian transitional justice process were not free of criticism. As Nassar, for example, states with regard to the stage of initiating transitional justice in Tunisia, Tunisian actors received contradictory advice from international experts (Nassar 2014, 70). A similar observation was made by one of my interview partners at a later stage in the process concerning organisations working with UNDP (quoted here for the purpose of illustration):

> The associations which work on transitional justice lack coordination. There is no coordination and collaboration between the different associations that work on transitional justice. [...] When the victims receive two leaflets on the same issue, there will be confusion. [...] Both [organisations that distributed information] are supported by UNDP.[78]

This not only has the potential to be confusing for the domestic actors involved in the process who rely on expert advice, but it may also lead to a "duplication of efforts in the assistance brought by the international community" (Nassar 2014, 70).

Despite Tunisian actors' understanding of transitional justice being shaped by international knowledge transfer, they did not always follow the international experts' recommendations. Letting a parliamentary selection committee choose truth commissioners without the participation of civil society is a clear example of when decisions in domestic politics did not follow what would conform to best practice in transitional justice.[79] Fostered by the initial participatory approach and its emphasis by Tunisian and international officials, civil society representatives developed a sense of entitlement with regard to participating as decision-makers, and not only in a consultative capacity.[80] Moreover, the international actors were sometimes perceived as being more supportive of the Tunisian government than of civil society because they were working with government agencies, such as the Ministry for Human Rights and Transitional Justice.[81] Because the government at the time was dominated by Ennahda, this led to the impression that one political side was receiving more support than the other:

> There is [...] an impression that when one part of Tunisian civil society remarks that certain intervening organisms are more pro-X or pro-Y, that would mean that they rather support [...] [the Islamist spectrum] because in fact at one moment, the Tunisian government was led by the Islamists, and UNDP would of course help the government and help the Ministry for Transitional Justice.[82]

These dynamics also played a part in the processual characteristic discussed below that shows the influence of conflict and frictions.

Championing a 'holistic approach'

The Tunisian transitional justice project is embedded in the paradigm of a holistic or integrated approach to transitional justice, as advanced by the ICTJ (2009) and the UN.[83] According to a holistic logic, it makes sense to address as many 'justice problems' as possible. This approach usually identifies four pillars of transitional justice that should feature in the process: truth, justice, reconciliation, and non-recurrence.[84] This holistic understanding of transitional justice was communicated to domestic actors in information material, workshops, and training sessions. While this provided discursive resources to actors who had previously been unable to access them, it also limited the possible shapes that transitional justice could take and steered the process in a particular direction. In the Tunisian case, one transitional justice expert remarked that some of their peers "preach the integrated approach like a gospel."[85] Within the project, various international actors prioritised different subjects within transitional justice.[86] Although this could help to avoid a duplication of efforts, it did not work out so well in Tunisia, according to Nassar (Nassar 2014, 70). However, it can also lead to a further expansion of efforts, because the different organisations try to have their 'pet issues' included in the transitional justice project. According to one of my interlocutors, this is why institutional reform was included in the Tunisian transitional justice law.[87]

As mentioned above, in this stage the Special Rapporteur for Truth, Justice, Reconciliation, and the Guarantee of Non-Recurrence, or rather the title of his office, played a significant role in shaping the discourse about what constitutes transitional justice in Tunisia. Because of the Special Rapporteur's prominence and visibility, the four pillars in the office's title frequently served as a reference for explaining transitional justice's purpose and 'proper' procedures. An understanding emerged among several of my Tunisian interlocutors that transitional justice would need to cover *each* of the four pillars to count as 'proper' transitional justice.[88] In combination with the holistic ideal, this led to an expansive approach to transitional justice that aimed to comprise all four pillars and involved the introduction of various measures that addressed a broad range of violations and covered a very long timeframe. Another interpretation was that these four aspects represent chronological steps in a transitional justice project.[89] Therefore, a teleological understanding of transitional justice processes emerged, accompanied by an expectation that processes of political and social change are controllable rather than contingent, at least when following certain rules.[90] From the perspective of the grievances and violations of the past that should be dealt with, in the Tunisian context it makes sense, for example, to cover socio-economic injustices within transitional justice – rather than political rights violations alone – and consequently to have a variety of measures included in the project. But as Rebekka Friedman and Andrew Jillions (2015, 141) critically remark, "[a] complementarity of means does not emerge organically." Given that transitional justice measures are often introduced in political situations in which a state's capacities are limited, the question is whether complementarity can be reached by the responsible institutions. One expert who was advocating for a pragmatic rather than a holistic approach believed that Tunisia's transitional justice institutions would be overstrained given the tasks they had to cover: "They could maybe do it if they were Sweden, but if they were Sweden they wouldn't need it."[91]

Conflict and friction

In this stage, conflict and friction continued to occur in a cross-cutting manner at various levels and between different combinations of actors in the transitional figuration. Friction did not occur in a unidimensional way, between domestic and international actors, for example (see also Kappler 2013), or between political and actors and civil society. It was multidirectional. Different civil society organisations, for example, did not necessarily share the same opinions on transitional justice, pursue the same goals, or even trust each other.[92] Alliances were formed across the figuration, driven by or fostering friction. Looking at the abovementioned example of emerging friction stemming from the perception that international actors were more supportive of the government than of civil society organisations, it becomes evident that unidirectional attributes are not sufficient to describe how conflict and friction drive and define processes of change.

Conflict and friction in transitional politics

Before the transitional law was adopted by the NCA, this stage was marked by conflict and frictions surrounding the government and the finalisation of the constitution, which was one of the reasons why the transitional justice law was put on hold by parliament for several months.[93] Since the revolution, the degree of stability in Tunisia has fluctuated as old and new political elites attempted to negotiate the cross-currents of a complex situation that was new to everyone: power differentials had significantly reduced compared with the period before the revolution, which can initially foster conflict

(Elias 1977, 130; 2006, 108). Tensions escalated again in the summer of 2013: "[S]treet politics, which occasionally turned violent, competed with – and eventually dominated – the formal institutional process" (Boubekeur 2015, 1). The constitution's one-year drafting period[94] proved overly ambitious, as the NCA did not manage to finalise the document within this timeframe. However, the opposition used this failure to challenge the government's legitimacy and to claim 'popular legitimacy' (based on support expressed in protests) as opposed to the 'electoral legitimacy' of the government (Boubekeur 2015). About sixty opposition NCA members left the assembly and staged sit-ins in front of parliament, calling for the government to resign, while the opposition also urged its supporters to hold nightly rallies outside the building. The assassination of two opposition politicians from the Popular Front – Chokri Belaid and Mohamed Brahmi – led to a further escalation of protests and, according to some analysts, brought the country to the brink of civil war (M'rad 2015; Boubekeur 2015). To resolve this deadlock and avoid the possibility of widespread violence, a quartet of civil society organisations[95] initiated and facilitated the National Dialogue, an elite conflict-resolution forum. Within the National Dialogue, the participating politicians managed to work out compromises on the major lines of political conflict. The technical details of how these compromises could be reflected in the constitution would then be specified within the NCA. It was in this context that the lustration clause relating to parliamentarians, which would have continued to exclude old-regime figures from running for office (draft Article 167 of the electoral law), fell victim to the rapprochement between Ennahda and Nidaa Tounes – a result of contacts between their respective party leaders Rachid Ghannouchi and Essebsi. Thus, the controversy around the clause led to friction between Ennahda's leadership and its rank-and-file membership, the latter being more in favour of keeping a lustration provision for Ben Ali-era officials (Marks 2015, 11).

The instability of this period helps explain why such a sensitive topic as transitional justice was put on hold. According to an ICTJ representative, the need for a transitional justice law only came back on to the policymaking agenda when President Marzouki's communication team published the *livre noir*,[96] which pilloried several personalities, journalists, and intellectuals for helping to create a positive image of the Ben Ali regime, based on records found in the presidential palace in Carthage. In doing so, Marzouki interfered in ongoing efforts of transitional justice and "did not respect the process" (Ghribi 2013). In this case, however, the friction the publication provoked clearly acted as a driver for the institutionalised transitional justice process to continue – if it was not to be disrupted by such controversial individual initiatives. Moreover, the transitional justice provisions themselves, in particular the disorganised execution of reparation provisions, also led to conflict and friction during this period, as manifested in the sit-ins at the Kasbah (El Gantri 2015), for example.[97]

Putting together the TDC

Looking at the transitional justice process first, one point of friction at this stage concerns the nomination of truth commissioners, both in terms of procedures and in terms of substance. First, as mentioned above, civil society representatives were not satisfied with the decision to exclude them from the selection process, particularly given their crucial role in the transitional justice dialogue and the drafting of the law. One civil society representative stated that "civil society was discarded."[98] To justify his resentment, he invoked the authority of the UN Special Rapporteur, de Greiff, who issued a report on Tunisia in 2013:[99] "Look at the de Greiff report. There are suggestions for choosing candidates, and civil society should have been involved."[100] This sentiment of exclusion led several civil society associations to boycott the truth commission by not sending applications to have their representatives considered for nomination to the commission.[101] Second, civil society actors were also highly critical that the same selection committee that nominated truth commissioners in the first place would decide on the response to any formal objections to their nominations, as there was effectively no possibility for legal recourse concerning the selection of truth commissioners. Civil society actors lodged a legal complaint against this provision with the administrative court, but it was rejected. This fostered the impression that the successful candidates had been decided on in advance.[102]

There was also friction over the substance of the nominations, that is, the actual nominees. Some of the objections to the nominees were more directed at the candidates personally and their alleged political opinions or affiliations, while others highlighted violations of the rules for selection as stipulated by the transitional justice law, which states that truth commissioners "may not [...] [h]ave held a parliamentary position or any position in the governments in the period extending from 1 July 1955."[103] Among the most controversial nominations was that of Khemais Chammari, who had been an MP during the Ben Ali era between 1994 and 1996 before being imprisoned for five years. His nomination, however, was justified by NCA members on the basis that he had not served his full term as an MP because of his imprisonment. As his name does not appear on the list of representatives of that time, the selection committee argued that the provision in the law would be a matter of interpretation and hence not apply to him.[104] A different reason that the nomination meeting met with resistance can be seen in the case of Khaled Krichi, who, as head of the Association of Political Prisoners, stated that former Ben Ali regime members imprisoned after the fall of the regime would need to be considered political prisoners as well. Since he was nominated as a victim representative and "this [perspective] was not really something that victims liked,"[105] his nomination was challenged. Similarly, by her own account, Oula Ben Nejma's nomination was objected to because of her husband's role as an advisor to Ennahda.[106] The various controversial nominations relate to the abovementioned pressure on parliamentarians to select 'partisan' members of the truth commission and the frictions accompanying the selection process. These were remarked on by civil society representatives and confirmed from within the parliamentary selection committee: "We have achieved [the nomination of the TDC members] with pain. [...] There was one party that only wanted partisan members."[107] Thus, frictions around the nomination process over procedures as well as substance set the course for the future relationship between (previously) active civil society figures as well as opposition forces and the new institution. These frictions also prompted the impression of partisanship and the resulting lack of trust that the commission had to fight against from the very beginning.

Friction within the truth commission

After the truth commissioners had been appointed to the commission, friction then emerged between the newly nominated members. During the consolidation phase, they had to decide on internal structures and equip themselves with bylaws. Leadership positions were distributed for the commission as a whole and for the sub-commissions. Since the truth commissioners elected the candidates for the various positions from among themselves, the posts were not necessarily distributed according to competencies in the respective subject matter. Instead, ideology and power struggles with respect to how best to position oneself may have played a role as well.[108] This led to dissatisfaction among those members who did not receive their preferred positions: they did not end up with responsibility in the sub-commissions they perceived to be most suitable for their skill-sets, or which would have best fit the functions they were nominated for. The representative of a victims' organisation, for example, thought that they would be best qualified to serve in the sub-commission for victims.[109] Members of the commission claimed that the Islamist/secularist divide was the dominant cleavage in provoking frictions and driving decisions and voting behaviour. However, an external consultant identified several other points of friction, for example between men and women and between lawyers and non-lawyers.[110] Thus, friction – and later more open conflict – within the truth commission was in part related to political/ideological struggles that were dominant in the country at that time, but it also developed due to dynamics that were particular to the commission.

In addition to the 'calculated' elections for leadership positions, the internal structuring itself gave evidence of power play and a striving for mutual oversight: parallel memberships in several sub-commissions allowed members or alliances of members to stay involved in several subject areas and prevented single members – potentially having responsibility for a certain topic – from becoming too powerful.[111] In general, frictions within the commission at this stage (and continuing in the next one) became even more obvious when looking at early defections, before the commission had even started to operate. One of the earliest commission members to defect, Noura Borsali, stated in a press interview: "I did not come to the TDC to fight a battle against internal dysfunctions."[112] These internal frictions slowed down the consolidation of the truth commission, leading to a perception of a further delay in transitional justice activities and 'idleness.'[113] This influenced the future operations of the commission as well as the public perception of its performance, which interlinked with societal cleavages.

Conclusion

The second stage, that of designing transitional justice, revealed an interplay between socio-technological, planned processes of change on the one hand and unplanned, spontaneous political and social dynamics on the other. Here, developments internal to the transitional justice process played a role, but equally important were reconfigurations regarding the future political architecture of the Tunisian state. There was a shift in understanding, taking the form of a labelling of transitional justice that restricted transitional justice to those activities falling within the official framework. While the trend towards seeking accountability continued, it did so in a more institutionalised manner. This shift in the understanding of transitional justice, and its increasing institutionalisation, interacted with heightened political polarisation and growing temporal distance from the revolution and led to changes in the understanding of victimhood: while the definition of victimhood was broadened, those who had previously enjoyed much attention and empathy, such as the 'martyrs and wounded of the revolution,' were not necessarily the prime focus of attention. There was a shift towards potential victims better positioned in institutionalised political structures. Parallel to the further institutionalisation of transitional justice, a counter-trend to the pursuit of accountability emerged, as exemplified by the abandonment of lustration clauses in the electoral law, which postponed lustration to a later point in time. This displayed a 'present-bias' in institutional politics – as well as a strong interlinkage between planned and unplanned political developments. This counter-trend is related to the intensification of conflict and friction between different political forces: since the institutionally led political transition was in deadlock, and sometimes violent unrest dominated on the street, transitional justice interplayed with acute crisis-solving measures that promoted deal-making and elite-consensus, which meant that accountability was not high on the agenda.

Frictions also intensified within the sphere of transitional justice, mainly because previously engaged civil society actors believed that they had been sidelined in the process. This stage was also marked by the growing engagement of international governmental and non-governmental organisations in the institutionalised transitional justice efforts. While the international community's engagement in transitional justice was mainly perceived as supportive rather than invasive, friction evolved around the level and manner of support, as well as the direction of the transitional justice project. The nomination of truth commissioners was as conflictive as the following consolidation phase of the commission would be. Thus, frictions have occurred in a multi-directional way between different actors in the transitional figuration, encouraging the formation of various alliances. These frictions set the course for the future characteristics and conditions of the TDC's operations, as well as for the perception of its work.

It is possible to draw further preliminary conclusions informed by Ferguson's work on development. Looking at what I would term the 'problem–capacity nexus' allows us to move from previously outlined specificities of the transitional justice field to the concrete processual developments in Tunisia. How and what kinds of institutionalised transitional justice efforts were introduced was co-determined by the 'justice industry' and depended on the socio-technological offer (what solutions were at hand) as well as political interests. While Ferguson (1994) found that development professionals invent 'development problems' for which they have solutions at hand but which do not necessarily correspond to actual problems, the 'problem–capacity nexus' in transitional justice in Tunisia may be skewed in a different direction. Transitional justice practice and scholarship have sought to identify 'transitional justice problems' more accurately by broadening their focus – and capacity – to include economic, social, and cultural questions, developing corresponding measures and privileging a holistic approach. However, this leads to capacity problems when transitional justice measures get "[o]verloaded with too many demands" (Andrieu 2010, 542). Consequently, different problems arise regarding the performance of transitional justice in two senses: how effectively it carries out its functions and how it is *perceived* to have carried out its functions.

Notes

1 See part on trials/legal measures for a description of the 2011 military trials.
2 In office from 2004 to 2011.
3 In office from 2001 to 2011. Previously served as director of national security from 1991.
4 First session of the public hearings of the TDC, personal observation, Tunis, November 2016.
5 A conflict resolution initiative headed by four civil society organisations to overcome the political deadlock and keep the constitution-writing process on track in the second half of 2013; see also the section on the perils of constitution-writing.
6 Sahbani remained in this position until his service was ended by governmental decree in June 2015. "Décret gouvernemental n° 2015–387 du 8 juin 2015, portant cessation de fonctions d'un chargé de mission"; available at www.pist.tn/jort/2015/2015F/Jo0482015.pdf (accessed 10 June 2018).
7 The following civil society groupings were represented in the technical committee: the Tunisian Network for Transitional Justice, the Tunis Center for Transitional Justice, the Tunis Center for Human Rights and Transitional Justice, the Independent National Coordination for Transitional Justice, and the Kawakibi Democracy Transition Center (Ministry for Human Rights and Transitional Justice 2013, 5).
8 Personal interview with civil society representative, member of the technical committee, Tunis, May 2014.
9 See the report by the Ministry for Human Rights and Transitional Justice (2013) as well as the video on the process published by the ministry; on file.
10 "But we are not used to these kinds of methods, consultations, etc." Personal interview with representative of Ministry of Justice, Tunis, March 2014.
11 Personal interview with former minister, Tunis, October 2015.
12 Personal interview with member of the technical committee, Tunis, April 2014. See also information on the website Justice Transitionnelle en Tunisie; available at www.justice-transitionnelle.tn/justice-transitionnelle/la-justice-transitionnelle-en-tunisie/le-dialogue-national-sur-la-justice-transitionnelle (accessed 10 June 2018; no longer active), and report by Ministry for Human Rights and Transitional Justice (2013, 19–20).
13 Personal interview with NCA member, member of the parliamentary selection committee for truth commissioners, Tunis, May 2014. See also Chapter 3 for dynamics that may have hampered and/or eventually fostered the law's adoption.
14 Here, the communitarian/collective aspect relates to redistribution but also acknowledges systematic political exclusion. Regions in the country's centre-west

were "politically and economically marginalized and systematically excluded from public investment in infrastructure, education and health" (Ottendörfer et al. 2017, 357).

15 Personal interview with civil society representative, Tunis, May 2014.

16 There is no further explanation for 'moral turpitude,' 'honour-related causes,' and to what posts the dismissal refers.

17 See discussion of exclusion from standing for NCA elections in Chapter 3.

18 This again is not further specified.

19 For a list of the nominees, see Tunisie14.tn (2014).

20 Personal interviews with truth commissioners, Tunis, March 2015.

21 While the ad hoc measures were not properly integrated into the planned project, there were some references to them within the institutionalised project. For further explanation, see the corresponding 'activities' part in Chapter 5.

22 One example of a Tunisian organisation that had been active in the field of transitional justice before the uprisings is the Kawakibi Democracy Transition Center. However, it was founded in Jordan in 2006 and only registered as civil society association in Tunisia after the uprisings.

23 Personal interview with head of Middle East department of an international NGO specialising in transitional justice, New York, March 2015.

24 The quartet was composed of the UGTT, UTICA, the Lawyers' Order (L'Ordre National des Avocats de Tunisie), and the LTDH.

25 In 2015, the four civil society organisations received the Noble Peace Prize for their mediation efforts. This successful initiative had been preceded by several unsuccessful attempts at dialogue. However, if not mentioned otherwise, in this book 'National Dialogue' refers to the quartet's successful initiative.

26 An Ennahda NCA member also described to me how many NCA members did not really understand parliamentary/committee work, since under Ben Ali the parliament had only been there to vote. Thus, it took some time until 'proper' committee work took place at all, which may have hindered the trust-building process. Personal interview with Ennahda NCA member, Tunis, April 2014.

27 Personal interview with representative of transitional justice NGO, Tunis, May 2014.

28 A notable exception that did not correspond to the majority situation in parliament was the consensus committee, an ad hoc parliamentary committee focused on finding compromise on contentious issues initiated by the president of the assembly, Ben Jafar. The allocation of seats on this body was different from the other parliamentary committees as the government parties did not have a majority. This committee and the different allocation of seats helped to bring a new dynamic into the deadlocked constitution-writing process.

29 Personal interview with civil society representative, Tunis, May 2014. This impression was confirmed in personal interviews with members of the parliamentary selection committee, Tunis, May 2014.

30 Personal interview with NCA member, Tunis, May 2014.

31 The "Livre Noir" is available online in Arabic at http://directinfo.webmanagercenter.com/2013/12/02/tunisie-le-livre-noir-disponible-en-ligne (accessed 15 December 2017).

32 Personal interview with member of the parliamentary selection committee, Tunis, May 2014.

33 Personal interview with truth commissioner, Tunis, March 2015.

34 Personal interview with civil society representative, Tunis, May 2014.

35 Personal interview with academic, Tunis, March 2015.

36 Ibid.; while Boubekeur (2015, 3) asserts that although "[o]riginally established as neighborhood committees to address the post-revolutionary security void and close to local UGTT chapters, the LPR [Leagues for the Protection of the Revolution] regrouped as political allies of Ennahda after it came to power and increasingly engaged in violent activities," other analysts in personal conversations did not agree with this assessment, at least not as a structural dynamic.

37 Personal interviews with a Tunisian journalist and a representative of LTDH, Tunis, March 2015, and Mdhilla, October 2015; several personal conversations with international journalists and NGO representatives, Tunis and New York, 2014–15.

38 Personal interview with human rights activist/journalist, Tunis, April 2014, see full quote below.

39 For the country's first free municipal elections in May 2018, former RCD officials were integrated in the electoral lists of both Nidaa Tounes and Ennahda and therefore returned to the forefront of politics (Wolf 2018).

40 Personal interview with political consultant, Amsterdam, June 2015.

41 Personal conversation with civil society representative, Tunis, April 2014.

42 "Why are the people not interested in this trial? [...] The fact that [Ben Ali] is being judged in absence has little impact on the Tunisians." Personal interview with civil society representative, Tunis, May 2014. "I think that the victims are not satisfied. But concerning Ben Ali, there is no interest to pursue trials against a person who is not there." Personal interview with representative of the Ministry of Justice, Tunis, April 2014.

43 Personal interview with civil society representative, Tunis, May 2014.

44 Personal interview with member of the technical committee, Tunis, April 2014. See also quote on p. 134.

45 UGTT, UTICA, LTDH, and the Lawyers' Order

46 Personal interview with representative of transitional justice NGO, Tunis, May 2014.

47 Several personal interviews with political and civil society actors, Tunis 2014–16.

48 Personal interview with human rights activist/journalist, Tunis, April 2014.

49 Article 43 lists a variety of areas that could require reform or vetting – politics, administration, economy, security, judiciary, media, education, and culture – and vaguely states that a committee should "[p]ropose practical suggestions to reform institutions that participated in corruption and violations [...] [p]ropose practical suggestions for vetting public administration and all sectors that require vetting."

50 This sentiment was expressed by several interview partners from politics and civil society, albeit using slightly different phrasing.

51 Personal interview with NCA member, Tunis, April 2014.

52 "That's not transitional justice. That's ordinary justice." Personal interview with NCA member, Tunis, May 2014.

53 "You know that transitional justice hasn't completely started. All the processes that have been [introduced], were in the general framework. Justice in a general manner." Personal interview with civil society representative, Tunis, April 2014."

54 "So, the transitional justice process as you know didn't start yet. We're still on the step of the nomination of the members of the transitional justice committee." Personal interview with NCA member, Tunis, May 2014.

55 Personal interview with representative of the Lawyer's Order, Tunis, May 2014.

56 Personal interviews with human rights activist, civil society representatives, representative of transitional justice NGO, Tunis, April/May 2014.

57 Personal conversation with civil society representative, Tunis, April 2014. According to the findings of the Bouderbala Commission (2012), the clear majority of those wounded or killed in the wake of the revolution were male and between the ages of eighteen and thirty-nine.

58 Personal interview with civil society representative, Tunis, May 2014.

59 'Young people' in this context does not necessarily mean people who are underage, but up to an age of about thirty. The age limit for truth commissioners, for example, is thirty, and I was told that initially it was envisaged that the age limit would be set even higher at thirty-five or forty. Personal interviews with civil society representative and representative of international transitional justice NGO, Tunis, May 2014. A privilege for older candidates has remained in the law, though: "In the case of equal number of votes, the older candidate shall be chosen" (Article 23, Organic Law on Establishing and Organising Transitional Justice, unofficial translation by the ICTJ). Over half of the Tunisian population is under thirty years old, so these regulations exclude a significant part of the population.

60 Personal interview with civil society representative, Tunis, May 2014.

61 Personal group interview with three former generals of the 'Barraket Essahel' group, Tunis, May 2014.

62 Personal observation in the Palais de Justice in Tunis on the day of Amami's trial. It was pointed out to me, by a foreign journalist who had worked in and on Tunisia for several years, that armed security forces had not usually been present in the courthouse since the revolution, and that this represented the return of an old regime-practice.

63 Personal interviews with academic, victim of Islamist violence, Tunis, March 2015; with civil society representative, Tunis, May 2014; several personal conversations concerning the first public hearings of the truth commission and the absence of stories of victims of Islamist violence.

64 It is worth noting here that justice conflicts and justice claims in the Tunisian transitional justice project initially remained within the boundaries of the nation-state, insofar as they were addressed towards national actors. While Tunisia joined the ICC in the early transition phase, discussions in interviews

about the potential deployment of international criminal justice have remained very hypothetical. Interdependence with international actors occurs with regard to definitions of justice, seeking justice, and providing justice.

65 See also quote above on sensitisation and neglect of embassies. Personal interview with representative of transitional justice NGO, Tunis, May 2014.

66 Personal interview with member of the technical committee, Tunis, May 2014.

67 'Al-adala al-intiqalia' in (simply transliterated) Arabic or 'justice transitionnelle' in French.

68 Several personal interviews, e.g. with representative of the Lawyer's Order and ministerial staff, Tunis, May 2014 and March 2015.

69 Several personal interviews/conversations with staff members of UN agencies and international NGOs.

70 Equity and Reconciliation Commission, established in January 2004 and running for one year from December 2004 until November 2005.

71 Several personal interviews with civil society representatives, truth commission members, Tunis, 2014/15.

72 Personal conversation with member of the technical committee, Tunis, September 2016.

73 Quote from personal interview with head of Tunisian NGO, Tunis, April 2014. Additionally, personal interviews with human rights activists, civil society representatives, representatives of international NGOs, truth commissioners, members of the technical committee, former minister, Tunis, April/May 2014, March 2015, October 2015. An example of a request for support would be the training of judges for specialised chambers. Personal interview with representative of transitional justice NGO and the Minister of Justice, Tunis, May 2014, March 2015.

74 Personal interviews and conversations with several transitional justice advisors, Tunis 2014–16 and New York 2015.

75 Personal interview with civil society representatives, member of the technical committee, Tunis, April 2014.

76 Personal interview with Tunisian representative of international human rights NGO, Tunis, May 2014. This also fits with personal observations at a workshop of the TDC in March 2015.

77 Several personal interviews and conversations, Tunisia, 2014–16.

78 Personal interview with TDC official, Kasserine, October 2015.

79 A transitional justice expert told me that they would have preferred the selection procedure to include civil society, that the law is not "perfect," but that they can "work with it." Personal conversations and interviews, Tunis 2014–16, New York 2015.

80 Personal interviews with former government minister and with civil society representative, Tunis, October 2015 and May 2014.

81 Personal interviews with representative of transitional justice NGO, Tunis, May 2014; and with member of the technical committee, Tunis, October 2015.

82 Personal interview with member of the technical committee, Tunis, October 2015.

83 A seminal document in the institutionalisation of transitional justice is the UN Secretary-General's report on 'the rule of law and transitional justice in conflict and post-conflict societies.' It states: "Where transitional justice is required, strategies must be holistic, incorporating integrated attention to individual prosecutions, reparations, truth-seeking, institutional reform, vetting and dismissals, or an appropriately conceived combination thereof" (UN Secretary-General 2004).

84 Sometimes complemented with cross-cutting issues, such as gender.

85 Personal interview, New York, April 2015.

86 Personal interview with representative of transitional justice NGO, Tunis, May 2014.

87 Informal conversation with transitional justice professional, Tunis, May 2015.

88 For example, personal interview with representative of the Lawyer's Order, Tunis, May 2014.

89 Personal interview with ministerial staff, relations with civil society and constitutional institutions, Tunis, March 2015.

90 In a personal conversation, a former staff member ensured me that the Special Representative does not share this perspective. March 2015.

91 Personal interview with transitional justice professional, New York, April 2015. See also Salehi (2021).

92 "[Civil society associations] would not be credible for other associations." Personal interview with truth commissioner, Tunis, March 2015.

93 Personal interview with representative of transitional justice NGO, Tunis, May 2014.

94 "Decree n° 2011–582," dated 20 May 2011, convening the electoral body for the election of the NCA; available at www.legislation.tn/sites/default/files/fraction-journal-officiel/2011/2011G/037/Tg20115823.pdf (accessed 10 June 2018). The political parties (eleven parties participating in the Ben Achour Commission, plus Ennahda) later reaffirmed their commitment to the one-year period in a written agreement (Pickard 2011).

95 UGTT, UTICA, LTDH, and the Lawyers' Order.

96 Personal interview with representative of international transitional justice NGO, Tunis, May 2014.

97 The Place de la Kasbah is in central Tunis, near the building that houses the Prime Minister's office. It has become a common place of protest since the revolution.

98 Personal interview with civil society representative, Tunis, May 2014.

99 Following his mission to the country in 2012, A/HRC/24/42/Add.1.

100 Personal interview with civil society representative, Tunis, May 2014.

101 Several personal interviews with civil society representatives and international transitional justice NGO, Tunis, 2014–15. Some of the interlocutors stated that they later regretted the decision.

102 Personal interview with representative of the Lawyers' Order, Tunis, May 2015.

103 Article 22, Organic Law on Establishing and Organising Transitional Justice, quoted from the unofficial translation provided by the ICTJ.

104 Personal interview with representative of transitional justice NGO, Tunis, May 2014. See also Ben Hamadi (2014).

105 Personal interview with representative of transitional justice NGO, Tunis, May 2014.

106 Personal conversation in the NCA immediately after Ben Nejma's hearing before the selection committee, Tunis, May 2014.

107 Personal interview with member of the parliamentary selection committee, Tunis, May 2014.

108 Personal interview with truth commissioner, Tunis, March 2015. Personal conversations with transitional justice professionals, Tunis and New York, March/April 2015.

109 Personal interviews with truth commissioners, Tunis, March 2015.

110 Personal interview with truth commissioners and conversation with international transitional justice professional, Tunis, March 2015.

111 Personal conversations with international consultant, Tunis, March 2015, and New York, April 2015.

112 Interview by Khalil Abdelmoumen in *Tunis Hebdo*, 17 November 2014; on file.

113 "In any case, we expect that they advance much better and at a greater pace." Personal interview with ARP member, Tunis, March 2015.

5

Performing transitional justice

This chapter focuses on the planned, institutionalised transitional justice project and its institutions in action. It shows how the planned transitional justice project interacted with political developments, dissects the interplay between these two elements, and demonstrates how transitional justice was *performed* in this setting. As will become clear, the processes I distinguish here analytically are deeply intertwined.

In order to do so, the chapter mainly concentrates on the TDC, its work, and the debates it gave rise to. It also touches upon the specialised chambers, as well as the reparations process. To some extent, vestiges of the ad hoc measures and activities that were implemented in the first stage and competed with the institutionalised process still played a role. But in general activities became less scattered as they were consolidated into the planned framework, and attention was mainly focused on the truth commission and activities that were concretely *labelled* as transitional justice. The truth commission was the first institution established within the planned transitional justice process to become operational. Its operation – and the friction and interplay with other processes it entailed – was the most prominent development during this stage. Therefore, the chapter focuses strongly on this institution but also includes other developments, such as the specialised chambers and the reparations process. These are intertwined with or emanate from the truth commission.

While this chapter covers some procedural aspects, a more detailed description of the truth commission's work and the activities that took place behind relatively closed doors can be found in the Appendix. These procedural aspects may be helpful to illustrate analytical arguments and may offer partial explanations to simple questions, such as why the truth commission did not make faster progress with its work. Looking at how sophisticated the process for examining each case was and how many steps a single file passed through, it becomes clearer why the process was taking so long and at least partly explains why the truth commission ran into difficulties in finishing its work on time.

Performing the planned transitional justice project

Starting the truth commission's operation, collecting dossiers, statement-taking

During this stage, the institutionalised transitional justice project gained traction because its centrepiece, the TDC, had now commenced its work. After the nomination of truth commissioners in mid-2014 and a period of administrative consolidation, which lasted around six months, the commission started its activities in late 2014. In mid-December of that year, the period for victims to present their cases (or dossiers) started in the TDC's headquarters in Tunis. While the reception of dossiers in the regional offices should have begun a month later, in early 2015, this was postponed because the first regional offices[1] did not open before late summer that year. The regional offices did specific sensitisation work to inform their local population about the purpose and activities of the truth commission, and about how to submit cases for consideration. Additionally, the commission had mobile units to receive dossiers all over the country (Jeune Afrique 2016).

The transitional justice law sets the period for cases to be presented at one year with the possibility of this being extended for a further six months (Article 40). This was an option the commission made use of. In the eighteen-month period, the TDC received over 60,000 dossiers lodged by people or entities claiming victimhood. The dossiers were then processed by the TDC, and if a case was deemed admissible, the claimant was invited to attend a closed hearing to give more information about the case (see the Appendix for a more detailed description of this procedure).

There were diverging procedures for arbitrage cases handled by a specific sub-commission. This sub-commission aimed for an admission of guilt from the alleged perpetrator of an abuse and had the power to negotiate a 'conciliation agreement' in cases of economic crimes.[2] Here, the state was usually a stakeholder and not the potential perpetrator. This sub-commission operated almost in parallel to the victim-centred process, and dossiers could be transferred to the arbitrage commission at any stage in the process. As a truth commissioner put it: "Basically, the arbitrage commission can come in at any time 'from the side.'"[3] Similarly, cases could also be transferred over to the sub-commission dealing with institutional reform and vetting.[4] In view of the prominence of the arbitrage process, and the pressure this sub-commission was under given the threat of competing legislation that would curtail its competencies, the sub-commission was actively looking for high-profile cases.[5] The first arbitration accord was reached with Ben Ali's son-in-law, Slim Chiboub, in May 2016. In hindsight, the arbitrage process was subject to critique, as it was perceived as non-transparent.[6]

Public hearings

At the end of 2016, the truth commission started to conduct public hearings. In these hearings, victims or their relatives gave (often very personal) accounts of what had happened to them. The first public hearings were livestreamed on national television and available over the internet, in Arabic as well as with French or English translation.[7] The public hearings covered a range of cases. I personally attended the first set of public hearings, which took place in November 2016 in a venue in the suburbs of Tunis that had previously belonged to Ben Ali's wife Leila Trabelsi. The hearings covered a broad array of issues. On the first day of the hearing, for example, seven victims shared their stories, representing four different kinds of abuse. They were from different parts of the country and had become victims at different points in time. Among them were mothers of 'martyrs of the revolution,' the mother and wife of a 'disappeared' person, and two men who had been political prisoners during the Ben Ali and Bourguiba eras respectively (Salehi 2016).[8] In the following months, several public hearings were held in Tunis and other parts of the country. Some hearings covered specific topics, such as sexual violence, cyber-dissidence, or corruption.

Remnants of ad hoc measures, specialised chambers, and reparations

Despite the start of the planned transitional justice project, the ad hoc measures continued to play a contingent role and intersected at various points with the planned process. The court of cassation annulled the judgments of the military court of appeals and referred the cases back to the court of first instance. This means that there was still no legal clarity for those who had been injured during the revolution and for relatives of the deceased. Moreover, the long-promised official, comprehensive list of martyrs had not materialised, meaning even more legal uncertainty – and potential inability to claim compensation – for the bereaved. The transitional justice institutions had competence over the 'martyrs and wounded of the revolution' cases. Thus, victims could file their cases with the truth commission and seek compensation within its framework,[9] and the specialised chambers could take over cases from the 'regular' justice system and even re-open cases that had already been heard.[10]

The back-and-forth between different institutions and the military and civil justice system led to victims and their bereaved relatives losing further confidence in the justice system. There was still hope that the transitional justice project, or specifically the specialised chambers, would be able to better deliver justice than previous legal proceedings. The mother of a 'martyr of the revolution' addressed the truth commission during the first public hearings: "You are the last piece of wood we cling to."[11] While the specialised chambers were formally established by decree in 2014, they only took up their first cases in mid-2018. At the time of writing in late 2020, no case has been finalised. The chambers struggle with challenges such as the defendants not appearing in court, and there are concerns that they do not meet legal standards.[12] It thus remains to be seen whether these chambers would be able to better fulfil victims' expectations.[13]

The reparations process moved at different speeds. The legal basis for the so-called Dignity Fund can be found in the transitional justice law of 2013, but the fund has long only existed on paper. In 2018, a governmental decree specified how the fund should be organised, managed, and financed,[14] and in mid-2020, under the Fakhfakh government, a commission was established to administer it. In the meantime, however, the TDC had sent out decision letters about reparations, according to a point system. One of my interview partners criticised the insensitivity of the procedure and worried that it would do more harm than good by failing to include proper explanations or follow-up for further developments and how to potentially access reparations (for an overview, see table 5.1).[15]

Interplay of planned and unplanned processes

Since the institutionalised transitional justice project was codified in the 2014 Constitution, it should have acquired a certain degree of autonomy from political change, or specifically from shifts in political preferences (see also Elias [1986] 2006). Nonetheless, this independence is limited, since the operation of the transitional justice institutions interacted with unplanned processes within the area of transitional justice and planned and unplanned developments in other fields. In disentangling this interaction, this section reiterates how the pursuit of transitional justice and the dynamics of transitional politics were intertwined, since "planned developments [...] interweave constantly with unplanned developments" (Elias 1977, 138–9; own translation).

Subtle challenges to the planned transitional justice project

In the 2014 elections to the ARP – in which candidates were not subject to the exclusion clauses that had applied in 2011 – Nidaa Tounes became the strongest party in parliament, and its leader, Essebsi, went on to win the presidential election.[16] Since Nidaa Tounes is a melting pot of old-regime figures and other secularist politicians who joined forces to contain Ennahda

Table 5.1 Table summarising measures and purpose for the stage of *performing transitional justice*

Justice measures; institutions	Area of responsibility	Activities	Challenges
TDC, including sub-commissions and regional offices	Political and economic crimes from 1955 to 2013; suggestions for institutional reform	File collection, hearings (closed and public), arbitration processes, urgent interventions, reparations	Rumours about its partisanship, internal struggles, challenges from the political sphere (both implicit, such as late budgets, and explicit, such as the 'economic reconciliation law')
General justice system	Judicial accountability	Martyrs and wounded cases, corruption and embezzlement cases	No trust
Specialised chambers	Judicial accountability	Trials related to transitional justice	Absence of defendants; lack of will/capacity to enforce
Dignity Fund	Reparation and compensation	Not yet operational	Making it operational, funding

(Boubekeur 2016, 116) through the "accumulation of experience" at the "centrist-democratic end of the spectrum,"[17] it did not come as a surprise that their support for the transitional justice project was limited. While there was no immediate attempt to abolish the TDC,[18] the Nidaa Tounes-led government, and Essebsi in particular, made several moves to hamper its work.[19]

Alongside these shifts in the political configuration, there was no longer any direct ministerial responsibility for transitional justice within the new cabinet, and no direct counterpart at the ministerial level for institutions or organisations involved in the transitional justice process to communicate and interact with. The different portfolios were scattered among different ministries.[20] The Ministry of Justice, for instance, retained responsibility for the specialised chambers but no longer saw itself as responsible for any other parts of the transitional justice project.[21] A new ministerial authority responsible for relations with civil society and constitutional institutions assumed responsibility for coordinating the operations of the truth commission, especially with regard to institutional reform, although the TDC is technically not a constitutional institution.[22]

Policymakers did not see transitional justice as a pressing issue. Parliament refused to take responsibility for the advancement of the transitional justice project, and the burden of 'performing transitional justice' was instead transferred to the TDC: "Actually, I will not hide that parliament is not too focused on the question of transitional justice and will leave that to the Instance [Vérité et Dignité; the French name for the TDC]. [...]."[23] However, parliament remained responsible for nominating new truth commissioners following any resignations. For this, there was again a special selection committee, as there had been in the NCA. Posts of truth commissioners remained vacant for extended periods of time, making it even more evident that the transitional justice project was not among the ARP's priorities. Within regular budgetary procedures, the ARP was also responsible for allocating the commission's budget.

Subtle moves to challenge the truth commission include a failure to promptly replace commissioners who had resigned[24] or delaying the allocation of the TDC's budget.[25] A civil society representative perceived these moves as designed to render the commission ineffective:

> They will also continue to give the impression that the process continues, that the TDC continues. Here, the TDC has problems, it is not us but it is the TDC that has problems. People present their resignations. Maybe other people will present theirs [...] maybe I say. So, we may let [the commission] work, but it is not doing anything.[26]

Thus, the planned process of change interplayed with the unplanned political dynamics from the new political figuration and power shifts after the elections, making the institutionalised project subject to challenges.

Obstructing transitional justice: the 'reconciliation law'

According to a senior Ennahda politician, President Essebsi's attitude towards the transitional justice project could be summarised with the sentence: "We must leave the dead alone."[27] Thus, the President was not interested in dealing with the repressive past. One of the most direct moves affecting the truth commission's competence and potentially hindering its work was the President's legislative initiative for a so-called 'reconciliation law' (first dubbed the 'economic' and later the 'administrative' reconciliation law) that contained amnesty provisions. It impinged on the commission's mandate on economic crimes and corruption, as well as its mandate for vetting civil servants, and in its original form would have rendered the truth commission's arbitrage mechanism obsolete. Although unplanned from a transitional justice point of view, this initiative represented a planned attempt at change that fuelled unplanned political and social dynamics in other areas.

During the time that the discussion of this draft law dragged on prior to adoption, it was not only criticised by transitional justice professionals and civil society.[28] Politicians who considered themselves to have been part of the *ancien régime* – having been active in the RCD, if not necessarily part of the clientelist system of the Ben Ali/Trabelsi-clan – also expressed their scepticism of the draft law. In interviews, Nidaa Tounes MPs, for example, explained the importance of disclosing the names of those involved in corruption and embezzlement and the amounts of money in question, as well as making money flows transparent. These politicians were afraid that there would be a widespread assumption that there was some kind of 'joint liability' of all ex-RCD members for crimes of the clan and argued that full disclosure was the only way to show who had *not* been involved.[29]

Other actors in the transitional figuration held ambivalent positions: while UGTT officials and regional chapters joined protests against the new law (Ottendörfer et al. 2017), the leadership remained vague in its stance, neither entirely opposing the reconciliation initiative nor supporting it in the form initially proposed (Chahla 2015). Ennahda was also ambivalent about the law. Thus, cleavages regarding the quest for accountability for corruption and economic crimes were not clear-cut between government and opposition, between politics and civil society. The stances even differed within parties.

The 'reconciliation law' faced fierce opposition from the grassroots campaign 'Manich Msamah' (I will not forgive)[30] and initially did not pass parliament (for an overview of the law's history, see Lincoln 2017).[31] However, after being reintroduced several times, an amended version, renamed the 'administrative reconciliation law,' was eventually adopted by the ARP in September 2017. This version is much less far-reaching in its undermining of transitional justice than the version initially drafted by the presidency. However, a senior Ennahda politician posited that in Essebsi's view it had become important for him personally to succeed in having *any* version of the law passed so that his own authority would not be undermined.[32]

The former president's initial failure to have the law passed by parliament shows that the transitional justice project enjoyed some degree of autonomy from political actors' preferences. It also shows, however, how the interplay between two planned initiatives, in combination with spontaneous political and social dynamics, produced an altered law that nobody had initially intended. Unplanned political and social dynamics such as protests, or the President's need to demonstrate his authority, influenced how the institutionalised, socio-technological process was altered or revised.

Is 'the system' still in place? On the role of historical continuities

Already in 2014, before the NCA decided against a lustration paragraph in the new electoral law and paved the way for a return of former members of the old regime to official politics, several of my interview partners from politics and civil society remarked that the entire system did not suddenly vanish with the ouster of Ben Ali: "The fall of Ben Ali – that was only the fall of the head of the corrupt regime. That was not the fall of the entire corrupt regime. Hence, the corrupt regime still exists."[33]

Dismantling the system of favouritism and corruption would require political will and new authorities that were adequately staffed and resourced; it would also require cooperation between the justice system and the civil service.[34] The reconciliation law was to the advantage of members of the business elite, as well as civil servants, who might still benefit under the amended version. Given that there was no clean slate in Tunisia, the civil service's cooperation in tackling corruption, past and present, and vetting the public sector was very unlikely. In this regard, the institutionalised transitional justice project was influenced by the unplanned dynamics of pitting different structures against each other.

Directly related to the question of the 'system's' persistence, and another good example of the immanent dynamic and the partial autonomy (Elias 1978, 165) that institutionalised transitional justice developed from changing political preferences, is the public hearing on corruption in May 2017. Ben

Ali's nephew, Imed Trabelsi, who has been imprisoned since 2011, gave testimony[35] which was recorded in prison and aired on national television as part of a public hearing (Huffpost Maghreb 2017b). Trabelsi explained how the system had worked under Ben Ali and how the clan around the President had built quasi-monopolies for diverse goods. The smooth functioning of the system had been dependent on the involvement of ministers, high-level civil servants, and customs officers. As well as apologising for his involvement, he also stated that the fall of the regime had not been the end of operations for 'the system': "[T]here was a revolution, but nothing has changed to my knowledge. I receive my echoes and the same system [of corruption] is still operational" (quoted in Huffpost Maghreb 2017b; own translation).

Although the details revealed by Trabelsi did not come as a surprise, the hearing took place at a particularly important moment: the government had just reintroduced the reconciliation law to parliament, political factions were debating the conditions of their support,[36] and civil society was mobilising against the law, most prominently within the framework of the 'Manich Msamah' campaign.

Trabelsi's testimony consequently ran counter to the presidency's intention of selling its own legislative initiative as the measure the country needed for 'reconciliation' and therefore as being preferable to the institutionalised transitional justice project. The testimony instead made the President and his allies look as if they were seeking to cover up crimes committed by the country's business elite. The reconciliation law initiative was already perceived by those concerned with transitional justice as a "massive whitewashing operation"[37] even before Trabelsi came forward. However, the testimony of someone so directly involved in the old regime's clientelist networks had resonance among a different and much wider audience. For those who were generally sceptical, and saw institutionalised transitional justice measures as biased or as an 'Ennahda project,' it provided another degree of credibility to the corruption and favouritism revealed by the transitional justice process. It also countered the criticism that only victims, and not perpetrators, were able to speak at the public hearings, and that the audience was only hearing one side of the story.[38] It is noteworthy here that in hindsight those who gave testimony at the public hearings were also dissatisfied with the lack of perpetrator testimonies. Drawing on a TDC survey among those who testified, a truth commissioner noted that, for the victims, the missing perpetrator testimonies were like the missing piece of a puzzle: "The 'why' is missing. They don't know why the perpetrators did what they did."[39]

The temporal overlap between the testimony and the passage of the law interacted with competing action from the presidency in an unplanned manner and strengthened the institutionalised transitional justice project.

Despite the divergent political preferences of the ruling factions, and attempts at obstruction, the example of the Trabelsi hearing shows that the planned project acquired at least some independence that allowed it to pursue its mandate and agenda.

Rumours around the truth commission and its president, and resulting contention

As in the previous stage, the work of the transitional justice project in general and the TDC in particular generated rumours and conspiracy theories that influenced how they were perceived and the level of support or rejection they received. The process was often described as "biased"[40] and the truth commission members as partisan. Ben Sedrine was again at the centre of the rumours and criticism. She was described as a polarising figure: "There are people who are with [her] and people who are against [her]."[41] Ben Sedrine was said to hold an enormous amount of power within the commission, which was described to me as an "authoritarian structure [...] effectively [being] in the hands of Sihem Ben Sedrine."[42] According to one of my interview partners, this ruling style and Ben Sedrine's refusal to "accept second opinions" suggested "that thousands of files would not be studied."[43]

Assessments of Ben Sedrine 's role and performance also drew on gendered tropes. One interview partner found that "Sihem [Ben Sedrine] tries to build this mystic image about her. Like the goddess Athena."[44] Athena in Greek mythology is the protectress of the city and the goddess of war, wisdom, practical reason, and handicrafts who shared the responsibility for the sphere of war with Ares. However, Athena was morally and militarily superior, since "she represented the intellectual and civilized side of war and the virtues of justice and skill [...]. She ultimately became allegorized to personify wisdom and righteousness" (Encyclopaedia Britannica 2018). Therefore, for some, Ben Sedrine gave the impression of being morally superior and better able to fight for justice than others who may also be designated to do so.[45] This fits well with several first- and second-hand accounts that people from in- and outside the commission were annoyed by Ben Sedrine's alleged self-righteousness.[46]

There were also rumours about how Ben Sedrine came to occupy her role and her behaviour prior to becoming a truth commissioner. These range from the abovementioned allegations of her not paying the journalists who worked for her when she ran a radio station[47] to the assumptions that Ben Sedrine was chosen to become the TDC's president because she would be susceptible to blackmail[48] or because (Ennahda) politicians knew that she would be divisive and that was what they intended.[49] This assumption did not take into account that Ben Sedrine had been elected to this post by her fellow truth commissioners.[50] However, rumours about her personal integrity explain the strong polarisation and antipathy towards her occupying the position – and this in turn affected attitudes towards the truth commission as a whole. These unplanned social and political dynamics interacted with the planned process, since they raised questions about the TDC's integrity, legitimacy, and capacity to deliver justice. These factors made it harder for the truth commission to fulfil its mandate and to argue for its continued existence and need for strong budgetary and political support. Ben Sedrine's integrity was also called into question after the truth commission had ceased to operate, with several interview partners stating that she had singlehandedly altered the final report.[51]

The final stages and aftermath of the truth commission

While I wrote above that there were no direct attempts to abolish the truth commission, it should be noted that there were efforts to hinder the extension of its mandate. The initial mandate lasted for four years with the possibility for renewal for another year. The transitional justice law stipulates that the TDC could prolong its mandate with a qualified or reasoned decision (*décision motivée*), which would then need to be submitted to parliament at least three months before the expiration of its mandate. But it does not specify who can decide whether a decision is reasoned or not. In interviews and conversations in 2015, several interlocutors involved in Tunisian politics and civil society, as well as international transitional justice professionals, raised the question of whether parliament would renew the mandate, therefore clearly assuming that the ARP would be competent to take a decision on the matter. In early 2018, then, the truth commission submitted its decision to prolong its own mandate to the ARP. In doing so, it insisted that it was in fact the commission's decision alone, and that the formal requirement to submit the decision to the ARP for approval did not imply that it fell within the competency of the assembly to decide on any extension to the mandate. The administrative court that reviewed the matter issued a statement that it could not interfere in the legislative sphere and therefore could not prevent the ARP from voting on the matter. In a vote boycotted by most ARP members for procedural reasons, the decision was then taken that the TDC's mandate would not be extended. In the parliamentary session, the president of the assembly was asked to recuse themselves, since there were accusations that he had been incriminated by the TDC and that his decision could therefore be subject to bias. He refused to do so. At that point, it seemed unlikely that the TDC would be able to continue its work beyond May 2018, which would have meant that it would have been unable to finish its task. In late May, however, the Ministry of Relations with Constitutional Bodies, Civil Society, and Human Rights itself moved to extend the TDC's mandate until the end of 2018. Thus, the planned process interacted with the unplanned dynamic of an unclear legal and administrative situation, as well as with the political dynamics that were responsible for the difficulties involved in extending its mandate in the first place and for having blocked the establishment of a constitutional court that might have been able to decide on the matter.

The TDC produced a final report, submitted it to the 'three presidencies,' and made it public in March 2019. At the time, Tunisia was preparing for parliamentary and presidential elections, and transitional justice, as a controversial issue, was not high on the political agenda. The process stalled, and it was unclear whether there would be any follow-up by state institutions. However, with the changes in the political landscape – the demise of Nidaa Tounes, which lost eighty-three seats, and the change in the presidency and the government after the 2019 elections – the process gained traction once again, and in June 2020 the final report was finally published in the country's official gazette. Thus, despite an obvious dependency on political dynamics and power struggles, these late developments again show that the planned transitional justice process developed its own momentum to some degree.

Non-linearity, trends, and counter-trends

This stage was marked by two dominant trends, a further shift in transitional justice activities and attention towards the planned project and declining political support for seeking accountability. Therefore, in this third stage, it is consequently possible to identify simultaneous trends and counter-trends at various levels (Elias [1986] 2006, 104). First, while there was a general shift of attention towards the institutionalised project, at a governmental level the project did not receive the degree of institutionalisation that it had received in the previous phase. Additionally, while the planned transitional justice project gained traction and the truth commission started its work, there were attempts to curtail the main transitional justice institutions' competencies and to introduce competing legislation. In the new political figuration based on elite compromise and allowing old-regime figures 'back in,' there was a decline in political support for the transitional justice project and for seeking accountability.

As mentioned above, in the 'in-between-time' before the 2019 elections, when new actors entered the political scene and the previously dominant camp logic was of less importance, transitional justice was not high on the agenda, and the process had stalled after the TDC submitted its final report.

After the elections and the cumbersome process of forming a government, there was some movement under the Fakhfakh government, with the TDC's final report being published in the country's official gazette and a commission being set up to administer the Dignity Fund. While at the beginning of its tenure some interview partners expressed concerns that transitional justice might not be high on the agenda of the Mchichi government, others expressed a more optimistic outlook a few months later. These dynamics again show the entanglement and interplay of the transitional justice project with the political transition more generally.

Important here were changes of actors and power shifts in the political figuration as well as actors changing their preferences. In Tunisia, both dynamics were relevant, since there was a reconfiguration of political power after the 2014 elections, with Nidaa Tounes – and with it some of the 'old elites' – becoming more powerful, and relevant actors such as Ennahda's leadership changing their preferences in the course of forming new political alliances. In the run-off to the 2019 elections and the period that followed, it is again possible to observe changes in the political landscape and reconfiguration of power: Nidaa Tounes declined in importance, and the new president, Saied, as well the subsequent governments seemed to be somewhat more willing to move forwards with the transitional justice project. Elias claims that processes can develop autonomy from specific individual actors (Elias [1986] 2006, 109) but not entirely from them, and this was reflected in the advancement of the transitional justice project, which shows how institutionalised processes of change develop a dynamic that is partly, though not entirely, independent from non-linearity and shifts in power constellations and political preferences.

Since trends in transitional justice have been outlined in the section on activities, and counter-trends became visible in the interplay between planned and unplanned processes, this section will concentrate on pinpointing non-linearity in, and counter-trends to, transitional justice and accountability.

Closing of the 'revolutionary window of opportunity'

Let us now revisit the first stage, when *initiating transitional justice* was possible because of the specific post-revolutionary figuration that opened a window of opportunity to establish measures of accountability. Power shifted intermittently away from those actors who were entangled in old-regime structures and would consequently be opposed to transitional justice measures that would hold them or their allies accountable for past wrongs. The momentum of the revolutionary spirit was used by those in power at that time, specifically the 'Troika' government and the NCA, to have transitional justice included as an integral part of the new Tunisian constitution.

In the third stage of *performing transitional justice*, the revolutionary window of opportunity for accountability gradually closed. This is both the cause and effect of the decision to allow old-regime figures back into politics. While political cleavages between established forces directly after the revolution and those who had previously been oppressed and were new to the political scene went deep, and there was the political will as well as the structural opportunities to seek accountability and to institutionalise these efforts, this changed over time, as became apparent during this stage:

> You see that at the beginning there was a clear decision to dissolve the RCD, the ruling party [...].
> They were discharged from their positions under Ben Ali, revoked etc. and put in prison. Then, slowly, slowly these people started to be released [...].
> And this has created the sense that there is a political taxonomy, a trend of whitewashing the old regime and allowing them to come back.[52]

A human rights activist remarked that those figures implicated in the old regime who wanted to return to politics had "gained time" and "passed the most difficult period."[53] So while a return to the forefront of politics had previously seemed unlikely (Salehi 2014, 107), this stage would ultimately allow them to return to the political process.

The cleavages between the political camps – mainly between Islamists represented by Ennahda and the old structures represented by Nidaa Tounes – narrowed: after an intensification of political conflict in 2013 was overcome through the National Dialogue, the trend was increasingly in the direction of political compromise or elite 'deal-making' (see Marzouki 2015; Dihstelhoff and Sold 2016). As a consequence, those who had initially had an interest in seeking accountability, and thereby excluding their opponents from the political process, now started collaborating with those they had wanted to see held to account ("There was a marriage contract between Beji Caid Essebsi and Rached Ghannouchi"[54]). Ennahda's leadership therefore refrained from pushing for further accountability measures. This trend towards political compromise was partly grounded in the volatile economic and security situation: "There has been nostalgia, there has been a bit of a revisionist spirit in Tunisia following the socio-economic and security problems. So, the trend has changed a bit."[55]

In the period from the dissolution of the Ministry for Human Rights and Transitional Justice in early 2014 to the termination of the *chargé de mission*'s service in mid-2015, along with the changes in the composition of the government,[56] there was a gradual downgrading of transitional justice as a governmental priority. The responsibility for transitional justice within the government is no longer based at one government agency. Thus, there is no direct interlocutor for the institutions, which complicates their coordination with political institutions and can hinder the execution of their tasks. This institutional disintegration of transitional justice at the *governmental* level represents a counter-trend to the ongoing institutionalisation of transitional justice.

This counter-trend became even more obvious as President Essebsi and Prime Minister Youssef Chahed stayed away from the first set of public hearings organised by the TDC in November 2016, as did the president of the ARP (Mohammed Ennaceur, Nidaa Tounes).[57] Essebsi justified his absence with a statement from his office that he does "not need to be present at all events" (Directinfo 2016; own translation), adding that the transitional justice process was 'inherited' from the 'Troika' and the NCA. Moreover, allegedly, the transfer of the hearings from central Tunis to a suburb was not due to renovation works at the original venue, as had originally been claimed. Rather, this supposedly happened because President Essebsi did not want to have the hearings in the city centre with the "Tunisia 2020" investment conference in sight.[58] At this conference, Tunisia was to present its development plan to international investors, hoping for funding for large-scale infrastructure projects.

Returning to the notion of the 'revolutionary window of opportunity,' there was a slight re-opening around and after the 2019 elections. Saied, who won the presidential election, ran on a 'revolutionary' platform, as did some parties that emphasised their will to 'protect the revolution.'[59] As president, Saied showed some openness towards the transitional justice issue. The Fakhfakh government included Ayachi Hammami, a lawyer, human rights activist, and former member of the Ben Achour Commission, as minister for human rights and relations with constitutional bodies and civil society, who was advancing the issue and, as one civil society representative put it, "helped to put pressure on the government."[60] In that period, the truth commission's final report, which had been at the three presidencies for over a year, was finally published in the country's official gazette. This was an important step, as another civil society representative remarked: "Now it can't be erased from history."[61] However, at least partly due to the COVID-19 pandemic, the report and its official publication did not receive much attention.[62]

Fakhfakh had to step down after only a few months in office and a technocratic government under the leadership of Mchichi took over. Here, civil society representatives already identified a counter-trend to the previous short-term advancement of transitional justice efforts, as government officials were not willing to engage with them: "He didn't meet with transitional justice and human rights groups, but he met with other people. That's not a good sign."[63] This counter-trend became even more pronounced through a number of legal initiatives that would alter the course of transitional justice and were aimed at abandoning efforts for justice and accountability (Belhassine 2020). As with the previous reconciliation law, these initiatives again show a tendency to instrumentalise the notion of reconciliation, using it in a sense that implies there was no further need to pursue transitional justice. However, in October 2020 Prime Minister Mchichi nominated Abderrazak Kilani to lead the General Authority of Resistance Fighters, Martyrs, and Wounded of Revolution and of Terrorist Operations. Since Kilani, as the former chairman of the National Bar of Tunisia and a UN ambassador, is a highly respected figure in law and politics, my interview partners interpreted this as a sign that Mchichi actually cares about transitional justice.[64] Thus transitional justice in Tunisia continues to be marked by non-linearity and simultaneous trends and counter-trends including in the period after the TDC ended its work.

Simultaneous renunciation and discursive consolidation

One prominent example of a counter-trend to the planned efforts of the institutionalised transitional justice project, and the planned efforts for seeking accountability, is the abovementioned reconciliation law. The initial version of the bill would have created competing competencies to tackle cases of alleged corruption, embezzlement, and economic crimes and would have decisively curtailed the TDC's competencies in these areas. Corrupt businessmen could have gotten out of legal trouble by paying money into a so-called development fund, but this would not have helped to dismantle the underlying "wheelwork of corruption" (Guellali 2017a).

After it failed to pass parliament several times, an amended version of the law was eventually adopted by the ARP that limits its reach to the 'administrative' sphere, effectively the civil service and public sector. Essentially, it foregoes any chance of vetting or reforming state institutions (Guellali 2017b). Discursively, the so-called 'reconciliation law' played an ambiguous role. On the one hand, it was sold as a non-vindictive piece of legislation, since, as one MP stated, "Vengeance is not in our character as a people."[65] But it could also be interpreted as abandoning accountability and as symbolising a lack of empathy for those who had been marginalised and had suffered under the system of corruption and favouritism, and thus as a counter-trend to transitional justice (see also Elias [1986] 2006, 116–17). "The problem in Tunisia is [...] there are the parties that are attached to power. Ennahda and Nidaa want reconciliation without justice. The others [oppositional parties and civil society] want justice before reconciliation."[66] 'Reconciliation,' previously understood as an objective of transitional justice, was reframed and increasingly used as a discursive tool to express opposition to the institutionalised project and accountability measures.[67] Framing the bill as a reconciliation initiative, and thus explicitly using transitional justice terminology, was an attempt to divert attention from and undermine the institutionalised transitional justice process. But it also shows that transitional justice *language* became part of the discursive repertoire of Tunisian elites (Salehi 2019). Hence, it is possible to identify a simultaneous trend and counter-trend: a renunciation of institutionalised transitional justice despite further discursive consolidation, through appropriation and *reinterpretation* of the notions entailed by the concept.

Ennahda's alternations

The counter-trend of eroding transitional justice was developing at the same time as the planned process was unfolding and as its related institutions became operational. These different processes and opposing trends were partly advanced by the same set of political actors in the transitional figuration. Ennahda in particular played an ambiguous role. Initially, the party was a driving force behind seeking accountability, compensating victims, and institutionalising transitional justice. It also shaped the composition of the truth commission and the design of the transitional justice project. While the party's support for seeking accountability and the institutionalised transitional justice process was not abandoned outright, it gradually became less consistent. One of my interview partners described transitional justice as a "bait" with which Ennahda had to engage while having no interest in it being successful: "Sixty-thousand people is a lot of votes."[68] In this stage, the non-linearity in Ennahda's policy became even more pronounced, both with regard to the *substance* of transitional justice and with regard to the *institutionalised components* of the process.

As part of the elite compromise, Ennahda's leadership had already abandoned the quest for the lustration of parliament in 2013, a decision pushed by Rachid Ghannouchi against the will of the party base (Marks 2015), which found it very hard to accept the failure to exclude former RCD members.[69] Legal clarity on the issue emerged only in mid-2014, when the corresponding article in the electoral law – Article 167 – failed to receive the necessary votes in parliament. Yet despite Ghannouchi's lobbying for the article not to pass, the decision was very tight. The article failed to pass by only one vote, since most Ennahda MPs voted in favour of the article and against the leadership's position (Marks 2015).

After the 2014 election, Ennahda joined the Nidaa Tounes-led government, although initially with only one symbolic ministerial post.[70] According to one dissenting Nidaa Tounes member who had not been part of the old regime, this "conservative–conservative alliance" was perceived to be leading "to [the] exclusion of all progressive forces" and the "recurrence of the mafia state."[71] A human rights activist described the parties as "two sides of the same coin."[72] Technically part of the governing coalition, Ennahda found it increasingly hard to adopt stances that were not in the interests of the members of Nidaa Tounes. Thus, rather than offering clear support, even Ennahda members voiced criticism vis-à-vis the truth commission: "In any case, we expect that they advance much better and at a higher speed."[73] Thus, transitional justice partly fell victim to what Nadia Marzouki (2015) refers to as "Tunisia's rotten compromise" between the two major political camps.

After Prime Minister Habib Essid lost a no-confidence vote in parliament and Chahed assumed the post in August 2016, a 'national unity government' comprising even more parties was formed. Ennahda's role in the government, and therefore also the closeness of the alliance, grew slightly with this reshuffle. The party received three ministerial portfolios, while Nidaa Tounes struggled with internal problems and defections.[74] The no-confidence vote was preceded by the 'Carthage Agreement,' sponsored by the presidency from its headquarters in the Tunis suburb of Carthage, which set out the priorities for the new national unity government. The agreement was signed in July 2016 by nine political parties and major associations. Scrutinising the ever closer collaboration of the major political forces in the country, Julius Dihstelhoff and Katrin Sold found that such an agreement could be criticised on the grounds that it leaves little space for oppositional control, personalises decision-making channels instead of relying on democratic procedures, leads to the avoidance of controversial topics, and institutionalises political strategies that were previously meant as measures to be taken in times of crisis (Dihstelhoff and Sold 2016).

However, despite the rapprochement between Ennahda and Nidaa Tounes and the gradual abandonment of accountability norms, several prominent Ennahda figures, including Ghannouchi, attended the first public hearings of the TDC in November 2016, thereby signalling their support for the institutionalised process. The leaders of Nidaa Tounes were absent, but the secretary-general of the powerful labour union the UGTT did attend, as did several prominent figures from the political left, such as the leader of the Popular Front (a leftist electoral alliance), indicating broader interest and support.[75] Thus, Ennahda's position was non-linear. It alternated between supporting and abandoning transitional justice and accountability and between allying with and dissociating itself from the old regime.

Disagreements within the party have also come to the fore. In November, Rachid Ghannouchi, the president of Ennahda and since November 2019 the speaker of the ARP, strongly criticised the truth commission and called for "global national reconciliation" and a new law to "close" the issue of transitional justice (Belhassine 2020). As well as provoking an open letter from five former truth commissioners,[76] a senior Ennahda politician described Ghannouchi's initiative as a personal one that the parliamentary group only heard about from the media.[77] Confronted with the same question about the initiative from the party leader, another Ennahda politician remarked that transitional justice was "not a commodity, but something that we have to do."[78] Thus, while reconciliation in general would be desirable, it should not be traded off against seeking truth, holding perpetrators to account, and providing compensation to those who suffered from violence, repression, and marginalisation. The politician was thereby trying to downplay the inconsistency in the messaging that Ennahda politicians have provided about transitional justice.

Trends in perceptions of the transitional justice process

This section outlines trends in the perception of transitional justice based on what was voiced in interviews and personal conversations, as well as in the media and on social media. There were two parallel but diverging trends: criticism of the institutionalised project and criticism of the obstacles in its path. Criticism of the project was to a large extent personalised and directed against truth commission members, particularly the leadership of the commission. The truth commission was often perceived as 'partisan,' with the legitimacy of the process also being questioned.[79] One argument was that it offered "small measures for big problems"[80] and that it would be unable to fulfil its task. The body's legitimacy was also called into question on the grounds that its members and their actions as commissioners were far from 'impeccable.' As mentioned above, there were plenty of rumours of interests and loyalties that might be driving their actions, as well as accusations of actual malpractice. Additionally, the impression that the commission's leadership believed itself to be above the law did not help to build trust in the project but enforced the impression of an autocratic style[81] that meant the commission was no better than old-regime institutions and simply represented different interests. Allegations of corruption, especially with regard to the opaque arbitrage process and "deals behind the scene,"[82] reflected similar sentiments. Another example was the lack of transparency on urgent interventions and the possibility of receiving ad hoc material support. No clear criteria were publicly announced, and according to one of my interview partners, the commission fired a judge who was not willing to sign off urgent interventions for people who were ineligible, a step that was opposed by some of the commission's members.[83] A lack of transparency and infighting also impeded the development of "societal ownership" of the truth commission and by extension the institutionalised transitional justice process – as one transitional justice professional put it, "these are the things that are remembered, the infighting, the lack of transparency, the problem with arbitration and Sihem's personality."[84] This general perception was not helped by the decision of former truth commissioners to run for parliament in 2019, allegedly with the aim of gaining legal immunity.[85] Two of the commissioners who were elected joined the parliamentary committee responsible for transitional justice, which another MP described as a conflict of interest.[86] According to a transitional justice professional, the decision of Zouheir Makhlouf to join Qalb Tounes, which they described as a "corrupted party," undermined the TDC's credibility even further. They recounted "painful remarks" about how "independent commissions take money and don't deliver," with the TDC being used as an example.[87]

Simultaneously in this stage, attempts at obstructing or hollowing out the transitional justice process, such as the reconciliation law initiative, were met with criticism and protest. This was expressed through the 'Manich Msamah' protests as well as in statements by civil society representatives, for example opposing the new law because of its unconstitutionality: "Because you can't impose a law that's against the constitution."[88] In addition, the public hearings may have contributed to making the commission's work more visible, and perceived more positively, by confronting the broader public with details of the country's history. By covering a broad range of violations, and a variety of victims from different generations and ideological backgrounds, the hearings were able to provide contact points for different parts of society.[89] Several interview partners emphasised the importance of the public hearings and their contribution to a more positive perception of the TDC's work. In hindsight, a truth commissioner found that: "The best gain, the fruit of our work, were the public hearings. The victims made them a success. They gained sympathy."[90] However, some of those who gave testimony did not perceive them quite as positively, especially when they were subsequently disappointed with how the truth commission treated them or handled their cases: "The victims told us that we used them at the public hearings."[91]

The specialised chambers started taking on cases in mid-2018, and thus efforts towards justice and accountability moved forwards while the TDC faced challenges in extending its mandate. Thus, we can again see simultaneous trends and counter-trends here. Moreover, the start of the trials again helped to bring attention to the transitional justice process. However, the specialised chambers found it difficult to bring the accused into court to attend their trials, and the security forces did not cooperate in enforcing their appearance. This impaired the perception of the trials as a potential avenue to bring about justice and hold perpetrators to account. One transitional justice professional remarked that the specialised chambers delivered a "poor performance," that they were like "theatre, a *mise en scène* as if they were public hearings."[92]

Thus, as mentioned above, there were simultaneous trends and counter-trends that criticised and defended the legitimacy of the institutionalised transitional justice process. Therefore, in this stage there was neither a clear advancement nor a retreat of accountability norms but simultaneous movements in both directions, confirming that norms or standards of transitional justice, of seeking accountability for past abuses, can be reversed.

International interconnectedness

Although this third stage in the process, that of *performing transitional justice*, was influenced by international expertise, as in the stage of *designing transitional justice* in Tunisia, there was an important difference in that domestic initiatives partly countered the internationally supported, institutionalised project.

Continuous transfer of knowledge and resources

The institutionalised transitional justice process was informed and supported by international expertise drawn from governmental and non-governmental organisations. This manifested in workshops and training sessions but also in technical support and the provision of financial resources for the operation of the transitional justice institutions.[93] Examples include the training of judges for the specialised chambers provided by the UNDP, technical support for the implementation of the public hearings by the ICTJ, and Avocats Sans Frontières' support in preparing the documentation for Kasserine to claim the status of 'victim region.'[94] International actors were also involved in drafting the commission's final report in various ways, ranging from helping with money and specialists and providing knowledge on data collection methodologies[95] to drafting entire sections of the report.[96] The ICTJ also continued to hold workshops and consultations after the truth commission ended its work.[97]

Foreign politicians and delegates from embassies frequently visited the TDC to express their support of the institution. Members of the TDC also visited other countries and the headquarters of international organisations and frequently spoke on panels and roundtables on transitional justice and/or Tunisia.[98] Hence, international knowledge transfer did not happen unidirectionally but rather as circulation, since Tunisian actors shared – and continue to share – insights that might be relevant in other contexts.

Between technical support and advocacy

As outlined above, international transitional justice professionals aimed to avoid giving the impression that they were taking sides in the process. However, the organisations involved nevertheless advocated for the transitional justice project to proceed and to comply with certain international standards, which they themselves to a large extent defined. This standpoint was contentious, since it was shared by some domestic actors but not by others. It therefore put these international actors in a certain political 'corner' because a transitional justice project conducted in this manner inevitably served the interests of some domestic actors more than others.

As one staff member of a transitional justice NGO remarked (not specific to the Tunisian context), international transitional justice experts found themselves reflecting on this dilemma: "At the beginning, we just wanted to provide technical assistance. But then we realised that this is not possible, when you are pushing for a human rights agenda, which is a political issue. Now we're more outspoken about that." Most Tunisian interview partners assessed the partnership as valuable: "[T]hey are very cooperative [and] respect all our choices,"[99] a truth commissioner stated about working with international organisations and NGOs, adding that international support lends the truth commission credibility. Several other interview partners emphasised that international experts, especially from the ICTJ, provided valuable knowledge in terms of content and techniques for "how to do the work."[100] While there is indeed criticism that the international transitional justice professionals, particularly those from ICTJ but also from other organisations, such as Avocats Sans Frontières, were too dominant in Tunisia "and didn't leave space for local NGOs,"[101] there are also voices who appreciate the organisation's work and advocacy: "ICTJ helped every time there was a problem."[102]

Apart from questions of ownership and agency, there was also criticism that the technical support was not done well. For example, one interview partner voiced criticism towards an international NGO's decision to let a "super junior"[103] consultant work on a part of the final report that would have required substantial technical expertise, as well as political sensitivity, and that especially the latter was lacking.

Another line of criticism directed at international actors was the 'unconditional support' offered to the TDC, which helped "much more the president [of the commission] than the Instance [i.e. the TDC] itself."[104] As a consequence of this stance, a member who resigned contends that the international community forestalled some necessary reforms at the truth commission.[105] There was also criticism that "donors continued to fund something that is failing" when the truth commission did not work well because they "needed to present it as a success."[106] UNDP in particular has been criticised: "They provided money, but not oversight."[107] Similarly, OHCHR allegedly tried to prevent expert criticism of the report.[108]

Thus, international support and advocacy continued to play a role in this stage, and the related discussions mirror wider political dynamics in the transition. Consequently, in this last stage, when there was limited political will, any further engagement in transitional justice was necessarily also advocacy, even when it came in the form of technical support, because it helped to keep the issue on the agenda in a political climate in which those in power hoped to wait it out: "Let time do the job and let people forget."[109]

Facing potential backlash

In several conversations with international consultants to the Tunisian transitional justice project, it became clear that they were willing to work with the project in the form in which it had been established, even if they viewed it as far from perfect. During the truth commission's consolidation phase, an NGO representative stated that "[the transitional justice law] is not really an excellent law, not a bad law, it's [...] you know, it's good, we can work with it. It's a compromise."[110] Given the fading political momentum that had made initiating and institutionalising a transitional justice project possible in the first place, the dominant assumption among international transitional justice professionals was that altering its founding law in an attempt to reform the truth commission could endanger the entire project. Any attempt to change the law would also run the risk that a new version, which would need to be passed by parliament with a very different composition than the NCA, would not be 'better' but 'worse.'[111] This could, for example, be in terms of mandate, competencies, or material resources – or that the opportunity would even be used to dismantle the truth commission entirely.[112]

Although (or maybe because) domestic cleavages and standpoints on transitional justice became less clear over time, especially with the tendency towards elite deal-making between the two dominant political camps, international actors' stances became more pronounced – even if their actual position did not change. This is because the sensitivity of the subject matter changed over time and advocacy for a transitional justice project aiming at accountability became more controversial.[113] The ICTJ especially became more vocal in criticising political agendas and policy initiatives and publicly declared its opposition to the President's 'reconciliation law.' While ICTJ President David Tolbert had already commented on the draft law when it was first introduced in 2015, at the time of its re-introduction into parliament the organisation joined other Tunisian and international civil society organisations in openly declaring their opposition to the law (see e.g. Bel-hassine 2016; ICTJ 2017). International NGOs that work on related issues such as human rights likewise took stances in this debate. Through its Tunisia researcher Amna Guellali, Human Rights Watch in particular highlighted some of the legal implications of the draft law and their potential consequences for the overall transition (Guellali 2017b).

What is more, international actors also had to navigate the internal quarrels within the truth commission. 'Side-taking' in the internal conflicts, or the impression thereof, was hardly avoidable. A simple example causing discontent was the question of which commissioners international actors chose to work with.[114]

Related to the backlash over the human rights situation more generally, during this stage and even before the two major terrorist attacks in the first half of 2015,[115] the political and security situation became more volatile and served as a justification for repressive politics. International human rights actors noted potential trends that pointed to a return of authoritarian practices including human rights abuses and restrictions of freedoms: "[O]bviously this has alarming implications for the human rights situation because we see more and more arrests. We see a return of former regime practices. We see a return of former regime figures."[116]

Representatives of an international organisation who were concerned about this tendency stated that they hoped to send a signal to the Tunisian government by despatching high-level figures to Tunis to discuss the human rights situation in the country. This was intended to show that the international community was not only concerned about the country's security situation but also about respect for human rights and the non-recurrence of repression.[117]

Lastly, it should briefly be mentioned that 'the international' does not always serve as a protector of transitional justice; it depends on the sector and the interests involved. The economic situation, and international intercon-nectedness at the economic level, was for instance used to justify a potential backlash relating to accountability. The transitional justice project was repeatedly framed as not being helpful in attracting badly needed foreign investment (Guellali 2017b). Thus, as mentioned above, the government reportedly did not want the public hearings to take place in the centre of Tunis with the 'Tunisia 2020' international investment conference taking place shortly afterwards, since transitional justice efforts were seen as having the potential to convey a negative image of Tunisia as an unstable country.[118]

This section has shown the crucial influence of international intercon-nectedness by demonstrating the continuous influence of international norms and knowledge, as well as the tension between technical support and advocacy that international transitional justice professionals find themselves in when faced with changing political conditions. The unplanned dynamics of potential backlashes over justice, accountability, and human rights influenced how international actors positioned themselves in the transitional justice figuration and expressed further support for the institutionalised project. Their position within the transitional justice figuration changed, even if their absolute position did not.

Conflict and friction

This stage of *performing transitional justice* was marked by conflict and friction that served as defining and driving components of social and political processes of change. As we have seen in the previous parts of this chapter, conflict and friction are among the main drivers of social processes (Elias [1986] 2006, 106). They bring about unplanned dynamics that interact with planned processes of change and are sometimes responsible for the development of diverging trends and counter-trends and define the character of international interconnectedness. This next section therefore serves the purpose of bundling and highlighting these aspects to point out the importance of conflict and friction in characterising the processual developments.

Friction between the truth commission and political and civil society spheres

In this stage, conflict and friction developed between the transitional justice institution, namely the TDC, and the political sphere (parts of the government, but also parts of parliament), as well as within the truth commission itself. This had consequences for the truth commission's ability to carry out its work, since these dynamics can be disruptive, and for the perception of its integrity.

With the changes in the political figuration, including power shifts and changing political preferences, transitional justice became subject to even more pronounced frictions of a political origin. This brought about challenges to the institutionalised transitional justice project. Although it was codified in the Tunisian constitution, and although the transitional justice law foresees "financial and administrative independence" (Article 16) for the TDC, parliament and the government could still take decisions that would influence the commission's ability to work. The commission's budget had to be approved by parliament and provided with the necessary funding. Some measures, such as budgetary restrictions or complications (e.g. delays in delivering the budget),[119] as well as the general lack of communication with the truth commission,[120] were perceived as a sign of a lack of political will for transitional justice and as fostering frictions. In the same vein, the ARP was responsible for nominating substitutes for truth commissioners who had resigned, a task that it did not treat with any urgency.[121] This ran the risk that the commission would become unable to function, because the law had set the quorum for valid decisions at two-thirds of its members (Article 59). Even more directly, measures provoking frictions between the political sphere and the truth commission relate to legislation that would curtail the commission's competencies, such as the reconciliation law. In addition, there was also a conflict over whether parliament was able to vote to extend the TDC's mandate, as mentioned above.

There were also frictions of a more personal or emotional origin. There was said to be a personal 'feud' between Tunisian President Essebsi and the president of the TDC, Ben Sedrine, with Essebi publicly stating that "Ben Sedrine [...] is unbearable, she is a 'disease.'"[122] Some have assumed that it was this personal animosity that triggered the President's initiative of the economic reconciliation law: "I think it's not a question of efficiency [as suggested by Essebsi], but it's a question of settling a problem between Beji and Sihem."[123] Similarly, Ben Sedrine was also accused of using the transitional justice process to settle personal scores.[124] Thus, this is reminding us about Elias's point on the (non-)rationality of bureaucratic measures.

Unilateral decisions taken by the truth commission's president fuelled various conflicts of a political and emotional origin. With regard to relations with the government, Ben Sedrine's attempt to seize the presidential archives without previous discussion or negotiation provoked outrage and questions about the commission's role, competence, and legitimacy. In the following example, a history professor explained why in his opinion the 'archive incident' was not conducive to trust in the TDC, since it let the people question the motives of its president. Although he acknowledged that the TDC was entitled to have access to the archives, he criticised the commission for overstepping its area of competence by not following proper rules of procedure. The lengthy quote below illustrates that there was also discontent over the idea that all rules and regulations existing in the Tunisian state prior to the revolution had become void:

> That's a desperate initiative, and it points to contempt of the archival rules. You imagine, the text [of the law], Article 40,[125] it says it authorises the commission, or the Instance [i.e. the TDC]. If someone [...] you present yourself, you say 'I'm a victim' etc. what's the role of the Instance? That's to look for the file. [...] But one does not take all the archives and put them in a different place. One cannot do that. So, this is [...] but this is contempt. It makes you think [...] so, in a modern country, which has a law on archives, not only in history. It has established these archives in 1975, but the law was updated in 1988 and it regulates [...] it regulates how the archives are managed. [...] So, it's because of this that I say that this behaviour hides badly a desire for vengeance, a desire for vengeance.[126]

This emphasises again that 'the past is not another country.' Indiscriminately ignoring or undermining existing provisions and competences alienated even those generally sympathetic to transitional justice and caused frictions beyond the cleavage between supporters and victims of the old regime.[127] Another issue pertaining to archives occurred towards the end of the TDC's mandate. According to two of my interview partners, there was disagreement among the truth commissioners about what to do with the victims' files and their testimonies and whether and in what way there could be a distinct memory institution.[128] Yet while the paper files were handed over to the National Archives, the digital files emerging from the TDC's secret hearings were handed over to the presidency of the republic, according to one of my interview partners because of a fight between the TDC's president and the director of the National Archives. Victims expressed fear about the recordings being handed over to the presidency.[129] This is highly problematic in a context in which victims trusted the TDC with their statements and in which it is unclear who will be in power, have access to the files, and the purposes for which they will use them.

Additionally, conflict and friction between the political sphere and actors from within the transitional justice figuration[130] have been grounded in the government's inaction and delaying tactics. This includes initially not publishing the TDC's final report, not enforcing the presence of the accused at the trials of the specialised chambers, and delays in setting up the Dignity Fund.

Internal conflicts and friction

The TDC's composition, which was already a matter of contention in the previous stage, proved far from harmonious. Several of its members had already resigned in the consolidation phase, and relationships became more frictional during the operational phase. These frictions again had different origins, with blurry lines between what was more political and what was more emotional.

This became noticeable most obviously when the commission's vice-president, Zouheir Makhlouf, unsuccessfully tried to remove Ben Sedrine from her post by sending a letter containing accusations against her to the president of the ARP (Réalités 2015). Makhlouf was then dismissed from the TDC, a decision which was overturned by the administrative court. After his re-instatement by the court, the conflict escalated, and he was physically prevented from entering the TDC's building and his office to continue his work as truth commissioner (Huffpost Maghreb 2016). In the run up to this escalation, there were, for example, allegations that Ben Sedrine had taken financial decisions alone – decisions which should have been authorised by the plenary of the TDC. This antagonised other commission members because they had been sidelined over those decisions. They were also worried that this would cause the commission trouble with the financial oversight authorities, since a similar incident happened with the president of the first ISIE, the electoral commission for the NCA elections, who was accused of mismanagement.[131] In hindsight, a parliamentarian stated that they should have paid more attention to the accusations voiced by Makhlouf: "It turned out that the things he mentioned about the commission were true and I regret that we didn't listen more to him."[132]

One line of conflict that was frequently mentioned in interviews was the rivalry between the TDC's president, Ben Sedrine, and the women's commissioner, Ibtihel Abdellatif. The rifts were reportedly so strong that the commissioners did not talk to each other.[133] Ben Sedrine allegedly tried to prevent Abdellatif from joining prestigious international events or taking on public-facing work.[134] According to various interview partners, Ben Sedrine also removed the chapter on women and sexual violence from the TDC's final report before it was submitted.[135] This could have serious consequences, as the issue of sexual violence might not receive the attention it deserves and the women concerned could be denied justice and dignity. Concretely, in combination with widespread logging of sexual violence as torture by statement-takers,[136] if the Dignity Fund actually becomes operational then women would potentially receive less compensation than they would be entitled to if the crimes against them had been recorded correctly.[137]

The final report was not approved and submitted by all remaining commissioners. In addition to the general legal problem of having a commission that does not meet its quorum, which meant that "everything the IVD [i.e. Instance Vérité et Dignité – the TDC] did carried some sort of illegality to it,"[138] the report kept being changed after the mandate expired. Several interview partners attributed the changes made to the report to the TDC's president, Ben Sedrine, and assessed this as highly problematic.[139]

In a different vein, based on research at two regional offices in Gafsa and Kasserine, I observed two further dynamics relevant for analysing friction in the process. First, a conclusion I draw with caution – at least in the immediate aftermath of them being opened, it seemed as if the regional offices were less affected by the conflicts and frictions in Tunis and could focus more on pragmatic, operational activities: "[F]or the regional offices, there are no problems because all the problems are in the centre in Tunis."[140] However, interaction and communication between the regional offices and headquarters seemed to be frictional as well. Staff at the regional offices did not feel well informed about decisions taken in Tunis, and their questions often remained unanswered.[141]

Although a civil society representative in Gafsa stated that those working in the TDC's regional office mostly owed allegiance to either Ennahda or Nidaa Tounes,[142] interviews with regional office directors provided more of a 'technocratised' than a 'politicised' impression. Both office directors, in Gafsa and Kasserine, were bureaucrats temporarily transferred to the truth commission who were appointed to their posts through a national *concours* – a competitive process used by the public sector. They did not have backgrounds as victims, activists, or in human rights work. Nor did they mention any political affiliation when asked about their backgrounds. Although they considered the transitional justice process to be important, and their task as contributing to the TDC fulfilling its mandate, they described themselves as being more driven by civic duty or a change in career than by political commitments. Thus, from their perspective, the frictions between the truth commission and the political sphere were a distraction from 'getting work done':[143] "I'm with the TDC and its objectives, its role. Other things don't concern me. The problems of the politicians, the blockage [...] that doesn't concern me. I have work to get done and a role to do."[144] When asked about political support or obstacles locally, and the frictions surrounding the transitional justice process, which became evident from research in Tunis, a director of a regional office stated that it was important to differentiate between local politicians' personal opinions as 'Kasserinois' (i.e., inhabitants of Kasserine, a marginalised region, who were likely to be in favour of the transitional justice project) and their stance as party politicians (against the project).[145]

While these internal frictions had a disruptive effect on the institutionalised transitional justice project and, as mentioned above, the infighting will likely be remembered as a defining feature of the truth commission, it also brought about new dynamics. For example, while internal struggles had the effect of undermining the truth commission's credibility, they also encouraged the perception that the TDC is not a one-sided, partisan body but comprises different perspectives. However, given the strong linkage of the commission with its president,[146] the former effect may prevail.

Friction between state forces and civil society

This stage was also marked by conflict and friction between the government or state forces and civil society. This conflict was felt both in driving the dynamics of transitional justice and in defining the broader political climate. With repeated attempts by the presidency to get the reconciliation law passed by parliament and to obstruct the institutionalised transitional justice project, there was explicit mobilisation against the law, with 'Manich Msamah' activists being especially vocal.[147] As well as demonstrations, the movement also used 'naming and shaming' tactics, such as "publishing the names of corrupt businessmen along with an estimate of the illegal profits they have made over the years" (El Hachimi 2020, 905). Mohamed El Hachimi (2020,

904) describes this kind of mobilisation and political engagement as "*In-politics-outside-parties* tendency" (emphasis in the original).

Second, contentious action increased in particular in the country's south and centre, with the size of the protests in early 2016 exceeding the record numbers of the years of the revolution (2010/11) and spreading to the capital for the first time since the uprisings (Vatthauer and Weipert-Fenner 2017, I, 2). Central to the protesters' demands has been the quest for social justice, not so much with regard to compensation for the marginalisation the regions had suffered in the past but their current economic situation, which is blighted by unemployment and lack of perspective. The protests have been fuelled by long-standing structures and practices including the ongoing distribution of public-sector jobs through corruption and clientelist networks that have their origins in the Ben Ali era: "[J]obs are still either channelled to political clients or to the ones who can afford to pay" (Salehi and Weipert-Fenner 2017).

These structures were built over several decades and with the extensive involvement of RCD cadres. Yet Ennahda's emergence as a crucial player in the political system did not lead these structures to be dismantled or bring an end to nepotistic practices: "Nahda reproduced the same system during its government […] the two years of government […] the same system we had with the single party. It was copy-paste of the same type of practice."[148]

Thus, many people believe that "[t]he structures remained the same, only the individuals occupying and governing them changed" (Schmitter and Sika 2017, 449). It was against this backdrop that the 'Fech Nestanew?' (What are we waiting for?) campaign started mobilising against the 2018 budget law (El Hachimi 2020, 905) and economic austerity. As spokesperson Henda Chennaoui explained in a media interview: "In 2014, nothing happened. In 2015 either, neither in 2016, nor in 2017. The political class showed no sign that it was doing anything. That's why we called our campaign 'What are we waiting for?'" (Matarese 2018).

These dynamics demonstrate the ongoing conflictive potential in transitional Tunisia, which regularly culminates in violent clashes, as well as emphasising the broader societal importance of 'dismantling the system,' even if transitional justice is not directly addressed. The very fact that it is not directly addressed, however, indicates that the institutionalised transitional justice project is not perceived as a relevant avenue for achieving justice for every actor in the transitional figuration. While one of my interview partners criticised those involved in the transitional justice project – especially the truth commission – for operating "as if they were […] in a vacuum" and ignoring "so much [that] has been done outside of transitional justice,"[149] there have been some efforts to broaden the discussion. For example, an event organised by the ICTJ on reparations in November 2020 included a representative from the Kamour Movement, which is located in the Tataouine region and calls for greater levels of employment in the oil sector, thus, exactly one of these protest movements that had not previously linked their quests for social justice to transitional justice.[150]

Conclusion

This stage of *performing transitional justice* reveals the interplay between socio-technological and planned processes of change with unplanned political and social dynamics. By exploring this interaction, the chapter has again emphasised how important it is to look at transitional justice processes in relation to their interaction with political and social change, that is, with *transitions* more generally.

This chapter showed how political support for the Tunisian transitional justice project has not been linear, and the political will for seeking account-ability has fluctuated over time. At certain points, the same actors who initially appeared to be committed to the goals of the transitional justice process later appeared to have renounced them, while some actors seemed to hold both positions at the same time. This is particularly apparent in the case of Ennahda, which fluctuated between supporting transitional justice and accountability and appearing to abandon that goal – especially in response to shifting power structures and new political alliances, which after the 2014 elections involved figures who had been prominent members of, or closely linked to, the old regime. Political dynamics now leaned more towards elite deal-making than pursuing accountability. Together with the election results, this logic determined the reconfiguration of political power and subsequent decision-making. In the run-up to and after the 2019 elections, then, there was again a shift in the power structures and dominant political logic. This again opened a window of opportunity for transitional justice to some degree, as the new government and president were more willing to move forwards with issues that had previously stalled, such as the publica-tion of the TDC's final report.

This stage also reveals how institutionalised processes can develop dynam-ics that are partly independent of actors and their political preferences. Despite declining support for the project on a political level after the 2014 elections – or maybe even beforehand with the National Dialogue when the political logic of elite deal-making gained dominance – fixing transitional justice in the constitution prevented the presidency under Essebsi, and the governments dominated by Nidaa Tounes, from pursuing their impunity agenda undisturbed. The project was able to continue thanks to its institutionalisation, some degree of popular support, as well as the cooperation of prominent figures that lent more legitimacy to the process – by testifying in public hearings, for example.

The changes in domestic political preferences and the non-linearity in political support for transitional justice also influenced the dynamics of international interconnectedness. Due to the changing positions of domestic actors and a changing context, international actors found themselves in a position of being more vocal advocates of the project and critics of government policies than had previously been the case, without changing their absolute positions towards the project.

The dynamics of change analysed in this stage were again driven and defined by conflict and frictions at various levels. Here, both internal and external dynamics were decisive, since they influenced how the truth commission was able to 'perform' its task of transitional justice. While internal frictions and conflict led to a decline in trust in the body and seriously hampered its functionality, external ones provoked more direct challenges to the project, with both serving to tie up the commission's limited capacities. This stage again highlights the political power of technocratic measures, since administrative moves such as not replacing members who had resigned, failing to provide the budget on time, or delaying the publication of the final report could have the consequence of hampering the work of the truth commission and the process of transitional justice.

'Performing' in this stage can be understood here in its double meaning of (1) either carrying out, respectively accomplishing something, and perhaps implying an assessment of quality; or (2) implying an outward orientation in the sense of presenting or staging. In this stage, transitional justice was also 'performed' through outward-oriented measures that were carried out despite the political and social challenges the truth commission and the transitional justice project more generally were facing. As mentioned above, the notion of performance allows us to grasp "processes of emergence" (Amicelle, Aradau, and Jeandesboz 2015, 298) and the notion of those processes constituting something "it is purported to be" (Butler 1990, 34).

I close with a preliminary conclusion that is more of an outlook. Policy 'success' is a matter of interpretation, as is policy 'failure' (Mosse 2005, 8–9, 18–20). Such a policy-oriented judgement may "obscure project effects" (Mosse 2005, 19) beyond the simple distinction of success or failure. The performance of transitional justice in Tunisia may therefore have had constitutive consequences, even if it did not proceed exactly as initially intended. This is because planned, internationalised processes of change usually interact with unplanned dynamics, often driven by friction, leading to non-linear pathways and unintended consequences.

Notes

1 The law provides for regional offices to be opened in all twenty-four governorates, but the commission only managed to open nine regional offices (Sidi Bouzid, Sfax, Kasserine, Gafsa, Sousse, Le Kef, Jendouba, Medenine, Gabès) (TDC 2019, 48). I visited the offices in Gafsa and Kasserine (in October 2015 and Kasserine again in August 2016) shortly after they had opened and started their work.
2 See Articles 45–50 of the transitional justice law.
3 Personal interviews with truth commissioner, Tunis, 24 and 26 August 2016.
4 Ibid.; at the time of writing in late 2020, this procedural aspect has not yet played a prominent role in the process.
5 Personal interview with head of the arbitrage sub-commission, Tunis, March 2015.
6 Video interview with Tunisian transitional justice professional, June 2020.
7 At the first public hearings, all testimony was delivered in Arabic, with the exception of one victim, Gilbert Naccache, who spoke in French, having lived in France for several decades.
8 Tunis (Sidi Dhrif suburb), 17–18 November 2016.
9 If they received compensation within a different framework, this should be set off against potential compensation from the structured transitional justice process. Personal group interview with three members of the sub-commission responsible for reparations, Tunis, March 2015.
10 Personal interview with the Minister of Justice, Tunis, March 2015. Article 42 of the transitional justice law states that "[t]he cases referred shall not be opposed by the principle of res judicata." Thus, the principle that there should be no double jeopardy is not applied here.
11 Personal observations, Tunis/Sidi Dhrif, November 2016; translation by professional interpreter.
12 Phone interviews with international and Tunisian transitional justice practitioners, activist, and politician. May, June, and November 2020.
13 For a detailed study of victims' participation in the transitional justice structures and their expectations, see Andrieu, Ferchichi, and Robins (2015).
14 "Décret gouvernemental n° 2018–211 du 28 février 2018, fixant les modalités d'organisation, de gestion et de financement du fonds de la dignité et de la réhabilitation des victimes de la tyrannie"; available at https://legislation-securite.tn/sites/default/files/law/Décret%20gouvernemental%20n°%202018-211%20du%2028%20février%202018.pdf (accessed 12 July 2021).
15 Phone interview with transitional justice professional, May 2020.
16 The political system was also one of the contentious issues discussed in the National Dialogue. Here, Ennahda was unable to prevail with its preference for a more parliamentary system; the opposition instead secured a more presidential system. Thus, in 2014 the president was not elected by parliament (as they were before by the NCA) but directly in a two-stage electoral process. There was no direct Ennahda candidate running for president, but former president

Marzouki was widely associated with Ennahda, since he was the president of the 'Troika' government.

17 Personal interview with Nidaa Tounes politician, ARP member, Tunis, October 2015.

18 In March 2018, parliament decided not to grant the TDC an extension. In May 2018, there was a ministerial decision to grant this extension until the end of 2018.

19 An ARP member who was involved in the process from the beginning speaks of intentional sabotage. Phone interview, November 2020.

20 Personal interview with head of Tunisian branch of international human rights NGO, Tunis, March 2015.

21 Personal interview with the Minister of Justice, Tunis, March 2015.

22 There is a difference between a constitutional institution and an institution established by the constitution. The TDC is the latter type, and thus the ministry would not be responsible for the TDC by default. Personal interview with ministerial staff, Ministry for Relations with Civil Society and Constitutional Institutions, Tunis, March 2015. It should be noted here that at the time of the interview, the ministry was still in its consolidation phase and was still figuring out what issues would fall under its portfolio. In January 2016, the ministry also officially took over responsibility for human rights.

23 Personal interview with ARP member, Tunis, March 2015.

24 There were several resignations from the TDC, starting in the early stages of the commission's tenure.

25 Since Nidaa Tounes had won a parliamentary majority in the 2014 elections, it would be able to push for things to happen or hold them back. In personal interviews, truth commission staff and members perceived these moves as consciously challenging transitional justice, something the parliamentarians denied. Tunis, March 2015.

26 Personal interview with law professor and member of the technical committee, Tunis, October 2015.

27 Personal interview with former government minister, Tunis, October 2015.

28 Several personal interviews in Tunisia, 2015–16.

29 Personal group interview with Nidaa Tounes MPs, Tunis, October 2015. Though it is likely that my interview partners had benefitted in one way or another from their RCD party membership, they definitely did not perceive themselves as part of the inner circle who had profited from the clan's economic activities. This fits with Allal's analysis that even former supporters turned against the regime's leadership as a result of the increasing kleptocracy (Allal 2012).

30 See Belhadj and Kurze (2021) for details of how the campaign mobilised.

31 Whether the law is compatible with the transitional justice provisions in the constitution is debatable. The law, however, was adopted before a judicial advisory body had delivered its legal opinion on the matter. Moreover, since the constitutional court was not yet functional (which remains the case at the time of writing in late 2020) a provisional body then decided on the new law's

constitutionality. Staffed with an even number of members, there was a tie in its vote on the question, which meant the matter was referred for a decision to the President – who had initiated the law in the first place.

32 Personal interview with senior Ennahda politician, Tunis, October 2017.

33 Personal interview with NCA member, Tunis, April 2014. This point was also made in interviews by civil society representatives.

34 Personal interviews with ministerial staff and anti-corruption official, Tunis, March and October 2015.

35 A recording of the hearing is available here: www.youtube.com/watch?time_continue=1&v=auboOE9Awtk (in Arabic) (accessed 7 July 2021).

36 See e.g. reports on the stances of Afek Tounes (Huffpost Maghreb 2017a) and Ennahda (Mekki 2015).

37 Personal interview with former minister for human rights and transitional justice, Tunis, October 2015.

38 This criticism, voiced in the press and in personal conversations after the first public hearings in November 2016, does not take into account the question of whether perpetrators were/are willing to give testimony. For example, *La Presse* also voiced criticism because the victims did not forgive the perpetrators during this first hearing and blamed the TDC and especially its president, Ben Sedrine, for having allowed a historical moment to be wasted (Abdelkrim Dermech in *La Presse*, 20 November 2016; on file).

39 Phone interview, December 2020.

40 Personal interview with former member of the truth commission, Tunis, March 2015.

41 Personal interview with Tunisian staff member of international NGO, Tunis, March 2015.

42 Personal interview with former member of the truth commission, Tunis, March 2015.

43 Phone interview with ARP member, September 2020.

44 Personal interview with representative of transitional justice NGO, New York, April 2015.

45 I made several attempts to interview Ben Sedrine, but my appointments were repeatedly cancelled at short notice. This is of course understandable, since she has a very busy schedule. However, I do regret that I cannot include her perspective in my analysis. The reason that I discuss her role in such detail here is because she was a recurrent topic in my interviews, usually brought up by my interview partners. When asked to comment on the attention she receives, a former minister and MP noted that "personalisation in Tunisia is very strong. That's due to the history of Tunisia." He put this into the context of the concentration and personalisation of power since independence: "When we were small, we thought that 'Bourguiba' was not only the name of the president, but that the function of the presidency itself would be called 'Bourguiba.' [...] Thus, it is completely normal that when we aim to attack the TDC, we find it easier to attack its president." Personal interview, Tunis, October 2015.

46 Several personal conversations (formalised interviews and informal talks), 2014–16.

47 Several personal conversations (formalised interviews and informal talks) with different actors ranging from Tunisian journalists to international NGO workers, Tunis and other places 2014–16.

48 Personal interview with lawyer (outspoken critic of the TDC), Tunis, August 2016.

49 Phone interview with Tunisian transitional justice professional, June 2020.

50 Some of the criticism, including some that could be described as misogynist, carried echoes of the Ben Ali years, when opposition figures including Ben Sedrine had been targeted by negative rumours.

51 Phone interviews with several transitional justice professionals, truth commissioner, May–December 2020.

52 Personal interview with representative of international NGO, Tunis, May 2014.

53 Personal interview with labour and human rights activist, Tunis, October 2015, my emphasis.

54 Personal interview with civil society representative, Mdhilla, October 2015.

55 Personal interview with ARP member, former high-level transitional justice official, Tunis, October 2015.

56 First, when the technocratic government took over from the 'Troika' following the National Dialogue, and second the change in government after the elections in late 2014.

57 Personal observation, Tunis/Sidi Dhrif, November 2016, monitored through media reports.

58 Personal conversations, Tunis, November 2016.

59 This is not necessarily connected to an overall progressive platform, neither for Saied nor, for example, the Islamo-populist Al Karama coalition.

60 Phone interviews with civil society representatives, September 2020.

61 Phone interview, September 2020.

62 Phone interview with the president of the parliamentary committee for 'martyrs and wounded of the revolution,' implementation of the general amnesty law and transitional justice, November 2020.

63 Phone interview with civil society representative, September 2020.

64 Phone interviews with two ARP members, among them the president of the parliamentary committee for 'martyrs and wounded of the revolution,' implementation of the general amnesty law and transitional justice, November 2020.

65 Personal interview with NCA member, Tunis, April 2014. Statement not directly related to economic reconciliation law but meant more generally.

66 Personal interview with civil society representative, Mdhilla, October 2015.

67 E.g. personal interview with law professor and member of the technical committee, Tunis, October 2015.

68 Phone interview with Tunisian transitional justice professional, June 2020.

69 Personal interview with Ennahda politician, Tunis, May 2014.

70 As Ennahda was the second strongest party in the coalition, one post did not reflect its electoral strength.

71 Personal interview with Nidaa Tounes politician, ARP member, Tunis, October 2015.

72 Personal interview with labour and human rights activist, Tunis, October 2015.

73 Personal interview with ARP member, Ennahda, Tunis, March 2015.

74 In interviews next to a party meeting in 2015, several Nidaa Tounes MPs described struggles over internal party procedures. There were two different visions of how to determine the participants of the next party congress, at which the future leadership would be elected. The party's secretary-general at that time, Mohsen Marzouk, wanted to democratise the procedure and for congress participants to be elected at the local level. His rival, the President's son Hafedh Caid Essebsi, however, wanted to keep the existing structures in place, meaning that the party's executive bureau would be chosen by regional coordinators and not by elected delegates. Personal interviews with Nidaa Tounes MPs, Tunis, October 2015. Marzouk resigned from his post in December 2015 and founded a breakaway party (Machrou Tounes) in March 2016.

75 Personal observation, Tunis/Sidi Dhrif, November 2016.

76 Open letter from 17 November 2020 written by Mohamed Ben Salem, Hayet Ouertani, Adel Maizi, Khaled Krichi, Sihem Bensedrine. French version on file with the author.

77 Phone interview, November 2020.

78 Phone interview, December 2020.

79 Several personal interviews with politicians and civil society representatives, Tunis, 2014–15.

80 Personal interview with lawyer (outspoken critic of the TDC), Tunis, August 2016.

81 Personal interviews with former truth commissioners, an academic, and international consultants, Tunis/New York, 2015; phone interview with politician, September 2020.

82 Video interview with transitional justice professional, June 2020.

83 Phone interview with truth commissioner, December 2020.

84 Phone interview with transitional justice professional, June 2020.

85 Ibid.

86 Phone interview with ARP member, September 2020.

87 Video interview with transitional justice professional, June 2020.

88 Personal interview with president of human rights NGO, Tunis, October 2015.

89 Several personal conversations with Tunisians from November 2016 onwards, as well as statements on social media after various public hearing sessions. (These are not representative, since the selection of the accounts I read on Facebook and Twitter is biased towards those that are politically active and part of a wider transitional justice figuration.)

90 Phone interview with truth commissioner, December 2020.

91 Ibid.

92 Video interview with transitional justice professional, June 2020.

93 This is usually not directly provided by the donor states to the institutions but channelled through, for example, UNDP. Personal conversations, Tunis, 2015.

94 The file was submitted by the Tunisian NGO Forum Tunisien pour les Droits Economiques et Sociaux; available at http://www.asf.be/wp-content/uploads/2015/06/ASF_TUN_R–gionVictime_201506_FR.pdf (accessed 10 June 2016).

95 Phone interview with truth commissioner, December 2020.

96 Phone interview with transitional justice professional, June 2020.

97 See, for example, conference entitled "How to Fund and Design Reparations Programs," Tunis/online, 18–19 November 2020.

98 One example of a trip abroad with a public appearance was a visit of the TDC to Germany in September 2015, organised by the German Foreign Office and the UNDP. Here, two representatives of the TDC (President Ben Sedrine and Adel Maizi) spoke at a panel discussion entitled "The Cumbersome Search for Justice: Dealing with the Past and Political Change in Tunisia" (in German, own translation) alongside a representative of the German Foreign Office and a researcher from the German Institute for International and Security Affairs (SWP). Personal observation, Berlin, September 2015.

99 Personal interview, New York, April 2015, and personal interview with truth commissioner, Tunis, March 2015.

100 Phone interviews with civil society representatives, May 2020. See here also Chapter 3 and Seabrooke (2014) on discussions about who is best equipped to do the work.

101 Phone interview with transitional justice professional, May 2020.

102 Phone interview with civil society representative, May 2020.

103 Phone interview with transitional justice professional, May 2020.

104 Personal interview with former truth commissioner, Tunis, March 2015.

105 Ibid.

106 Video interview with Tunisian transitional justice professional, June 2020.

107 Phone interview with transitional justice professional, May 2020.

108 Ibid.

109 Phone interview with ARP member, November 2020.

110 Personal interview with representative of transitional justice NGO, Tunis, May 2014.

111 'Better' is mostly understood in the sense that a review of the law would reduce its 'flaws' and make it more specific and less prone to hijacking by those seeking to push a different political agenda.

112 Several personal conversations (formalised interviews and informal talks) with international consultants to the transitional justice process, Tunis 2014–16, New York 2015.

113 See also the researcher's position in the conceptualisation of process-concurrent research as a double helix (see fig. 0.2). Similarly, the international actor's position could also change in relation to subject matter and context, even if it did not change absolutely.

114 Personal interview with transitional justice professional, New York, May 2019.

115 Both the attack in Tunis's Bardo museum in March and the one at a beach resort in Sousse in June were carried out by Tunisians said by investigators to be associated with the so-called Islamic State (IS or ISIS). Both of the attacks targeted foreign tourists. As a consequence, various countries, including the UK, issued travel warnings that effectively stopped their tourists visiting Tunisia, and cruise companies cancelled stops at Halq al-Oued (La Goulette) port near Tunis, choosing alternative Mediterranean destinations. I was in Tunis on the day of the Bardo attack and was able to observe the reaction of ordinary people, which was on the one hand calm (and not panic-driven), but on the other hand marked by anger towards the attackers and a sense of despair, partly because it was clear that the attack would affect the tourism sector, which had just started to recover after the revolution. Personal observation and conversations, Tunis, March 2015.

116 Personal interview with Tunisian representative of international human rights NGO, Tunis, May 2014.

117 Personal interview with representatives of an international organisation, New York, April 2015.

118 Personal conversations in the course of the first public hearings, Tunis, November 2016.

119 Personal interview with staff member of the TDC, Tunis, February 2015. By contrast, an ARP member stated that the TDC's budgetary expectations were unrealistic and that the delay in allocation was due to the commission failing to deliver its first budget proposal on time. Personal interview, Tunis, March 2015.

120 Personal interview with member of the TDC, Tunis, March 2015.

121 Personal interview with ARP member, former high-level transitional justice official, Tunis, October 2015.

122 Available at www.youtube.com/watch?v=j9pyEtBx91g (accessed 10 June 2016); translation by Sihem Hamlaoui (research assistant).

123 Personal interview with state official, Tunis, October 2015.

124 Video interview with transitional justice professional, June 2020.

125 Article 40: "The Commission shall enjoy the following powers which shall enable it to complete its tasks: Have access to public and private archives, regardless of all restrictions contained in the applicable legislation."

126 Personal interview with academic, Tunis, March 2015.

127 See also letter of Tunisian historians directed at the TDC regarding the rewriting of history available at www.gnet.tn/temps-fort/tunisie/-reecriture-de-lhistoire-les-historiens-montent-au-creneau/id-menu-325.html (accessed 3 June 2018).

128 Video interviews with transitional justice professional, May and June 2020.

129 Video interview with transitional justice professional, June 2020.

130 Professionals, but also civil society or those affected by the inaction.

131 Personal interview with truth commissioner, Tunis, March 2015.

132 Phone interview with ARP member, September 2020.

133 Phone conversation with transitional justice professional, May 2020.

134 Video interview with transitional justice professional, June 2020.

135 Several phone and video interviews with transitional justice professionals and a truth commissioner between May and December 2020.

136 According to my interview partner, this was done on the orders of the TDC's president. Phone interview, December 2020.

137 According to the TDC's point system, women get sixty-five points for torture and seventy-five points for rape. Phone interview with truth commissioner, December 2020.

138 Phone interview with transitional justice professional, June 2020.

139 Phone and video interviews with transitional justice professionals and truth commissioner, May–December 2020.

140 Personal interview with head of regional office, Kasserine, October 2015.

141 Personal research visit and interviews with several staff members, Gafsa and Kasserine, October 2015 and August 2016.

142 Personal interview with civil society representative, Mdhilla, October 2015.

143 Personal interviews with TDC's regional heads of office, Gafsa and Kasserine respectively, October 2015.

144 Personal interview with head of regional office, Gafsa, October 2015.

145 Personal interview with head of regional office, Kasserine, October 2015.

146 In their open letter of November 2020, the five former truth commissioners criticise the use of the term 'Commission "Bensedrine"' for the TDC as demeaning language inherited from the dictatorship. French version on file with the author.

147 The movement's Facebook page is available at www.facebook.com/manichmsame7/ (accessed 2 December 2020).

148 Personal interview with NCA member, Tunis, April 2014.

149 Phone interview with transitional justice professional, May 2020.

150 Hybrid event entitled "How to Fund and Design Reparations Programs" (Tunis/online) streamed on ICTJ's Facebook page, 19 November 2020.

Conclusion

The introduction of transitional justice measures has become a standard practice for countries undergoing a transition from violent, repressive rule towards a more peaceful and democratic future – or at least that is usually the proclaimed aim. Transitional justice emerged as a global norm and an intersecting field of scholarship and practice through the emergence of a common knowledge base, a transitional justice figuration with origins in the human rights community, and a set of measures that make up the transitional justice 'toolbox.' Since 2010, the scope of transitional justice has broadened beyond physical human rights violations and atrocities towards a more holistic approach. The field of practice has also professionalised, often provoking discussions about the tensions between technocratic approaches and the inherently political nature of transitional justice. As transitional justice travels to different contexts, the normative concept may resonate differently, be reconfigured, and vernacularised. However, transitional justice efforts are contentious, and it is not surprising that they trigger controversies in the societies in which they are applied, given that they emerge from conflict in the first place. Moreover, the assemblage of different ideas that charge and challenge power structures may also produce frictions that drive internationalised processes of change.

Both dynamics can be observed in Tunisia. Transitional justice was introduced as a standard practice shortly after the fall of the authoritarian regime. An inclusive, consultative transitional justice dialogue, carried out with extensive international involvement, informed the drafting of a comprehensive transitional justice law in line with a holistic approach to transitional justice that aimed to address various parts of society, seeking accountability for a diverse set of crimes and offering redress for numerous grievances. The violations and grievances addressed in the text of the law range from political human rights violations to economic crimes and socio-economic marginalisation.

But transitional justice was also embedded in contestation, because it both emerged from and fostered conflict. In March 2018, the contested nature of transitional justice, at least in the form it assumed in Tunisia, culminated in a legally questionable parliamentary vote to abolish the TDC after its initial four-year term. The central transitional justice institution was thus denied an extension of its mandate, despite an extension having been provided for in the law. For about two months, it looked as if the truth commission would not be able to finish its work. At the end of May 2018, however, the Ministry for Relations with Constitutional Bodies, Civil Society, and Human Rights decided to extend the mandate until the end of the year, in effect overruling the parliamentary vote. After the expiration of this extended mandate, the TDC submitted its final report to the 'three presidencies' and published a version on its website in March 2019. This was followed by a period of political inaction that stalled the transitional justice process. Even those measures that moved forwards, the specialised chambers, suffered from a lack of political will, given that the security forces refused to enforce the attendance of the accused at trials and nothing was done about that. In 2020, then, transitional justice regained its momentum to some degree with the publication of the TDC's final report in Tunisia's official gazette (and thereby its official recognition by the government) and some administrative moves, such as establishing a commission to administer the Dignity Fund. However, at the same time there were pushes from some political actors, among them Abir Moussi who is close to the old regime, but also Ennahda's Rachid Ghannouchi (Belhassine 2020), for a new 'reconciliation law' that would imply abandoning justice and accountability.

In a context in which Tunisia's approach to transitional justice was carefully planned and internationally commended for being inclusive and comprehensive, these conflictive, non-linear developments raise the question of how and why all of this happened. Although this book does not aim to give an authoritative answer to that question, it can offer some clues to understand the *how* and *why* of the developments of the transitional justice process in Tunisia.

To investigate these questions, I developed an analytical framework drawing on Elias's social-theoretical approaches to processes of change to structure my empirical analysis of transitional justice in Tunisia. Working on the assumption that social and political change is contingent rather than 'structureless history' or teleological and predetermined (Elias 1977, 147), four characteristics were identified that shape internationalised processes of change, such as transitional justice: the interplay of planned, institutionalised processes of change with unplanned/spontaneous dynamics; the non-linearity of processes of change; international interconnectedness and interdependence; and the driving and defining function of conflict and friction. The book thus offers a novel theoretical perspective for the analysis of transitional justice and opens up new avenues for the application of Elias's theory of social processes.

To conclude this book, I will proceed in three steps. First, I will revisit the findings of the empirical analysis. Then, I will outline the contribution to various knowledge areas that the book offers. Finally, I will provide an outlook and avenues for future research.

Characteristics of transitional justice in process

This book divided transitional justice in process in Tunisia into three analytically informed stages: *initiating*, *designing*, and *performing* transitional justice. To showcase the empirical findings of this study, these stages were temporally defined for heuristic reasons but cannot be delineated that clearly otherwise. Together, they span the period that began with the first ad hoc initiatives for justice in transition in 2011–12, through the design of a planned transitional justice project (2012–14), to conclude with the performance of transitional justice, which began in mid-2014. The book covers developments until the end of 2020. By revisiting the empirical findings of this study by focusing on the characteristics of transitional justice in process, I aim to highlight their conceptual and argumentative implications.

Interplay of planned processes of change with unplanned dynamics

Let us first return to the argument that planned processes of change do not usually proceed exactly as planned but are subject to interplay with unplanned processes – social and political dynamics that influence the eventual course the process of change will take (Elias 1977). In the first stage, and in a very timely manner after the fall of the Ben Ali regime, transitional justice was initiated through ad hoc measures, such as military trials for human rights violations during the uprisings, civil trials for economic crimes, investigation commissions and compensation measures, as well as the earliest efforts to institutionalise the process, which was marked by the preliminary engagement of international transitional justice professionals and the establishment of a Ministry for Human Rights and Transitional Justice. However, in this stage, transitional justice had not yet been introduced as a planned project that was separate from other measures of transitional governance; nevertheless, the latter often had a transitional justice dimension in that the transitional authorities began to address issues of justice in connection with past abuses and malpractice. Apart from the abovementioned investigation commissions, this particularly applies to the new electoral legislation, which functioned as a means of lustration and resulted in an NCA largely free of old-regime figures.

Thus, there emerged an unplanned interweaving of transitional justice and transitional governance measures that were institutionalised, albeit often still grounded in old-regime legislation and structures, but not coordinated. They meshed with each other and interacted with the fluctuating political and social dynamics of transitional Tunisia – where periods of relative calm were repeatedly interrupted by public protests. Here, the power shifts after the fall of the regime brought about new political figurations. Some of those who had previously been marginalised within the political system, especially Islamists, gained powerful positions. However, anxiety about Ennahda's political intentions and a potential "hidden radical agenda" (Boubekeur 2016, 113) fostered an Islamist–secularist divide. Thus, in a setting in which there was no clean slate, especially with regard to the judiciary, the post-revolutionary power structures determined the window of opportunity for accountability.

The second stage of designing transitional justice was mainly marked by two interacting dynamics: a further institutionalisation of transitional justice and a volatile, violent, and highly polarised political context. Regarding the former, a planned project was designed in a participatory process with the support of international transitional justice professionals. Nonetheless, given the power constellation at that time and the distrust between the different political and societal camps, transitional justice began to be seen by many as an Ennahda project that would mainly benefit the party's constituencies. A sense emerged that it would represent a kind of 'victor's justice,' a perception that is still relevant at the time of writing in late 2020, especially with regard to the reparations process and the lack of political willingness to push it forwards.[1]

'Street politics,' which occasionally turned violent, and competing claims for legitimacy brought the constitution-writing process to a halt. An elite crisis-solving mechanism, the National Dialogue, brought about a political rapprochement between the leaderships of competing political camps and gave rise to the initial changes that allowed members of the old regime to return to the political stage, indicating that the post-revolutionary figuration could not be fixed immutably. Moreover, since transitional justice was not the most pressing issue on the political agenda, its institutionalisation – and hence the planned project – stalled during the deadlocked constitution-writing process. Thus, while transitional justice was indeed beginning to be institutionalised, the process interacted with the unplanned dynamics of power shifts within the political figuration, narrowing the window of opportunity for accountability.

In the third stage, that of performing transitional justice, the main institution of the planned transitional justice project, the TDC, became operational. As the political cleavages had further narrowed, deal-making between the political elites now became a vital means of political decision-making. The goal of accountability slipped further and further down the political agenda, and planned, institutionalised transitional justice faced even more opposition, including from those actors who had previously advocated for it. In this stage, transitional justice developed a limited degree of independence from shifting power structures and political preferences; despite an attempt to introduce competing planned processes of change – or to wait it out – transitional justice was continuously performed in Tunisia, in some instances despite it running counter to the political preferences of the ruling factions. Accordingly, one important insight from my research is that the planned transitional justice project, which is often described as depoliticised or technocratic, is deeply entangled with and dependent on politics. A technocratic, planned project is not a sign of depoliticisation but rather a particular manifestation of politics.

I would briefly like to mention here that after the 2019 elections, the political climate again became more favourable towards transitional justice. However, transitional justice, as in most other instances of life and politics, interacted with the unplanned dynamics brought about by the 2020 COVID-19 pandemic, which required so much attention that there was little room left for other political and socio-economic projects.[2]

Non-linearity, trends, and counter-trends

Let us now come back to the point that processes of change are usually not linear, and that they may indeed be directional, yet not *uni*directional (Elias 1977, [1986] 2006). Antipodal developments, impulses, pushes in different directions, and opposing trends may be interlinked, and processes of change may be reversible. The non-linear, reversible developments are often results of, or accompany, shifts in power. These are likewise not necessarily absolute but can be temporal, relative adjustments, which may again be subject to change.

In the first stage of initiating transitional justice, there was a general unwillingness (on a political as well as societal level) to accept a 'business as usual' approach towards old-regime figures and practices. The power constellations in the political figuration allowed for the pursuit of accountability for human rights violations and economic crimes and to initiate transitional justice. However, these early retributive measures mainly targeted the political leadership, not the underlying, deeper structures of the system.

And while there was widespread empathy for those who had suffered under dictatorship and during the uprisings, there was also mistrust of the Islamists, especially among those with secular convictions, and their suffering was not taken seriously in these political and social circles. To some degree, this may be related to the perception that those newly in power were perpetuating old-regime, nepotistic practices and thus forfeiting their group's claims to victimhood. Yet opposing trends could also be observed in those instances in which the will for accountability and the pursuit of transitional justice seemed explicit. The involvement of old-regime institutions in these early accountability measures gave the impression of a performance of justice, without a deeper commitment to dismantling the system.

Already in the second stage, then, despite the trend of further institutionalising transitional justice, counter-trends to the pursuit of accountability became more pronounced than in the first stage. This can be seen in the decision to commute the sentences handed out to high-level regime figures, with the exception of Ben Ali, on charges connected with the violence used against protesters, so that they could be released from prison, reinforcing the perception that the judiciary was still serving the interests of the 'system' and that the dismantling of deeper structures was not being pursued. Furthermore, with the growing importance of elite compromise and deal-making in Tunisian politics, which paved the way for a partial return of members of the old regime to political life, transitional justice became less of a priority and measures for acute conflict-resolution essentially functioned as a counter-trend to the pursuit of justice and accountability. This was accompanied by a shift in the understanding of what transitional justice meant and entailed. While previously the ad hoc measures were commonly understood to be part of transitional justice, with ongoing institutionalisation they were excluded from this understanding. What was labelled transitional justice increasingly shifted towards the planned project and was decoupled from the more fundamental idea that it was about seeking justice and accountability in transition.

In the third stage, it is possible to observe the simultaneous performance of transitional justice within the structures of the planned project after the truth commission took up its work and a decline in the political will to bring about justice and accountability. Challenges to transitional justice came from the political sphere, since power in the political figuration shifted away from those who had initially pushed for the planned project, and the latter had also changed their political preferences so that transitional justice was no longer a priority. Moreover, the TDC's legitimacy and ability to deliver justice was increasingly brought into question. The commission continued its work despite these challenges and was able to counter the declining political will to a certain extent by performing outward-oriented tasks such as public hearings. After the commission's mandate came to an end, the trend pointed towards 'waiting transitional justice out': the project was neither driven forwards nor actively abolished. However, with another shift in the political figuration and in power structures, some progress was made in the pursuit of transitional justice, leading to a sense of optimism among my interview partners that this trend would continue.

Across the three stages, it became evident that the political will to seek justice and accountability was not linear, that transitional justice was not a teleological process, and that trends and counter-trends emerged and evolved simultaneously or successively. Thus, my results tie in with debates in the transitional justice scholarship that criticise the teleological appeal and strong goal-orientation of the concept.

International interconnectedness

Although it may seem like a truism in a study that is concerned with internationalised processes of change, let us revisit the implications of international interconnectedness. Internationalised processes of change are shaped by the interplay and interdependencies of domestic and international processes (Elias [1981] 2006a) and by the circulations of norms, ideas, and knowledge; as well as by the fluid, processual nature of figurations that transcend state boundaries.

Concerning transitional justice in Tunisia, international interconnectedness was an essential feature of the processual developments across all three stages. The first stage was generally marked by increased donor attention and activities providing both financial and technical support to the country in transition. In this stage, transitional justice expertise started to flow in as well. International transitional justice organisations, both governmental and non-governmental, began cooperating with domestic actors from civil society and politics, exploring opportunities and advocating for a more institutionalised approach to transitional justice, in line with international standards. These different actors therefore formed an internationalised transitional justice figuration that was marked, over the stages, by changing preferences, fluid alliances, and shifting positions of power.

In the second stage, the role of international transitional justice professionals and dominant approaches became even more important in designing transitional justice. The ICTJ, UNDP, and OHCHR, in particular, closely accompanied the participatory transitional justice dialogue and drafting of the transitional justice law and transferred knowledge about transitional justice – including international knowledge, ideas, and standards – to domestic actors through workshops and training. They thereby co-determined the socio-technological offering that would shape institutionalised transitional justice in Tunisia, essentially following a holistic approach. These norms, ideas, and knowledge, however, resonated with domestic ones, which were appropriated and reconfigured. While domestic actors generally welcomed international support, this stage revealed the thin line between support and interference, which was noticed by both domestic and international actors. In this respect, international transitional justice professionals together with domestic actors – mainly from civil society but to a lesser extent from politics as well – advocated for the transitional justice project to proceed. However, since the domestic political priority was acute conflict resolution, the search for accountability and justice was compromised.

During the performance of transitional justice, there was a continuous transfer of knowledge and resources from international transitional justice professionals and donors. While continuing the work they started in the previous stage, international actors found themselves in a situation in which they could not draw a clear line between the provision of technical support for the institutionalised transitional justice project and advocacy work. While this line may have been contested before, it definitely became more and more blurry. Since there was a political backlash against seeking accountability and the planned project – in the form of direct challenges or strategies of waiting it out – when doing advocacy work for transitional justice to proceed in a certain manner, international transitional justice professionals were forced to take a clearer position. Thus, although their initial, absolute position towards the transitional justice project did not change, shifting political preferences among domestic actors meant that their relative positions did.

Here, one important lesson is that international actors, in transferring norms, ideas, and knowledge and defining the socio-technological offering, significantly shaped the planned transitional justice project. Nonetheless, there was no 'top-down' transfer of global ideas to a local context but rather an appropriation and reconfiguration of what was on offer. Moreover, my results show that no clear domestic–international divide was shaping transitional justice in process in Tunisia; instead, there were shifting and cross-cutting alliances within the internationalised transitional justice figuration.

Conflict and friction

Let us finally return to the argument that conflict and friction are important drivers and defining components for internationalised processes of change that can be both disruptive and productive (Elias 1977, 1978, [1986] 2006, [1987] 2003). They influence power structures and the changes that power structures undergo – and in turn may be triggered *by* these changes and dynamics. This particularly holds for transitional justice, as it emerges from and is embedded in conflict.

The first stage, in which transitional justice was initiated, was marked by transitional struggles at different levels. They mostly concerned the future shape and political architecture of the Tunisian state, as well as questions of inclusion and exclusion and access to power. These struggles materialised in frictional encounters and open conflict within the transitional institutions, mainly within the NCA, as well as protests and violent clashes on the street, most often between police and protesters. Frictions also emerged in transitional justice, mainly between political actors and civil society, over early institutionalisation efforts. While the government established the Ministry for Human Rights and Transitional Justice, much of civil society was sceptical about this move, fearing a political instrumentalisation of the issue, and instead pushed for the codification of transitional justice in law.

The stage of designing transitional justice was characterised by cross-cutting conflict and friction in the transitional figuration. Conflict on the street and in parliament influenced transitional justice insofar as the issue became less of a priority and it was put on hold in parliament, with the lustration clause for future elections to parliament falling victim to the resolution of transitional conflict. Looking at transitional justice more concretely, alliances formed across different actor groups, since political preferences were not necessarily aligned by role or status. However, when parliament eventually took up the issue of transitional justice, friction intensified between political and civil society actors, since parts of civil society felt sidelined by decisions to amend the law and keep the prerogative of nominating truth commissioners within the NCA. Although international actors initially supported the involvement of civil society actors in the nomination procedure, they refrained from putting pressure on the politicians to secure this. Concurrently, friction evolved between parts of civil society and international transitional justice professionals, since some segments of civil society interpreted the non-interference of international actors in the matter as support of the government over civil society. Towards the end of this stage, then, the formation and consolidation of the truth commission proved frictional, as members were concerned with their position within the commission's internal power structures.

When transitional justice was performed, frictions and conflictive dynamics evolved between the TDC, the political system, and civil society. With further shifts in power and political preferences, the truth commission increasingly faced challenges from the political sphere. These challenges were subtle – for example, parliamentary or governmental inaction with regard to transitional justice issues – or more direct, such as the introduction of legislation that would curtail the truth commission's competencies. Moreover, the attitude of the TDC's president was perceived as off-putting (or 'authoritarian') for civil society actors as well as fellow truth commissioners, going against inclusive ideas of transitional justice. This was a factor contributing to internal frictions between commission members that influenced the set-up, working ability, and external perceptions of the commission. These conflictive lines among the members cut across political preferences, professional background, and gender.

Thus, transitional justice emerged from conflict in Tunisia, and it brought about new frictions and conflict among actors that were felt both in a productive and disruptive manner. One important lesson we can draw from the Tunisian case is that conflict and friction – and in turn alliances – do not need to be linear, 'horizontal,' or 'vertical' but can be cross-cutting between different actor groups and subject to change.

Contribution to knowledge

As well as the empirical information related to the Tunisian case, the present study contributes to theory development in international politics and conflict studies and to the field of transitional justice. It also offers some ideas for the transfer of its findings to other cases, as well as to policy. Since these contributions are scattered across different parts of this book, I would like to highlight here what we can take away from my study for knowledge in different areas.

What does the study teach us about the Tunisian case?

This book complements existing research into transitional justice in Tunisia by providing new data and deep empirical insights, and also by covering more recent dynamics. It offers new insights on different levels, from the broader political and social dynamics in which transitional justice is embedded to dynamics that are internal to the 'transitional justice bubble' and the TDC.

The study's unique contribution lies in the approach it takes in investigating the processes of change related to transitional justice in Tunisia. By analysing the interplay of different political and social processes, it situates the transitional justice process within a broader political and social context and enhances our understanding of certain dynamics – such as why the TDC is so contested in Tunisia, despite it having adopted such a wide approach to victimhood – within the transitional justice process itself. The study's inclusion of a variety of actors, rather than focusing on one political or social group, allows analysis of different perspectives that are often treated as separate from each other, as well as the relationships and dynamics between them. Here, the present research spans across the Islamist–secularist, politics–civil society, government–opposition, and domestic–international divides. It shows that these divides are artificial categories and that breaking them up allows for a more nuanced narrative, since alliances are built, and frictions occur, in a cross-cutting manner. In addition to the actors that are usually directly involved in transitional justice and based in the capital, the study also includes the perspectives of actors who are not directly occupied with transitional justice but who are nonetheless decision-makers or opinion-shapers, as well as perspectives from the interior regions.

Another empirical contribution stems from the insights generated through research into processes that are still unfolding, which provides unique perspectives on a particular timeframe. These will offer a valuable baseline for future studies that research the Tunisian transitional justice process during the same timeframe but in hindsight, that is, with larger temporal distance.

What implications does the study have for theory development?

The present study developed a theoretical framework for analysing internationalised processes of change, highlighting the interplay of planned, socio-technological efforts with unplanned, spontaneous dynamics. The framework contends that besides this interplay, internationalised processes of change are characterised by their non-linearity and opposing trends, the crucial role of international interconnectedness, as well as the driving and defining role of conflict and friction.

Let me briefly recall what has already been outlined in the introduction to this book: one prominent strand of transitional scholarship deals with questions of what transitional justice should do and achieve and therefore focuses strongly on the normative goals, outcomes, and effects of transitional justice measures, for example, peace, human rights, democracy, and political institutions – both from quantitative and qualitative perspectives (see e.g. Crocker 1999; Olsen, Payne, and Reiter 2010a, 2010b; Wiebelhaus-Brahm 2010; De Greiff 2012; Salehi and Williams 2016; Kochanski 2020a, 2020b). Another strand focuses more on the role of domestic and international political dynamics and the transition part of transitional justice (see e.g. McGrattan 2009; Subotić 2009; Jones and Bernath 2017; McAuliffe 2017b; Cronin-Furman 2020). This book contributes to the second strand. In order to challenge an "understanding that society [develops] more or less 'automatically' towards a better social order" (Elias 1978, 151) when transitional justice measures are introduced, it is important to put processual dynamics at the centre of social scientific enquiry (Elias 2006b) in transitional justice. Exploring how transitional justice relates to processes of political and social change and putting the justice and the transition part in conversation with each other can help us to understand questions of *how* and *why* (Elias

1977, 138) transitional justice processes develop, certain goals become prominent, and effects come about. This book aims to contribute to such a research agenda by analysing transitional justice through a process lens.

Regarding the concrete realm of transitional justice, a process-theoretical perspective allows us to deepen our understanding of transitional justice in relation to other political and social dynamics. It theoretically captures the issue beyond the normative deliberations and goal-oriented questions that often underpin theoretical assumptions and ideas in transitional justice research. While one strand of transitional justice theory is often concerned with what transitional justice *should* mean and entail or with the possible *consequences* of transitional justice measures, this study contributes to the literature that seeks to capture the *how* and *why* of processual developments in transitional justice and thereby to the strand in transitional justice research that is more concerned with domestic and international political dynamics. My book therefore introduces a novel theoretical approach into the study of transitional justice that contends that a process lens allows us to research transitional justice from a different perspective that might make it possible to research questions that have received less attention in the field. The approach allows for an inclusive analysis that does not need to decide between micro and macro levels, nor differentiate neatly between actors and structures, but instead allows for an integration of these different aspects into a single analysis.

While this book's analytical framework has been developed for the study of transitional justice processes, it could also be used to analyse other internationalised processes of change in which planned, socio-technological efforts interact with unplanned, spontaneous dynamics. The framework could either serve as a starting point for analysing similarly specific, planned reform projects – e.g. security or justice sector reform – or broader efforts at change, such as political or peace missions, of which transitional justice efforts often form a part. Moreover, the processual heuristic I propose in this book was borne out of the desire and necessity to research a process that did not yet have an endpoint. I therefore hope to contribute to the development of alternatives for researching processes in contexts for which classical process-tracing may not be the most suitable approach.

What conclusions can we draw for the field of transitional justice?

This study contributes to the literature that finds that the technocratisation and bureaucratisation of transitional justice is not an indicator of depoliticisation but fulfils deeply political functions (see also Ferguson 1994). A central point that emerges from the present research relates to the international 'justice industry' and the professional onset of transitional justice projects. Tunisia is a crucial case here, since the government at that time willingly collaborated with international justice actors to develop and implement a holistic transitional justice project that included an array of contemporary measures and ideas for which Tunisia provided a kind of testing ground. The study therefore argues that the fact that those in power had decisive influence on designing and performing transitional justice in the way it was done, and on institutionalising the process, privileged some political preferences and actors over others.

Complementary to scholarship on norm divergence and the 'hijacking' of transitional justice for political purposes (Subotić 2009, 2015) that relates to a reinterpretation of *imposed* transitional justice efforts, I find that *voluntary* transitional justice (i.e. the country invites the 'justice industry' to set up a process and was not required to do so) can equally be appropriated. This book argues that design and appropriation in this voluntary setting, then, are frictional processes shaped by shifting alliances that do not correspond to clear cleavages between international and domestic, or political and civil society actors. Rather, cleavages and alliances are more complex and dynamic. In this regard, the book also contributes to the debate over how the 'global' and the 'local' interact in transitional justice, which provides a more nuanced picture than simply assuming that international templates are imposed on domestic actors and that the latter's ideas and preferences are neglected.

Taking Ferguson's work as a point of departure, which found similar dynamics regarding the political functions of seemingly anti-political moves in the context of development policies, my findings indicate that the 'problem–capacity nexus' is skewed in a different direction with transitional justice. While Ferguson finds that development measures are introduced according to the knowledge and capacity of development professionals, with little connection to the actual problems in a particular context, a different nexus could be observed in the case of transitional justice in Tunisia. Here, the measures introduced corresponded to the capacities of transitional justice practitioners. But the measures and problems addressed as part of the holistic approach also fitted very well indeed with the historical, social, and political background, since socio-economic grievances were a major reason for the uprisings that toppled the authoritarian regime. However, international practitioners sometimes overlooked the limited capacity of the newly established political and transitional justice institutions, which were overburdened with the various tasks they aspired to complete in line with the holistic project. Thus, although the problems addressed and the measures applied fit the Tunisian context, and not only the capacities of international transitional justice professionals, the limited attention given to domestic institutional capacity led to a precarious 'problem–capacity nexus' as well (for an exploration of that argument in more detail, see Salehi 2021).

Moreover, again, the political nature of the transitional justice project, as well as of the holistic approach, is of importance here: a more far-reaching project – that potentially challenged the power and privilege of more people, but also seemed almost impossible to accomplish from the beginning in light of the existing capacities – provoked more challenges and was harder to accomplish in a shifting political climate than a less ambitious and more 'low-key' project would most probably have been.

What can we learn from the study for other cases in the MENA region and beyond?

The Tunisian case is unique and paradigmatic at the same time. It is paradigmatic in that it reflects the dominant dogma and approach of professional transitional justice at the time it was introduced. But it is also unique in that Tunisia was willing to welcome international transitional justice professionals and develop and adopt a holistic approach with their guidance and support. Thus, the results may provide relevant insights for other transitional justice projects introduced in a similar 'world-time-context' shaped by a similar approach to internationalised transitional justice, including a similar socio-technological offering of transitional justice measures. However, the results may not be directly transferable to other cases in which the domestic political actors in power are less willing to introduce a transitional justice project that conforms to international standards and dominant approaches.

A critical question that emerges regarding the transferability to other cases relates to the criticism that transitional justice is essentially 'templated' and does not differentiate sufficiently between contexts. Considering any transfer of my results to cases in which the social and political set-up differs significantly, or with a past that is marked by very different forms of violence and repression than in Tunisia, I would contend that it is vital to differentiate between the rather generic characteristics of analysis developed in this study and the concrete dynamics in Tunisia. The latter may offer valuable insights for similar settings – e.g. dealing with a highly repressive past, a transition from authoritarian rule, and the legacy of widespread economic marginalisation and corruption – or certain aspects that may not be specific to these settings, such as frictions between different parts of the 'justice industry.' The generic characteristics, however, may indeed offer helpful clues for transitional justice in a range of different contexts as they encourage one to ask how planned processes of change interplay with unplanned ones, to pay attention to the non-linearity of these processes and to identify opposing trends, to analyse the implications of international interconnectedness, and to explore the cross-cutting nature of conflict and friction that drives, defines, and emerges from transitional justice processes.

If we look at the MENA region, it is possible to identify similar grievances to those that we have seen in Tunisia – requests for change, an end to political oppression, economic marginalisation, and corruption and nepotism, as well as demands for justice and accountability.

In February 2019, for example, mass protests erupted in Algeria when President Abdelaziz Bouteflika announced that he would run for a fifth term. As Anne Wolf points out:

> The protest movement, triggered by the prospect of a fifth term for the ailing president, soon came to focus on a set of wider grievances. These included rampant poverty and unemployment, especially of university graduates, alongside political exclusion and, last but not least, growing popular dislike for the *hogra*, the term Algerians use to describe the contempt they feel directed by the ruling class towards ordinary people. (Wolf 2019, 708)

One researcher focusing on Algeria argues that the 'deep state' in Algeria runs even deeper than in Tunisia, and thus dismantling the repressive, marginalising structures will be even harder.[3]

In Lebanon, a series of protests in 2019/20 also combined socio-economic demands with quests for accountability for the ruling class and an end to corrupt, nepotistic practices and the abolition of the sectarian order. Calls for justice and accountability intensified both domestically and internationally[4] after the enormous explosion at the Beirut port in August 2020 that can be traced back to the negligence and irresponsibility of political leaders and for which, at the time of writing, it seems no one will be held accountable. As Ibrahim Halawi (2020) points out, the consociational power-sharing agreement that has defined the Lebanese political system for decades and has often been praised as inclusionary – and labelled as a 'reconciliation agreement' (see e.g. Salehi 2020) – has become a manifestation of "cartel-like politics, with a small group of sectarian elites – often married to and partnered with business elites – monopolizing state and economic privileges" (Halawi 2020, 132). It therefore functions in a counter-revolutionary manner, blocking avenues for change.

One lesson that we can draw from the Tunisian case is that change, justice, and accountability need a window of opportunity and that provisions for justice and accountability and the corresponding institutions need to be enshrined in law to stand a chance. Even then, it will be hard for the institutions to deliver on their promises without sustained political support. Strong international support, both politically and in the provision of resources and expertise, is crucial. Moreover, without structural change and dismantling 'the system' not only superficially, but at a deeper level, the grievances that provoke uprisings and quests for change will not disappear. On the contrary, they will perpetuate themselves, producing new generations of citizens that also feel marginalised but whose grievances are not covered by a transitional justice process with a limited mandate that mainly covers 'the past.' Thus, we can learn from Tunisia that using 'revolutionary windows of opportunity' to introduce transitional justice processes that help uncover violence, repression, and marginalisation may be worthwhile for exactly this purpose, it can only be a start in dismantling violent, repressive structures that are built on nepotism and corruption.

Beyond the MENA region, the Tunisian case also offers valuable insights into certain aspects of conflicts and their resolution. I would like to briefly point to two examples here: Ethiopia and the Central African Republic. My decision to include the Ethiopian case in this conclusion predates the outbreak of the Tigray conflict in November 2020, which of course changes dynamics and questions of urgency, yet I think it is still worthwhile to discuss the point I want to draw attention to. In February 2019, the Ethiopian parliament issued a proclamation to establish a reconciliation commission[5] with a mandate to focus on "reconciliation, peace and national cohesion" but with "no broad-based political consensus on the mandate" (Dersso 2019) behind it. However, as a peacebuilding practitioner working on Ethiopia told me, the reconciliation commission was not in a particularly strong position and demands for a national dialogue became more prominent.[6] In October 2020, then, a consortium of different actors (the Political Parties' Joint Council, Destiny Ethiopia, and Yehasab Ma'ed (Plate of ideas) in concert with the Ministry of Peace) made their initiative for a national dialogue public (Abdu 2020). The outbreak of the Tigray conflict has intensified demands for a national dialogue (International Crisis Group 2020), which is logical in the current situation of acute conflict. However, looking at the demands for such a forum in conjunction with the Tunisian case, we may want to pay attention to the new political dynamics short-term conflict resolution measures bring about and how these might set the course and potentially close routes for longer-term conflict resolution measures such as the reconciliation commission. As I have shown in this book, many of my interview partners link the lack of political support for the TDC and transitional justice in general back to the 2013 National Dialogue and the ensuing shift in the dominant political logic towards elite deal-making. Therefore, my research supports the argument of Dawit Yohannes and Meressa Dessu (2020, 20) insofar as it is important to link a national dialogue process with other political processes, including the National Reconciliation Commission.

Insights we can draw for the Central African Republic stem from one of the book's other findings. Like Tunisia, the draft law for establishing a

Truth, Justice, Reconciliation, and Reparation Commission was preceded by broad national consultations (Grilhot 2019) that resulted in a similarly ambitious mandate: the truth commission was to deal with a sixty-year timeframe, spanning from 1959 to 2019 (Leberger 2020). Thus, like Tunisia, the mandate predates the independence of the Central African Republic from French colonial rule. It also foresees the process covering a broad range of violations committed by a variety of actors, including "state or private institutions, such as the army, police, justice, education, the financial sector, the media, political parties and their affiliated movements, religious denominations, associations, armed groups and other organizations" (Leberger 2020). Unusually for a national truth commission, it also provides for investigations into foreign military interventions. Like in Tunisia, the initial mandate is four years with the possibility of a one-year extension, but the commission is only made up of eleven commissioners (Leberger 2020). Thus, without wanting to imply that the commission is "doomed to fail,"[7] the Tunisian case may offer lessons for the limits of transitional justice, as one of my interview partners pointed out.[8] The ambitious mandate in combination with the timeframe it operates in and limited financial resources raises some questions about the 'problem–capacity nexus' (see Chapter 4 in this book and Salehi 2021). Does the mandate fit the relevant 'justice problems' in the country? And does it fit the capacities of domestic actors and institutions?

Going beyond the scope of this book, the analytical framework developed in this study may also be applicable to a wider array of internationalised processes of change beyond transitional justice. It could, for example, be transferred to other planned, internationalised conflict resolution processes, such as national dialogues, or democratic reform initiatives. And since transitional justice is seen as a core site for enacting broader international efforts at change, such as peacebuilding (Obradovic-Wochnik 2018) or political missions, the framework may also prove useful for analysing these larger internationalised processes of change through a processual lens.

What can we take away for policy?

Although this study does not aim to provide concrete policy recommendations, given that it is to a large extent concerned with planned efforts at change which can correspond to "government decisions" (Elias 1978, 146), and therefore to policies, it does have some policy implications. First, the book reiterates that policies cannot usually be assumed to proceed and be implemented as planned, since planned processes of change interact with unplanned social and political dynamics. Anecdotal evidence suggests that this is actually less banal than it sounds, since those who are involved in policy planning and implementation are often surprised by it. This can be seen in the following quote from a senior transitional justice professional: "We realised at some point that when the four principles don't work, this might have just different reasons depending on the political context."[9] Thus, although this goes against common project logics and funding provisions, it would be useful for those who plan and implement policies to bear in mind the strong likelihood that their plans may be subject to challenges and change. If challenges and changes are considered likely from the beginning, this can help actors prepare for them and be ready to adjust policies when appropriate.

In the case of transitional justice, this would also mean that policymakers need to pay attention to provisions that would have the beneficial effect of making it harder to roll back efforts and undermine newly created institutions. In Tunisia, transitional justice was even enshrined in the constitution, yet this did not prevent Tunisia's transitional justice policies being subject to political challenges. On the other hand, the political institutions that were needed to protect the process – a specific example would be the constitutional court – were not in place or did not possess sufficient authority.

My study also makes a case for reconsidering whether a holistic approach to transitional justice is necessarily always the best one. While the aim of designing a transitional justice project that addresses past grievances as holistically – and therefore as justly – as possible is laudable, this study suggests that it may be equally important to consider the ability of transitional institutions to actually implement such a holistic project. That is, if the goal is to avoid the production of new injustices, grievances, and mistrust of institutions, it is important to take into account the constraints in any specific situation when designing transitional justice policies.

Avenues for future research and outlook

Three main avenues for future research emerge from this study. The first directly concerns transitional justice in Tunisia. For the Tunisian case, future research could look at how transitional justice has developed beyond the timeframe covered in this study and the reasons for these developments. My study also provides the basis for scrutinising process-concurrent research results in hindsight and for analysing the longer-term implications and effects of transitional justice. Moreover, while I chose a broad range of interlocutors, this study is still mainly situated within the 'political scene,' among figurations of political and social elites, thus defining the scope of this book. It would therefore be worthwhile to conduct further research on transitional justice in Tunisia with a focus on other actors and sectors of the population.

One example would be to engage more with populations in the south and centre.

It would be particularly interesting to analyse other emerging/ongoing transitional justice processes against the backdrop of the results of this study and potentially gain comparative insights. Currently coming into consideration would be two cases that fall within a similar 'world time-context' as Tunisia's transitional justice process, a time period marked by a similar dominant approach in transitional justice research and practice, and in both of which the introduction of transitional justice measures is being driven by domestic governments and not solely imposed from the outside. The first of these is The Gambia. The Gambia's Truth, Reconciliation, and Reparation Commission, which has been active since October 2018, set out to publish its final report in mid-2021.[10] Like Tunisia, The Gambia is seeking justice for those affected by the country's repressive, authoritarian past. One interesting distinction between Tunisia and The Gambia is the commission's decision to prioritise public hearings, which according to one of my interview partners avoided some of the pitfalls of a lack of transparency, especially with regard to questions of economic crimes and corruption.[11] A further example is that of Colombia, where special transitional justice courts (the Special Jurisdiction for Peace) and an accompanying Commission for the Clarification of Truth, Coexistence, and Non-Repetition have been set up. In contrast to the Tunisian process, which has sought justice for the victims of authoritarian rule, Colombia is hoping to provide justice and accountability after decades of civil war. Another case currently underway that would be interesting to analyse against the backdrop of the Tunisian case is the transitional justice process in the Central African Republic, mentioned above. As I have already outlined, there are similarities with regard to the participative approach to mandate development, ambition/expansiveness of the mandate, and its reach pre-independence. Thus, it would be interesting to explore whether we can also see similarities in how the process plays out as it proceeds.

Lastly, as mentioned above, it would be worthwhile to apply the analytical framework developed in this study to other internationalised processes of change in order to gain new insights by studying them through a processual lens. This could be a useful approach for other narrowly defined, planned projects aimed at change, such as democratic reform initiatives or national dialogues, and broader efforts such as political or peace missions. For these, the results may be more diffuse when looking at these processes as a whole. But research could also help to break down larger efforts into smaller dynamics, which may in turn contribute to the bigger picture of how and why internationalised processes of change develop as they do. For this avenue of research, an array of cases could be considered and would need to be specified with regard to their relevance for a more precise research interest.

Outlook

I would like to close this conclusion with a short glimpse into more recent developments and a discussion of how transitional justice in Tunisia might proceed in the future.

If things proceed as planned, the Tunisian government should develop reforms based on the final report of the TDC. Notwithstanding questions of political will, the final report, according to one of my interview partners, is not of a consistent quality and mirrors the somewhat chaotic report-writing process several of my interview partners have described. Report-writing was marked by conflict between truth commissioners and by varying degrees of engagement and diligence. I have been told that some recommendations are better than others,[12] some are "boiler-plate,"[13] and some make more sense in the Tunisian context. Thus, even if the government develops policies in line with the findings of the TDC, it is open to question whether the report provides the best basis for them. Moreover, the biggest points of critique relate to the disappearance of the chapter on women and sexual violence, as well as the retrospective changes made after the report had been submitted. Whereas the former changes have the potential to deny victims justice, the latter would undermine the legitimacy of the report. With regard to reparations, my interview partners are pessimistic that the victims will receive what they have been promised: "They will probably not see a single dinar."[14] Although the issue is still seen as crucial and a commission for administering the Dignity Fund was established in mid-2020, my interview partners do not expect there to be enough political will, or the financial means, to actually pay money to the victims.[15]

What the final report does, however, is to link structures of oppression and marginalisation back to colonial rule. In this regard, "there is a revolutionary and radical notion in the report, radical in the sense of Angela Davis,"[16] as one of my interlocutors remarked. Thus, it is "'grasping things at the root'" (Davis 1984, 14). The report may provide a basis for further grappling with the legacy of colonial rule, which may help to overcome inequality within Tunisia but could also serve as an example for the engagement of transitional justice with the legacy of colonialism. In general, ideally, the report should open "up a debate and not close it."[17]

As I draw this conclusion to a close, I would like to come back to the quote at the beginning of this book that "The truth, whatever we do, is revolutionary."[18] Given the constitutive consequences that the performance of something as "it is purported to be" (Butler 1990, 34) can have, there is a strong likelihood that despite the manifold challenges the work of the TDC and performance of transitional justice in Tunisia may still 'crack open the past' and contribute to justice and accountability for those who have suffered from violence and grievances of different kinds.

Notes

1 Phone interview with member of the parliamentary committee responsible for transitional justice, November 2020.
2 Phone interviews with two parliamentarians, November 2020.
3 Phone conversation with Algeria researcher, May 2020.
4 See e.g. www.ohchr.org/EN/NewsEvents/Pages/DisplayNews.aspx?NewsID=26163&LangID=E, www.ictj.org/news/ictj-joins-14-prominent-ngos-demand-accountability-and-non-sectarian-political-system-lebanon (accessed 17 December 2020).
5 Available at www.usip.org/sites/default/files/20190923-PROCLAMATION%20TO%20ESTABLISH%20RECONCILATION%20COMMISSION-AC.pdf (accessed 17 December 2020).
6 Personal conversation with peacebuilding practitioner, Berlin, September 2020.
7 This is criticism that I received when I first presented my empirical data from Tunisia on the matter at a conference in 2015.
8 Phone interview with transitional justice professional, May 2020.
9 Personal interview, New York, April 2015. A similar issue came up in an online consultation entitled "Civil Society & Inclusive Peace: A Reality Check" that took place from 27 February to 1 March 2018 organised by the Inclusive Peace and Transition Initiative (Geneva), Peace Direct (London), and the Global Partnership for the Prevention of Armed Conflict (The Hague), which I was invited to participate in.
10 See www.trrc.gm/updates (accessed 17 December 2020).
11 Phone interview with transitional justice professional, May 2020.
12 Phone interview with transitional justice professional, June 2020.
13 Phone interview with transitional justice professional, May 2020.
14 Phone interview with transitional justice professional, June 2020.
15 Several interviews with transitional justice professional and politicians, between May and December 2020.
16 Video interview with activist/relative of victim, November 2020.
17 Phone interview with transitional justice professional, June 2020.
18 Gilbert Naccache, Sidi Dhrif, November 2016.

Appendix

The working of the TDC

Treating the dossiers and statement-taking[1]

The dossiers handed into the commission were individually checked for admissibility at the selection (*tri* in French) department of the TDC, which would verify whether the file fell under the competency of the commission. The selection department determined whether the violations that were filed fulfilled the following criteria: that they took place in the temporal mandate of the commission (1 July 1955 to the end of 2013), were committed by an organised entity such as the state (and not by a private person), and correspond to one of the thirty-three violations that the commission had identified. Victim categories comprised members of the political opposition, Islamists, and victims of the revolution. Afterwards, closed hearings (or statement-taking) with the potential victims[2] were conducted. A team of two statement-takers composed of one lawyer and one sociologist or psychologist[3] did the hearing with the victim or, on rare occasions, with a legal representative. The statements were checked against *mappings*, a dispatch in table form and a narrative report for eighteen specific topics produced by the 'mapping department' using only publicly available, external sources.[4] Material stored in closed archives, to which the TDC received special access rights, would only be used later by the 'analysis department' to verify the victims' claims and testimonies.

Exceptional treatment and urgent interventions

While the lengthy procedure described above was standard, and compensation should usually only be determined when all files had been treated, there was a quicker process for urgent cases and 'urgent interventions' for those in need. For instance, to speed up procedures for the elderly, statement-takers from Tunis conducted hearings in Kasserine before the regional office hired and trained local staff. These urgent cases could then be followed by an 'urgent intervention' if necessary. This means that victims who were considered in urgent medical or material need[5] could receive immediate assistance instead of waiting until the whole transitional justice project moved forwards to the definition and distribution of compensation measures.[6]

Divergence from the standard procedure was possible if a victim did not want to give testimony with local statement-takers in the regional offices, for instance because they were acquainted (which is more likely in smaller local communities than in Tunis). They then had the possibility of being heard in any other regional office or in the headquarters in Tunis.[7]

Public hearings

Attending the first hearings was only possible after obtaining accreditation. Given that the hearing room itself was relatively small – it could only house around three hundred people – there was an extra room for accredited journalists and a tent next to the venue with live broadcasting.

To observe both settings, I attended the first day in the hearing room and the second day in the tent. In the hearing room, the truth commission members faced the audience, while those giving testimony sat with their back to the audience, facing the panel of truth commissioners. Thus, sitting in the hearing room, one could only see the faces of the victims via the large screens in the room. It should be noted here that only seeing faces on the screen, and listening to the interpretation as I did, mediated emotions during the hearing. However, being in the hearing room, one could distinctly feel the different emotions of the victims and how they resonated with the audience. In the tent, the broadcasting showed the victims' testimonies and the commission members, but also sometimes the audience in the hearing room.

Notes

1   I made two visits in September 2016 to the different departments of the TDC (in the 'annexe' building as well as the main building), during which several staff members explained and demonstrated their work and the procedures in detail. Procedures in Kasserine (which can be slightly different) were explained and demonstrated to me at a visit in August 2016.

2   Technically, at this stage in the procedure a person's victim status has not yet been verified. However, I refer to those who have handed in their files at the TDC as 'victims' because this is the terminology commonly used at the commission. Several personal visits to the TDC's offices in Tunis, Gafsa, and Kasserine, 2015/16; with a specific visit to the 'Annex' building to observe procedures in September 2016.

3 There can be three statement-takers when one or two are still in training. Personal observation with explanation from statement-takers, Tunis, September 2016.
4 Personal observation and interviews with mappers working on Youssefists. Tunis, September 2016.
5 A bed or a fridge were mentioned as examples. Personal interview with regional TDC staff, Kasserine, October 2015.
6 At the end of August 2016, around one year after the opening of the regional office, twenty-two decisions for urgent interventions had been taken in Kasserine, fourteen of them were executed in full, four not completely, and four were ongoing. An urgent intervention can either be requested by the victim or proposed by the office. To avoid corruption, responsibility for a particular urgent intervention rotates among the staff members. Personal interviews with head of regional office and staff members, Kasserine, August 2016.
7 Ibid.

References

Abdu, Brook. 2020. "Consortium Plans National Dialogue." *Reporter*, 10 October. www.thereporterethiopia.com/article/consortium-plans-national-dialogue. Accessed 17 December 2020.

Aboueldahab, Noha. 2017. *Transitional Justice and the Prosecution of Political Leaders in the Arab Region: A Comparative Study of Egypt, Libya, Tunisia and Yemen*. Oxford and Portland: Hart Publishing.

Acharya, Amitav. 2004. "How Ideas Spread: Whose Norms Matter? Norm Localization and Institutional Change in Asian Regionalism." *International Organization* 58 (2): 239–75.

ACLED. 2015. "The Conflict Cycle in Post Revolutionary Tunisia, 2011–2014." ACLED Working Paper 7.

———. 2020. "Demonstrations Spike in Tunisia Despite COVID-19 Pandemic." https://acleddata.com/2020/06/29/demonstrations-spike-in-tunisia-despite-covid-19-pandemic. Accessed 5 August 2020.

Al Riahi, Leyla. 2016. "The Quest for an Alternative Economy: Social Activism in Tunisia as a Case in Point." Arab Forum for Alternatives and Rosa-Luxemburg-Foundation. www.afalebanon.org/en/publication/6725/the-quest-for-an-alternative-economy-social-activism-in-tunisia-as-a-case-in-point. Accessed 18 December 2020.

Alexander, Christopher. 1997. "Authoritarianism and Civil Society in Tunisia." *Middle East Report* 27 (205). www.merip.org/mer/mer205/authoritarianism-civil-society-tunisia. Accessed 16 June 2018.

———. 2010. *Tunisia: Stability and Reform in the Modern Maghreb*. London and New York: Routledge.

Allal, Amin. 2012. "Trajectoires 'révolutionnaires' en Tunisie." *Revue française de science politique* 62 (5): 821–41. doi:10.3917/rfsp.625.821.

———. 2013. "Becoming Revolutionary in Tunisia, 2007–2011." In *Social Movements, Mobilization, and Contestation in the Middle East and North Africa*, edited by Joel Beinin and Frédéric Vairel. Second Edition, 185–204. Stanford: Stanford University Press.

Al-Salihi, Al-Saghir. 2017. *Internal Colonization and Uneven Development: Marginalization in Tunisia as a Case in Point*. Tunis. Original in Arabic.

Amicelle, Anthony, Claudia Aradau, and Julien Jeandesboz. 2015. "Questioning Security Devices: Performativity, Resistance, Politics." *Security Dialogue* 46 (4): 293–306.

Amnesty International. 1991. "Newsletter." www.amnesty.org/download/Documents/NWS210041991ENGLISH.PDF. Accessed 10 June 2018.

———. 2011. "Tunisia in Revolt: State Violence during Anti-Government Protests." www.amnesty.org/download/Documents/32000/mde300112011en.pdf. Accessed 3 August 2021.

Anderson, Lisa. 2014. *The State and Social Transformation in Tunisia and Libya, 1830–1980*. Princeton: Princeton University Press.

Andrieu, Kora. 2010. "Civilizing Peacebuilding: Transitional Justice, Civil Society and the Liberal Paradigm." *Security Dialogue* 41 (5): 537–58.

———. 2016. "Confronting the Dictatorial Past in Tunisia: Human Rights and the Politics of Victimhood in Transitional Justice Discourses since 2011." *Human Rights Quarterly* 38 (2): 261–93. doi:10.1353/hrq.2016.0028.

Andrieu, Kora, Wahid Ferchichi, and Simon Robins. 2015. "'To Participate Is to Have Hope […]': Victim Participation in Tunisia's Transitional Justice Process." Kawakibi Democracy Transition Center, Impunity Watch & Center for Applied Human Rights. https://static.wixstatic.com/ugd/f3f989_94ee35b1387b4810a35dbbdc310d75f1.pdf. Accessed 3 August 2021.

Arbour, Louise. 2007. "Economic and Social Justice for Societies in Transition." *International Law and Politics* 40 (1): 1–27.

Arnould, Valerie. 2016. "Transitional Justice in Peacebuilding: Dynamics of Contestation in the DRC." *Journal of Intervention and Statebuilding* 10 (3): 321–38. doi: 10.1080/17502977.2016.1199476.

Arthur, Paige. 2009. "How 'Transitions' Reshaped Human Rights: A Conceptual History of Transitional Justice." *Human Rights Quarterly* 31 (2): 321–67.

Atalay, Zeynep. 2016. "Vernacularization of Liberal Civil Society by Transnational Islamist NGO Networks." *Global Networks* 16 (3): 391–411.

Autesserre, Séverine. 2014. *Peaceland: Conflict Resolution and the Everyday Politics of International Intervention*. New York: Cambridge University Press.

Ayadi, Mohamed, and Wided Matoussi. 2014. "Scoping of the Tunisian Economy." Learning to Compete Working Paper. Africa Growth Initiative, African Development Bank Group & UNU-WIDER (17).

Ayeb, Habib. 2011. "Social and Political Geography of the Tunisian Revolution: The Alfa Grass Revolution." *Review of African Political Economy* 38 (129): 467–79.

Barkan, Elazar. 2006. "Historical Reconciliation: Redress, Rights and Politics." *Journal of International Affairs* 60 (1): 1–15.

Baylis, Elena A. 2008. "Tribunal-Hopping with the Post-Conflict Justice Junkies." *Oregon Review of International Law* 10: 361–90.

Belhadj, Aymen, and Arnaud Kurze. 2021. "Whose Justice? Youth, Reconciliation, and the State in Post-Ben Ali Tunisia." *Journal of Human Rights* 20 (3): 356–72. doi:10.1080/14754835.2020.1868296.

Belhassine, Olfa. 2016. "Tunisie: la loi sur la 'réconciliation économique' refait surface, suscitant un nouveau tollé." https://www.justiceinfo.net/fr/28285-tunisie-la-loi-sur-la-reconciliation-economique-refait-surface-suscitant-un-nouveau-tolle.html. Accessed 3 August 2021.

———. 2020. "Tunisia's Transitional Justice at the Mercy of Politics." www.justiceinfo.net/en/reconciliation/46054-tunisia-transitional-justice-mercy-of-politics.html. Accessed 17 December 2020.

Bell, Christine. 2009. "Transitional Justice, Interdisciplinarity and the State of the 'Field' or 'Non-Field.'" *International Journal of Transitional Justice* 3 (1): 5–27.

Ben Hafaiedh, Abdelwahab, and I. W. Zartman. 2015. "Tunisia: Beyond the Ideological Cleavage: Something Else." In *Arab Spring: Negotiating in the Shadow of the*

Intifadat, edited by I. W. Zartman, 50–79. Athens and London: The University of Georgia Press.

Ben Hamadi, Monia. 2014. "Tunisie: Khemais Chammari a-t-il le droit d'être membre de L'Instance Vérité et Dignité?" Huffpost Maghreb, 5 May. https://web.archive.org/web/20190227142726/https://www.huffpostmaghreb.com/2014/05/05/tunisie-khemais_n_5265712.html. Accessed 3 August 2021.

Ben-Josef Hirsch, Michal. 2006. "Agents of Truth and Justice: Truth Commissions and the Transitional Justice Epistemic Community." In *Rethinking Ethical Foreign Policy: Pitfalls, Possibilities and Paradoxes*, edited by David Chandler and Volker Heins, 184–205. London: Routledge.

Berman, Chantal. 2019. "When Revolutionary Coalitions Break Down: Polarization, Protest, and the Tunisian Political Crisis of August 2013." *Middle East Law and Governance* 11 (2): 136–79. doi:10.1163/18763375–01102003.

Björkdahl, Annika, and Ivan Gusic. 2015. "'Global' Norms and 'Local' Agency: Frictional Peacebuilding in Kosovo." *Journal of International Relations and Development* 18 (3): 265–87. doi:10.1057/jird.2015.18.

Björkdahl, Annika, and Kristine Höglund. 2013. "Precarious Peacebuilding: Friction in Global–Local Encounters." *Peacebuilding* 1 (3): 289–99.

Blaise, Lilia. 2018. "Interview – Sihem Bensedrine: 'Je suis la gardienne d'un temple que l'on tente de saccager.'" Middle East Eye, 28 March. www.middleeasteye.net/fr/reportages/interview-sihem-bensedrine-je-suis-la-gardienne-d-un-temple-que-l-tente-de-saccager. Accessed 10 June 2018.

Bleeker, Mô. 2010. "Foreword." In *Transitional Justice: Global Mechanisms and Local Realities after Genocide and Mass Violence*, edited by Alexander L. Hinton, vii–viii. New Brunswick, NJ, and London: Rutgers University Press.

Boesenecker, Aaron P., and Leslie Vinjamuri. 2011. "Lost in Translation? Civil Society, Faith-Based Organizations and the Negotiation of International Norms." *International Journal of Transitional Justice* 5 (3): 345–65.

Bonacker, Thorsten. 2012. "Globale Opferschaft: Zum Charisma des Opfers in Transitional Justice-Prozessen." *Zeitschrift für Internationale Beziehungen* 19 (1): 5–36. doi:10.5771/0946-7165-2012-1-5.

Bonnefoy, Laurent. 2008. "L'illusion apolitique: adaptations, évolutions et instrumentalisations du salafisme yéménite." In *Qu'est-ce que le salafisme?*, edited by Bernard Rougier, 137–59. Paris: Presses Universitaires de France.

Boraine, Alexander L. 2006. "Transitional Justice: A Holistic Interpretation." *Journal of International Affairs* 60 (1): 17–27.

Boubekeur, Amel. 2015. "The Politics of Protest in Tunisia: Instrument in Parties' Competition vs. Tool for Participation." SWP Comments 13.

———. 2016. "Islamists, Secularists and Old Regime Elites in Tunisia: Bargained Competition." *Mediterranean Politics* 21 (1): 107–27.

Bouderbala Commission. 2012. "Résumé du Rapport de la Commission D'investigation sur Abuses: sur les abus enrégistrés au cours de la période allant du 17 Décembre 2010 jusqu'à l'acomplissmeent de son objet." Report on file.

Buckley-Zistel, Susanne. 2014. "Narrative Truths: On the Construction of the Past in Truth Commissions." In *Transitional Justice Theories*, edited by Susanne Buckley-Zistel, Teresa K. Beck, Christian Braun, and Friederike Mieth, 144–62. London and New York: Routledge.

———. 2016. "Frictional Spaces: Transitional Justice between the Global and the Local." In *Peacebuilding and Friction: Global and Local Encounters in Post-Conflict Societies*, edited by Annika Björkdahl, Kristine Höglund, Gearoid Millar, Jair van der Lijn, and Willemijn Verkoren, 17–31. Milton Park, Abingdon, Oxon: Routledge.

———. 2018. "Transitional Justice." In *the Oxford Handbook of International Political Theory*, edited by Chris Brown and Robyn Eckersley, 153–65. Oxford: Oxford University Press.

Bush, Sarah S. 2015. *The Taming of Democracy Assistance: Why Democracy Promotion Does Not Confront Dictators*. Cambridge: Cambridge University Press.

Butler, Judith. 1990. *Gender Trouble: Feminism and the Subversion of Identity*. New York and London: Routledge.

Byrne, Eileen. 2011. "Tunisia Clinches Deal on Road to Democracy: One-Year Constituent Assembly Will Write New Constitution." *Financial Times*, 13 September. www.ft.com/content/cf2bfefa-de1d-11e0-9fb7-00144feabdc0. Accessed 16 June 2018.

Campus France. 2018. "Chiffres Clés: Août 2018." https://ressources.campusfrance.org/publications/chiffres_cles/fr/chiffres_cles_2018_fr.pdf. Accessed 3 August 2021.

Carter Center. 2012. "National Constituent Assembly Elections in Tunisia: October 23, 2011; Final Report." www.cartercenter.org/resources/pdfs/news/peace_publications/election_reports/tunisia-final-oct2011.pdf. Accessed 3 August 2021.

———. 2014. "The Constitution-Making Process in Tunisia: Final Report." www.cartercenter.org/resources/pdfs/news/peace_publications/democracy/tunisia-constitution-making-process.pdf. Accessed 3 August 2021.

Cavatorta, Francesco, and Rikke H. Haugbølle. 2012. "The End of Authoritarian Rule and the Mythology of Tunisia under Ben Ali." *Mediterranean Politics* 17 (2): 179–95. doi:10.1080/13629395.2012.694043.

Chahla, Marwan. 2015. "La réconciliation économique ne pose pas problème à L'ugtt." *Kapitalis*, 16 September. http://kapitalis.com/tunisie/2015/09/16/la-reconciliation-economique-ne-pose-pas-probleme-a-lugtt. Accessed 10 June 2018.

Charrad, Mounira M., and Amina Zarrugh. 2014. "Equal or Complementary? Women in the New Tunisian Constitution after the Arab Spring." *Journal of North African Studies* 19 (2): 230–43.

Checkel, Jeffrey. 1998. "Norms, Institutions and National Identity in Contemporary Europe." ARENA Working Paper 98/16.

Chomiak, Laryssa. 2011. "The Making of a Revolution in Tunisia." *Middle East Law and Governance* 3 (1–2): 68–83.

———. 2017. "Tunisia: The Colonial Legacy and Transitional Justice." Centre for the Study of Violence and Reconciliation Report. https://media.africaportal.org/documents/Tunisia-Report-Electronic.pdf. Accessed 3 August 2021.

Chouikha, Larbi. 2010. "Évoquer la mémoire politique dans un contexte autoritaire: 'l'extrême gauche' tunisienne entre mémoire du passé et identité présente." *L'Année du Maghreb*, 427–40.

Chouikha, Larbi, and Eric Gobe. 2015. *Histoire de la Tunisie depuis l'indépendence*. Paris: La Découverte.

Clark, Phil, and Nicola Palmer. 2012. "Challenging Transitional Justice." In *Critical Perspectives in Transitional Justice*, edited by Nicola Palmer, Phil Clark, Danielle Granville, 1–16. Cambridge: Intersentia.

Crocker, David A. 1999. "Reckoning with Past Wrongs: A Normative Framework." *Ethics & International Affairs* 13 (1): 43–64.

Cronin-Furman, Kate. 2020. "Human Rights Half Measures: Avoiding Accountability in Postwar Sri Lanka." *World Politics* 72 (1): 121–63. doi:10.1017/S0043887119000182.

Davis, Angela. 1984. *Women, Culture & Politics*. New York: Vintage Books.

De Greiff, Pablo. 2012. "Theorizing Transitional Justice." In *Transitional Justice*, edited by Melissa S. Williams, Rosemary Nagy, and Jon Elster, 31–77. New York and London: New York University Press.

Dersso, Solomon A. 2019. "Ethiopia's Experiment in Reconciliation." www.usip.org/publications/2019/09/ethiopias-experiment-reconciliation. Accessed 17 December 2020.

Dihstelhoff, Julius, and Katrin Sold. 2016. "The Carthage Agreement under Scrutiny." Sada – Middle East Analysis. https://carnegieendowment.org/sada/66283. Accessed 3 August 2021.

Directinfo. 2016. "Beji Caid Essebsi: "L'ivd est indépendante, ne se soucie guère du président de la république." Directinfo, 23 November. http://directinfo. webmanagercenter.com/2016/11/23/beji-caid-essebsi-livd-est-independante-ne-se-soucie-guere-du-president-de-la-republique. Accessed 10 June 2018.

Diwan, Ishac. 2019. "Tunisia's Upcoming Challenge: Fixing the Economy before It's Too Late." www.arab-reform.net/publication/tunisias-upcoming-challenge-fixing-the-economy-before-its-too-late. Accessed 5 August 2020.

Duthie, Roger, and Paul Seils, eds. 2017. *Justice Mosaics: How Context Shapes Transitional Justice in Fractured Societies*. New York: ICTJ.

El Gantri, Rim. 2015. "Tunisia in Transition: One Year after the Creation of the Truth and Dignity Commission." ICTJ Briefing. www.ictj.org/sites/default/files/ICTJ-Briefing-Tunisia-TJLaw-2015.pdf. Accessed 3 August 2021.

El Hachimi, Mohamed. 2020. "Power Outside the Institutions: Debating the Metamorphosis of Non-State Actors in North Africa." *The Journal of North African Studies* 25 (6): 896–917. doi:10.1080/13629387.2019.1644921.

Elias, Norbert. 1977. "Zur Grundlegung einer Theorie sozialer Prozesse." *Zeitschrift für Soziologie* 6 (2): 127–49.

———. 1978. *What Is Sociology?* New York: Columbia University Press.

———. 1992. *Time: An Essay*. Oxford: Blackwell Publishers.

———. [1987] 2003. *Engagement und Distanzierung*. Frankfurt am Main: Suhrkamp.

———. [1986] 2006. "Figuration, sozialer Prozeß und Zivilisation: Grundbegriffe der Soziologie." In *Aufsätze und andere Schriften III*, edited by Norbert Elias Stichting Amsterdam, 100–17. Frankfurt am Main: Suhrkamp.

———. [1981] 2006a. "Soziale Prozeßmodelle auf mehreren Ebenen." In Norbert Elias Stichting Amsterdam 2006, 48–52.

———. [1939] 2006. *Über den Prozeß der Zivilisation: Soziogenetische und psychogenetische Untersuchungen*. Frankfurt am Main: Suhrkamp. Zweiter Band: Wandlung der Gesellschaft. Entwurf zu einer Theorie der Zivilisation.

———. [1981] 2006b. "Zivilisation und Gewalt: Über das Staatsmonopol der körperlichen Gewalt und seine Durchbrechungen." In Norbert Elias Stichting Amsterdam 2006, 72–117.

———. [1983] 2006. "Zur Diagnose der gegenwärtigen Soziologie: Vortrag Auf Dem 2. Kongreß für Angewandte Soziologie in Bochum." In Norbert Elias Stichting Amsterdam 2006, 375–88.

Elster, Jon. 2004. *Closing the Books: Transitional Justice in Historical Perspective*. New York: Cambridge University Press.

Encyclopaedia Britannica. 2018. "Athena: Greek Mythology." www.britannica.com/topic/Athena-Greek-mythology. Accessed 10 June 2018.

Erman, Eva. 2013. "The 'Right to Have Rights' to the Rescue: From Human Rights to Global Democracy." In *Human Rights at the Crossroads*, edited by Mark Goodale, 72–83. Oxford and New York: Oxford University Press.

Ferchichi, Wahid. 2011. "A Chronicle of Legislative Developments in the Aftermath of the Tunisian Revolution: A Revolution Seeks the Means to Succeed!" *Perspectives* 1 (2): 236–45.

Ferguson, James. 1994. *The Anti-Politics Machine: Development, Depoliticization and Bureaucratic Power in Lesotho*. Second Edition. Minneapolis: University of Minnesota Press.

Finnemore, Martha, and Kathryn Sikkink. 1998. "International Norm Dynamics and Political Change." *International Organization* 52 (4): 887–917.

Fletcher, Laurel E., Harvey M. Weinstein, and Jamie Rowen. 2009. "Context, Timing and the Dynamics of Transitional Justice: A Historical Perspective." *Human Rights Quarterly* 31 (1): 163–220.

Foucault, Michel. 1977. "Nietzsche, Genealogy, History." In *Language, Counter-Memory, Practice: Selected Essays and Interviews*, edited by Donald F. Bouchard, 139–64. Ithaca: Cornell University Press.

———. 1980. *Power/Knowledge: Selected Interviews and Other Writings 1972–1977*. New York: Vintage Books.

Fraihat, Ibrahim. 2016. *Unfinished Revolutions: Yemen, Libya, and Tunisia after the Arab Spring*. New Haven and London: Yale University Press.

Fraser, Nancy. 2005. "Reframing Justice in a Globalizing World." *New Left Review* 36: 69–88.

———. 2012. "On Justice: Lessons from Plato, Rawls and Ishiguro." *New Left Review* 74: 41–51.

Frazer, Owen. 2014. "Mediation Perspectives: The Tunisian National Dialogue." https://isnblog.ethz.ch/conflict/mediation-perspectives-the-tunisian-national-dialogue. Accessed 16 June 2018.

Freedom House. 2010. "Freedom in the World 2010: Tunisia." https://web.archive.org/web/20180117190738/https://freedomhouse.org/report/freedom-world/2010/tunisia. Accessed 3 August 2021.

———. 2012. "Freedom in the World 2012: Tunisia." https://web.archive.org/web/20181116155930/https://freedomhouse.org/report/freedom-world/2012/tunisia. Accessed 3 August 2021.

———. 2015. "Freedom in the World 2015: Tunisia." https://web.archive.org/web/20180202073620/https://freedomhouse.org/report/freedom-world/2015/tunisia. Accessed 3 August 2021.

Friedman, Rebekka, and Andrew Jillions. 2015. "The Pitfalls and Politics of Holistic Justice." *Global Policy* 6 (2): 141–50.

Gallien, Max. 2020. "Smugglers and States: Illegal Trade in the Political Settlements of North Africa." Dissertation, London School of Economics. http://etheses.lse.ac.uk/4116/1/Gallien__Smugglers-and-states.pdf. Accessed 18 December 2020.

Gana, Nouri. 2013. "Introduction: Collaborative Revolutionism." In *The Making of the Tunisian Revolution: Contexts, Architects, Prospects*, edited by Nouri Gana, 1–32. Edinburgh: Edinburgh University Press.

Ghribi, Asma. 2013. "Tunisia's 'Black Book' Strikes at Media Freedom." *Foreign Policy*, 6 December. http://foreignpolicy.com/2013/12/06/tunisias-black-book-strikes-at-media-freedom. Accessed 16 June 2018.

Giddens, Anthony. 1979. *Central Problems in Social Theory: Action, Structure, and Contradiction in Social Analysis*. Berkeley and Los Angeles: University of California Press.

Glenna, Maria. 2016. "Peace Consolidation and Conflict Resolution in Post-Authoritarian Countries." Master's thesis, American University, Washington, DC.

Gobe, Eric, and Larbi Chouikha. 2013. "Is the Tunisian Political Transition in Danger?" IEMed Mediterranean Yearbook. www.iemed.org/wp-content/uploads/2021/02/Is-the-Tunisian-Political-Transition-in-Danger.pdf Accessed 3 August 2021.

Goodale, Mark. 2013. "Human Rights *after* the Post-Cold War." In *Human Rights at the Crossroads*, edited by Mark Goodale, 1–28. Oxford and New York: Oxford University Press.

Goodhart, Michael. 2013. "Human Rights and the Politics of Contestation." In *Human Rights at the Crossroads*, edited by Mark Goodale, 31–44. Oxford and New York: Oxford University Press.

Gouëset, Catherine. 2011. "Ben Ali et la liste des 65 flatteurs." *L'Express*, 20 January. www.lexpress.fr/actualite/monde/afrique/ben-ali-et-la-liste-des-65-flatteurs_953972.html. Accessed 12 November 2017.

Gray, Doris H., and Terry Coonan. 2013. "Notes from the Field: Silence Kills! Women and the Transitional Justice Process in Post-Revolutionary Tunisia." *International Journal of Transitional Justice* 7 (2): 348–57. doi:10.1093/ijtj/ijt002.

Grewal, Sharan. 2016. "A Quiet Revolution: The Tunisian Military after Ben Ali." https://carnegieendowment.org/2016/02/24/quiet-revolution-tunisian-military-after-ben-ali-pub-62780. Accessed 16 June 2018.

———. 2017. "Tunisian Security Forces Rock the Vote." http://carnegieendowment.org/sada/68021. Accessed 16 June 2018.

Grilhot, Gaël. 2019. "Central Africans Discretely [*sic*] Consulted on Truth Commission." justiceinfo.net, 12 September. www.justiceinfo.net/en/truth-commissions/42348-central-africans-discretely-consulted-on-truth-commission.html. Accessed 18 December 2020.

Guellali, Amna. 2017a. "La réconciliation économique renaît de ses cendres." Nawaat, 10 May. http://nawaat.org/portail/2017/05/10/la-reconciliation-economique-renait-de-ses-cendres. Accessed 3 June 2018.

———. 2017b. "La Loi sur la réconciliation administrative, dangereuse pour l'avenir de la démocratie tunisienne." Middle East Eye, 21 September. www.middleeasteye.net/fr/opinions/la-loi-sur-la-r-conciliation-administrative-dangereuse-pour-l-avenir-de-la-d-mocratie. Accessed 10 June 2018.

Gutting, Gary. 2014. "Michel Foucault." http://plato.stanford.edu/archives/win2014/entries/foucault. Accessed 16 June 2018.

Hachemaoui, Mohammed. 2013. "Tunisia at a Crossroads: Which Rules for Which Transition?" SWP Research Paper. https://www.swp-berlin.org/publications/products/research_papers/2013_RP06_hmu.pdf. Accessed 3 August 2021.

Hajer, Maarten A. 2005. "Coalitions, Practices, and Meaning in Environmental Politics: From Acid Rain to BSE." In *Discourse Theory in European Politics: Identity, Policy and Governance*, edited by David Howarth and Jacob Torfing, 297–315. Houndmills, Basingstoke: Palgrave Macmillan.

Halawi, Ibrahim. 2020. "Consociational Power-Sharing in the Arab World as Counter-Revolution." *Studies in Ethnicity and Nationalism* 20 (2): 128–36. doi:10.1111/sena.12328.

Hartshorn, Ian M. 2017. "Organized Interests in Constitutional Assemblies." *Political Research Quarterly* 70 (2): 408–20. doi:10.1177/1065912917695190.

Hibou, Béatrice. 1999. "Tunisie: le coût d'un 'miracle.'" *Critique internationale* 4 (1): 48–56.

———. 2011. *The Force of Obedience: The Political Economy of Repression in Tunisia*. Translated by Andrew Brown. Cambridge: Polity.

Hinton, Alexander L. 2010. "Introduction: Toward an Anthropology of Transitional Justice." In *Transitional Justice: Global Mechanisms and Local Realities after Genocide and Mass Violence*, edited by Alexander L. Hinton, 1–22. New Brunswick, NJ, and London: Rutgers University Press.

———. 2018. *The Justice Facade*. Oxford and New York: Oxford University Press.

Huffpost Maghreb. 2014. "Ali Seriati, ex-directeur de la sécurité présidentielle sous Ben Ali libéré." Huffpost Maghreb, 17 May. www.huffpostmaghreb.com/2014/05/17/ ali- seriati-_n_5342336.html. Accessed 13 December 2017.

———. 2016. "Tunisie: Zouhair Makhlouf physiquement empêché de reprendre ses fonctions à L'instance Vérité et Dignité." Huffpost Maghreb, 25 April. https:// web.archive.org/web/20160801173924/https://www.huffpostmaghreb.com/ 2016/04/25/tunisie-zouhair-makhlouf_n_9771038.html. Accessed 3 August 2021.

———. 2017a. "'Afek Tounes soutient le projet de loi sur la réconciliation économique mais sous sonditions,' annonce Yassine Brahim." Huffpost Maghreb, 16 May. www.huffpostmaghreb.com/2017/05/16/afek-tounes_n_16643586.html (no longer active). Accessed 10 June 2018.

———. 2017b. "Instance Vérité et Dignité: Imed Trabelsi, gendre de Ben Ali, s'explique sur la corruption sous l'ancien régime." Huffpost Maghreb, 20 May. https:// web.archive.org/web/20180312125029/http://www.huffpostmaghreb.com/ 2017/05/19/imed-trabelsi_n_16715022.html. Accessed 3 August 2021.

———. 2018. "Pour Sihem Ben Sedrine, la prolongation du mandat de L'ivd est une 'décision' et pas 'une demande' faite à L'arp." Huffpost Maghreb, 6 March. www.huffpostmaghreb.com/2018/03/06/sihem-ben-sedrine-prolong_n_19365174. html (no longer active). Accessed 10 June 2018.

Human Rights Watch. 2015. "Flawed Accountability: Shortcomings of Tunisia's Trials for Killings during the Uprising." www.hrw.org/report/2015/01/12/flawed-accountability/shortcomings-tunisias-trials-killings-during-uprising. Accessed 16 June 2018.

———. 2018. "Tunisia: Parliament Shouldn't Undercut Transitional Justice: Extending Truth and Dignity Commission Term Vital for Victims." www.hrw.org/ news/2018/03/23/tunisia-parliament-shouldnt-undercut-transitional-justice. Accessed 10 June 2018.

International Center for Transitional Justice (ICTJ). 2009. "What Is Transitional Justice?" www.ictj.org/sites/default/files/ICTJ-Global-Transitional-Justice-2009-English. pdf. Accessed 16 June 2016.

———. 2011. "Focus: Solomon Islands: Transitional Justice Mechanisms in Solomon Islands." www.ictj.org/sites/default/files/ICTJ-SolomonIslands-Fact-Sheet-2011-English.pdf. Accessed 16 June 2018.

———. 2017. "ICTJ Denounces the Passage of Tunisia's New 'Administrative Reconciliation' Law That Grants Amnesties to Public Officials for Corruption." www.ictj.org/news/ictj-denounces-passage-tunisia%E2%80%99s-new-%E2% 80%98administrative-reconciliation%E2%80%99-law-grants-amnesties. Accessed 10 June 2018.

International Committee of the Red Cross. 2011. "Tunisia: Listening to Detainees Affected by the Prison Riots." www.icrc.org/eng/resources/documents/ interview/2011/tunisia-interview-2011-02-18.htm. Accessed 13 March 2018.

International Crisis Group. 2013. "Tunisia: Violence and the Salafi Challenge." Crisis Group Middle East/North Africa Report 137.

———. 2014. "L'exception tunisienne: succès et limites du consensus." Briefing Moyen-Orient et Afrique du Nord. https://d2071andvip0wj.cloudfront.net/the-tunisian-exception-success-and-limits-of-consensus-french.pdf. Accessed 3 August 2021.

———. 2016. "Tunisia: Transitional Justice and the Fight against Corruption." Middle East and North Africa Report 168. https://d2071andvip0wj.cloudfront.net/168-tunisia-transitional-justice-and-the-fight-against-corruption.pdf. Accessed 3 August 2021.

———. 2020. "Ethiopia's Clash with Tigray: Getting to a Ceasefire and National Dialogue." https://d2071andvip0wj.cloudfront.net/ethiopia-tigray-crisis-alert_0.pdf. Accessed 17 December 2020.

Jdey, Ahmed. 2012. "A History of Tunisia, January 14, 2011: The End of a Dictator and the Beginning of Democratic Construction." *boundary 2* 39 (1): 69–86.

Jeffrey, Alex, and Michaelina Jakala. 2015. "Using Courts to Build States: The Competing Spaces of Citizenship in Transitional Justice Programmes." *Political Geography* 47: 43–52.

Jeune Afrique. 2016. "Tunisie: L'instance Vérité et Dignité en chiffres." *Jeune Afrique*, 15 June. www.jeuneafrique.com/333831/politique/tunisie-linstance-verite-dignite-chiffres. Accessed 16 June 2018.

Jones, Briony. 2020. "The Performance and Persistence of Transitional Justice and Its Ways of Knowing Atrocity." *Cooperation and Conflict* 56 (2): 1–18.

Jones, Briony, and Julie Bernath, eds. 2017. *Resistance and Transitional Justice.* London: Routledge.

Judt, Tony. 1992. "The Past Is Another Country: Myth and Memory in Postwar Europe." *Daedalus* 121 (4): 83–118.

Justice Transitionnelle en Tunisie. "Le Dialogue National sur la justice transitionnelle." https://web.archive.org/web/20180408205330/http://www.justice-transitionnelle.tn/justice-transitionnelle/la-justice-transitionnelle-en-tunisie/le-dialogue-national-sur-la-justice-transitionnelle. Accessed 3 August 2021.

Kappler, Stefanie. 2013. "Peacebuilding and Lines of Friction between Imagined Communities in Bosnia–Herzegovina and South Africa." *Peacebuilding* 1 (3): 349–64.

Katzenstein, Suzanne. 2003. "Hybrid Tribunals: Searching for Justice in East Timor." *Harvard Human Rights Journal* 16: 245–78.

Kausch, Kristina. 2013. "'Foreign Funding' in Post-Revolution Tunisia." https://www.files.ethz.ch/isn/167265/WP_Tunisia.pdf. Accessed 3 August 2021.

Kazemi, Elham. 2019. "Transitional Justice in Tunisia: When Religion Meets State." *International Journal of Transitional Justice* 13 (3): 590–607. doi:10.1093/ijtj/ijz026.

Keller, Benjamin. 2015. "The Complex Case of Tunisia's Blocked Funds." swissinfo.ch, 6 April. www.swissinfo.ch/eng/returning-stolen-assets_the-complex-case-of-tunisia-s-blocked-funds/41360476. Accessed 16 June 2018.

Kennedy, David. 2016. *A World of Struggle: How Power, Law, and Expertise Shape Global Political Economy.* Princeton: Princeton University Press.

Kerr, Rachel. 2017. "Transitional Justice in Post-Conflict Contexts: Opportunities and Challenges." In *Justice Mosaics: How Context Shapes Transitional Justice in Fractured Societies*, edited by Roger Duthie and Paul Seils, 116–39. New York: ICTJ.

Ketelaars, Elise. 2018. "Gendering Tunisia's Transition: Transformative Gender Justice Outcomes in Times of Transitional Justice Turmoil?" *International Journal of Transitional Justice* 12 (3): 407–26. doi:10.1093/ijtj/ijy016.

Khatib, Lina. 2014. "Challenges of Representation and Inclusion: A Case Study of Islamist Groups in Transitional Justice." In *Transitional Justice and the Arab Spring*, edited by Kirsten J. Fisher and Robert Stewart, 131–50. Milton Park, Abingdon, Oxon: Routledge.

Kochanski, Adam. 2020a. "Mandating Truth: Patterns and Trends in Truth Commission Design." *Human Rights Review* 21 (2): 113–37. doi:10.1007/s12142–020–00586-x.

———. 2020b. "The 'Local Turn' in Transitional Justice: Curb the Enthusiasm." *International Studies Review* 22 (1): 26–50. doi:10.1093/isr/viy081.

Krause, Monika. 2014. *The Good Project: Humanitarian Relief NGOs and the Fragmentation of Reason*. Chicago and London: The University of Chicago Press.

Krichen, Aziz. 2016. *La Promesse du Printemps*. Bordeaux: Editions Script.

Kurze, Arnaud. 2019. "Youth Activism, Art, and Transitional Justice: Emerging Spaces of Memory after the Jasmine Revolution." In *New Critical Spaces in Transitional Justice: Gender, Art, and Memory*, edited by Arnaud Kurze and Christopher K. Lamont, 63–85. Bloomington: Indiana University Press.

Lachenal, Perrine. 2019. "Fake Martyrs and True Heroes: Competitive Narratives and Hierarchized Masculinities in Post-Revolutionary Tunisia." *Men and Masculinities* 24 (1): 1–19.

Ladisch, Virginie, and Christalla Yakinthou. 2020. "Cultivated Collaboration in Transitional Justice Practice and Research: Reflections on Tunisia's Voices of Memory Project." *International Journal of Transitional Justice* 14 (1): 80–101. doi:10.1093/ijtj/ijz037.

Lamont, Christopher K. 2013. "Transitional Justice and the Politics of Lustration in Tunisia." www.mei.edu/content/transitional-justice-and-politics-lustration-tunisia. Accessed 16 June 2018.

Lamont, Christopher K., and Héla Boujneh. 2012. "Transitional Justice in Tunisia: Negotiating Justice during Transition." *Politička misao* 49 (5): 32–49.

Lamont, Christopher K., and Hannah Pannwitz. 2016. "Transitional Justice as Elite Justice? Compromise Justice and Transition in Tunisia." *Global Policy* 7 (2): 278–81. doi:10.1111/1758-5899.12291.

Lamont, Christopher K., Joanna Quinn, and Eric Wiebelhaus-Brahm. 2019. "The Ministerialization of Transitional Justice." *Human Rights Review* 20 (1): 103–22.

Leberger, Grégory. 2020. "Central African Republic: Ambitious Truth Commission Plans." justiceinfo.net, 5 February. www.justiceinfo.net/en/truth-commissions/43733-central-african-republic-ambitious-truth-commission-plans.html. Accessed 18 December 2020.

Leebaw, Bronwyn A. 2008. "The Irreconcilable Goals of Transitional Justice." *Human Rights Quarterly* 30 (1): 95–118.

Levitt, Peggy, and Sally E. Merry. 2009. "Vernacularization on the Ground: Local Uses of Global Women's Rights in Peru, China, India and the United States." *Global Networks* 9 (4): 441–61.

———. 2011. "Making Women's Human Rights in the Vernacular: Navigating the Culture/Rights Divide." In *Gender and Culture at the Limit of Rights*, edited by Dorothy Hodgson, 81–100. Philadelphia: University of Pennsylvania Press.

Li, Tania M. 2011. "Rendering Society Technical: Government through Community and the Ethnographic Turn at the World Bank in Indonesia." In *Adventures in Aidland: The Anthropology of Professionals in International Development*, edited by David Mosse, 57–80. Oxford and New York: Berghahn.

Lincoln, Jennifer. 2017. "Manich Msamah and the Face of Continued Protest in Tunisia." www.jadaliyya.com/pages/index/27062/manich-msamah-and-the-face-of-continued-protest-in. Accessed 27 August 2017.

Linklater, Andrew. 2011. "Process Sociology and International Relations." *The Sociological Review* 59 (S1): 48–64.

Lundy, Patricia, and Mark McGovern. 2008. "Whose Justice? Rethinking Transitional Justice from the Bottom Up." *Journal of Law and Society* 35 (2): 265–92.

Lust, Ellen. 2011. "Why Now? Micro Transitions and the Arab Uprisings." Comparative Politics – Democratization Newsletter. https://themonkeycage.org/wp-content/uploads/2011/10/Ellen_Lust_final.pdf. Accessed 3 August 2021.

Mabon, Simon. 2020. *Houses Built on Sand: Sovereignty, Violence and Revolution in the Middle East.* Manchester: Manchester University Press.

Mabrouk, Mehdi. 2011. "A Revolution for Dignity and Freedom: Preliminary Observations on the Social and Cultural Background to the Tunisian Revolution." *The Journal of North African Studies* 16 (4): 625–35.

Madlingozi, Tshepo. 2010. "On Transitional Justice Entrepreneurs and the Production of Victims." *Journal of Human Rights Practice* 2 (2): 208–28.

Mandraud, Isabelle. 2011. "La Tunisie va connaître de Vraies Élections Libres." *Le Monde*, 20 April. www.lemonde.fr/tunisie/article/2011/04/20/la-tunisie-va-connaitre-de-vraies-elections-libres_1510254_1466522.html. Accessed 19 March 2017.

Marks, Monica. 2015. "Tunisia's Ennahda: Rethinking Islamism in the Context of ISIS and the Egyptian Coup." Rethinking Political Islam Series. Brookings Institution. www.brookings.edu/wp-content/uploads/2016/07/Tunisia_Marks_FINALv.pdf. Accessed 3 August 2021.

Martin, Jean-François. 1993. *Histoire de la Tunisie contemporaine: De Ferry à Bourguiba 1881–1956.* Paris: L'Harmattan.

Marzouki, Nadia. 2015. "Tunisia's Rotten Compromise." www.merip.org/mero/mero071015. Accessed 8 August 2015.

Masri, Safwan M. 2017. *Tunisia: An Arab Anomaly.* New York: Columbia University Press.

Matarese, Mélanie. 2018. "Tunisian Anti-Austerity Campaign Leader Says Social Contract Is Broken." Middle East Eye, 11 January. www.middleeasteye.net/news/tunisian-anti-austerity-campaign-leader-says-social-contract-broken. Accessed 5 May 2021.

McAuliffe, Pádraig. 2017a. "Reflections of the Nexus between Justice and Peace-building." *Journal of Intervention and Statebuilding* 11 (2): 245–60. doi:10.1080/17502977.2017.1287636.

———. 2017b. *Transformative Transitional Justice and the Malleability of Post-Conflict States.* Northampton, MA: Edward Elgar Publishing.

McEvoy, Kieran. 2007. "Beyond Legalism: Towards a Thicker Understanding of Transitional Justice." *Journal of Law and Society* 34 (4): 411–40.

McGrattan, Cillian. 2009. "'Order Out of Chaos': The Politics of Transitional Justice." *Politics* 29 (3): 164–72.

Meddeb, Hamza. 2015. "Rente frontalière et injustice sociale en Tunisie." In *L'etat D'injustice au Maghreb: Maroc et Tunisia*, edited by Irene Bono, Béatrice Hibou, Hamza Meddeb, and Tozy Mohamed, 63–98. Paris: Karthala.

Mekki, Thameur. 2015. "Amnistie contestée pour les délits économiques en Tunisie." *Orient XXI*, 10 November. https://orientxxi.info/magazine/amnistie-contestee-pour-les-delits-economiques-en-tunisie,1079. Accessed 10 June 2018.

Menzel, Anne. 2015. *Was vom Krieg übrig bleibt: Unfriedliche Beziehungen in Sierra Leone*. Bielefeld: Transcript Verlag.

———. 2020. "The Pressures of Getting It Right: Expertise and Victims' Voices in the Work of the Sierra Leone Truth and Reconciliation Commission (TRC)." *International Journal of Transitional Justice* 14 (2): 300–19. doi:10.1093/ijtj/ijaa011.

Merry, Sally E. 2006. *Human Rights and Gender Violence: Translating International Law into Local Justice*. Chicago and London: The University of Chicago Press.

Middle East Monitor. 2018a. "Tunisian Organisations Stress the Need for Transitional Justice." Middle East Monitor, 25 April. www.middleeastmonitor.com/20180425-tunisian-organisations-stress-the-need-for-transitional-justice. Accessed 10 June 2018.

———. 2018b. "Tunisia to Extend Truth and Dignity Commission's Mandate Until End of 2018." Middle East Monitor, 25 May. www.middleeastmonitor.com/20180525-tunisia-to-extend-truth-and-dignity-commissions-mandate-until-end-of-2018. Accessed 10 June 2018.

Middle East Watch, and International Human Rights Law Group. 1992. "Tunisia: Military Courts That Sentenced Islamist Leaders Violated Basic Fair-Trial Norms." www.hrw.org/legacy/reports/pdfs/t/tunisia/tunisia.92o/tunisia920full.pdf. Accessed 5 May 2021.

Miles, Matthew B., A. M. Huberman, and Johnny Saldaña. 2014. *Qualitative Data Analysis: A Methods Sourcebook*. Third Edition. Thousand Oaks, CA: Sage.

Millar, Gearoid. 2013. "Expectations and Experiences of Peacebuilding in Sierra Leone: Parallel Peacebuilding Processes and Compound Friction." *International Peacekeeping* 20 (2): 189–203.

Millar, Gearoid, Jair van der Lijn, and Willemijn Verkoren. 2013. "Peacebuilding Plans and Local Reconfigurations: Frictions between Imported Processes and Indigenous Practices." *International Peacekeeping* 20 (2): 137–43.

Ministry for Human Rights and Transitional Justice. 2013. "Report: National Dialogue on Transitional Justice in Tunisia: October 2013." Report on file with the author.

Moe, Louise W., and Anna Geis. 2020. "Hybridity and Friction in Organizational Politics: New Perspectives on the African Security Regime Complex." *Journal of Intervention and Statebuilding* 14 (2): 148–70. doi:10.1080/17502977.2020.1729618.

Mosse, David. 2005. *Cultivating Development: An Ethnography of Aid Policy and Practice*. London: Pluto Press.

M'rad, Hatem. 2015. *National Dialogue in Tunisia*. With the assistance of M. Ben Salem, K. Mejri, M. Charfeddine, B. Ennouri, and M. Zgarni. Tunis: Nirvana.

Mullin, Corinna, and Ian Patel. 2016. "Contesting Transitional Justice as Liberal Governance in Revolutionary Tunisia." *Conflict and Society* 2 (1): 104–24. doi:10.3167/arcs.2016.020111.

Murphy, Colleen, and Kelebogile Zvobgo. 2020. "Not a Moment but a Movement: The Case for Transitional Justice in the U.S." *Ms. Magazine*, 16 December. https://msmagazine.com/2020/12/16/movement-transitional-justice-united-states/?utm_source=twitter&utm_medium=social&utm_campaign=SocialWarfare. Accessed 18 December 2020.

Nader, Laura. 1997. "Controlling Processes: Tracing the Dynamic Components of Power." *Current Anthropology* 38 (5): 711–36.

———. 2010. "Epilogue: The Words We Use: Justice, Human Rights, and the Sense of Injustice." In *Mirrors of Justice: Law and Power in the Post-Cold War Era*, edited by Kamari M. Clarke and Mark Goodale, 316–31. New York: Cambridge University Press.

Nagy, Rosemary. 2008. "Transitional Justice as Global Project: Critical Reflections." *Third World Quarterly* 29 (2): 275–89.

———. 2014. "Transitional Justice as Global Project: Critical Reflections." In *Law in Transition: Human Rights, Development and Transitional Justice*, edited by Ruth Buchanan and Peer Zumbansen, 215–26. Oxford and Portland: Hart Publishing.

Nassar, Habib. 2014. "Transitional Justice in the Wake of the Arab Uprisings: Complexity and Standardization." In *Transitional Justice and the Arab Spring*, edited by Kirsten J. Fisher and Robert Stewart, 54–75. Milton Park, Abingdon, Oxon: Routledge.

———. 2020. "When the Transitional Justice Global Industry Meets Tunisia: On the Role of Internationals in the Country's Transitional Justice Process." Original in Arabic, English translation on file with the author. www.legal-agenda.com/article.php?id=6329. Accessed 10 July 2020.

National Report Submitted in Accordance with Paragraph 5 of the Annex to Human Rights Council Resolution 16/21, Tunisia. A/HRC/WG.6/13/TUN/1. UN Human Rights Council; Working Group on the Universal Periodic Review. 30 March 2012.

Nesiah, Vasuki. 2016. "Transitional Justice Practice: Looking Back, Moving Forward: Scoping Study." Impunity Watch. https://cad5e396-f48c-4e90-80f5-27ccad29f65e.filesusr.com/ugd/f3f989_3a7cc0f2c4574c5a9a5925e5fb4e0cbd.pdf. Accessed 3 August 2021.

Obradovic-Wochnik, Jelena. 2018. "Hidden Politics of Power and Governmentality in Transitional Justice and Peacebuilding: The Problem of 'Bringing the Local Back In.'" *Journal of International Relations and Development* (online): 1–22. doi:10.1057/s41268-017-0129-6.

Office Français de Protection des Réfugiés et Apatride. 2014. "Tunisie: la loi d'aministie générale du 19 Février 2011." www.ofpra.gouv.fr/sites/default/files/atoms/files/tunisie_loi_damnestie_generale_du_19_fevrier_2011.pdf. Accessed 5 May 2021.

Olsen, Tricia, Leigh Payne, and Andrew Reiter. 2010a. "The Justice Balance: When Transitional Justice Improves Human Rights and Democracy." *Human Rights Quarterly* 32 (4): 980–1007. doi:10.1353/hrq.2010.0021.

———. 2010b. *Transitional Justice in Balance*. Washington, DC: United States Institute of Peace.

Orford, Anne. 2003. *Reading Humanitarian Intervention: Human Rights and the Use of Force in International Law*. Cambridge: Cambridge University Press.

Ottendörfer, Eva. 2016. *Die Internationale Politik der Vergangenheitsaufarbeitung: Global–Lokale Interaktion in Timor-Leste*. Baden-Baden: Nomos.

Ottendörfer, Eva, Mariam Salehi, Jonas Wolff, and Irene Weipert-Fenner. 2017. "Labor Unions and Transitional Justice: An Exploratory Study on a Neglected Actor." In *Justice Mosaics: How Context Shapes Transitional Justice in Fractured Societies*, edited by Roger Duthie and Paul Seils, 344–69. New York: ICTJ.

Perkins, Kenneth. 2014. *A History of Modern Tunisia*. Cambridge: Cambridge University Press.

Pickard, Duncan. 2011. "Challenges to Legitimate Governance in Post-Revolution Tunisia." *The Journal of North African Studies* 16 (4): 637–52. doi:10.108 0/13629387.2011.639563.

———. 2015. "Al-Nahda: Moderation and Compromise in Tunisia's Constitutional Bargain." In *Political and Constitutional Transitions in North Africa: Actors and Factors*, edited by Justin Frosini and Francesco Biagi, 16–44. Routledge Studies in Middle Eastern Democratization and Government 7. London: Routledge.

Preysing, Domenica. 2016. *Transitional Justice in Post-Revolutionary Tunisia (2011–2013): How the Past Shapes the Future*. Wiesbaden: Springer.

Réalités. 2015. "Zouhair Makhlouf: 'Le Ministère Public doit ouvrir une enquête concernant la fuite de ma lettre adressée à Mohamed Ennaceur.'" *Réalités*, 26 August. www.realites.com.tn/2015/08/zouhair-makhlouf-le-ministere-public-doit-ouvrir-une-enquete-concernant-la-fuite-de-ma-lettre-adressee-a-mohamed-ennaceur. Accessed 10 June 2018.

Reporters Without Borders. 2010. "World Press Freedom Index 2010." https://rsf.org/en/world-press-freedom-index-2010. Accessed 10 June 2018.

Robinson, Isabel. 2015. "Truth Commissions and Anti-Corruption: Towards a Complementary Framework?" *International Journal of Transitional Justice* 9 (1): 33–50. doi:10.1093/ijtj/iju022.

Rowen, Jamie. 2017. *Searching for Truth in the Transitional Justice Movement*. Cambridge: Cambridge University Press.

Rubli, Sandra. 2012. "Transitional Justice: Justice by Bureaucratic Means?" swisspeace Working Paper 4/2012. https://www.files.ethz.ch/isn/154626/WP4_2012.pdf. Accessed 3 August 2021.

Salehi, Mariam. 2014. "Wahrheit und Gerechtigkeit." *Internationale Politik* (6): 102–8.

———. 2016. "Tunisia: Performing Justice in Difficult Times." www.opendemocracy.net/en/north-africa-west-asia/tunisia-performing-justice-in-difficult-times. Accessed 3 August 2021.

———. 2019. "Droits de l'homme bien sûr! Human Rights and Transitional Justice in Tunisia." In *Accessing and Implementing Human Rights and Justice*, edited by Kurt Mills and Melissa Labonte, 137–59. Milton Park, Abingdon, Oxon: Routledge.

———. 2020. "Designing Transitional Justice: Problems of Planning Political & Institutional Change in Volatile Political Contexts." In *Challenges to the Middle East North Africa Inclusionary State*, edited by Marc Lynch and Bassel Salloukh, 41–5. POMEPS Studies 37.

———. 2021. "Trying Just Enough or Promising Too Much? The Problem–Capacity-Nexus in Tunisia's Transitional Justice Process." *Journal of Intervention and Statebuilding* (online). https://doi.org/10.1080/17502977.2021.1882756.

Salehi, Mariam, and Irene Weipert-Fenner. 2017. "Tunisia's Struggle against Corruption: Time to Fight, Not to Forgive." https://web.archive.org/web/20181001184140/https://www.opendemocracy.net/north-africa-west-asia/tunisia-s-struggle-against-corruption-time-to-fight-not-to-forgive. Accessed 3 August 2021.

Salehi, Mariam, and Timothy Williams. 2016. "Beyond Peace vs. Justice: Assessing Transitional Justice's Impact on Enduring Peace Using Qualitative Comparative Analysis." *Transitional Justice Review* 1 (4): 96–123.

Sammari, Emna. 2020. "La Justice Transitionnelle en Tunisie: L'instance Vérité et Dignité entre loi et pratique." In *Justice et Réconciliation dans le Maghreb Post-Révoltes Arabes*, edited by Eric Gobe, 155–84. Hommes et sociétés. Paris: Karthala.

Schmitter, Philippe C., and Nadine Sika. 2017. "Democratization in the Middle East and North Africa: A More Ambidextrous Process?" *Mediterranean Politics* 22 (4): 443–63. doi:10.1080/13629395.2016.1220109.

Schwedler, Jillian. 2013a. "Puzzle." Newsletter of the American Political Science Association Organized Section for Qualitative and Multi-Method Research 11 (2).

———. 2013b. "Spatial Dynamics of the Arab Uprisings." *PS: Political Science & Politics* 46 (2): 230–4. doi:10.1017/S104909651300019X.

Seabrooke, Leonard. 2014. "Epistemic Arbitrage: Transnational Professional Knowledge in Action." *Journal of Professions and Organization* 1 (1): 49–64.

Sharp, Dustin N. 2013. "Interrogating the Peripheries: The Preoccupations of Fourth Generation Transitional Justice." *Harvard Human Rights Journal* 26 (1): 149–78.

———. 2014. "Addressing Dilemmas of the Global and the Local in Transitional Justice." *Emory International Law Review* 29 (1): 71–117.

———. 2015. "Emancipating Transitional Justice from the Bonds of the Paradigmatic Transition." *International Journal of Transitional Justice* 9 (1): 150–69.

———. 2019. "What Would Satisfy Us? Taking Stock of Critical Approaches to Transitional Justice." *International Journal of Transitional Justice* 13 (3): 570–89. doi:10.1093/ijtj/ijz018.

Shaw, Rosalind. 2007. "Memory Frictions: Localizing the Truth and Reconciliation Commission in Sierra Leone." *International Journal of Transitional Justice* 1 (2): 183–207.

Shaw, Rosalind, and Lars Waldorf, eds. 2010. *Localizing Transitional Justice: Interventions and Priorities after Mass Violence*. Stanford: Stanford University Press.

Schwartz-Shea, Peregrine, and Dvora Yanow. 2012. *Interpretive Research Design: Concepts and Processes*. New York: Routledge.

Sikkink, Kathryn. 2011. *The Justice Cascade: How Human Rights Prosecutions Are Changing World Politics*. New York: W. W. Norton & Company.

Soss, Joe. 2018. "On Casing a Study versus Studying a Case." *Qualitative and Multi-Method Research* 16 (1): 21–7. doi:10.5281/ZENODO.2562167.

Stepan, Alfred. 2012. "Tunisia's Transition and the Twin Tolerations." *Journal of Democracy* 23 (2): 89–103. doi:10.1353/jod.2012.0035.

Subotić, Jelena. 2009. *Hijacked Justice: Dealing with the Past in the Balkans*. Ithaca: Cornell University Press.

———. 2012. "The Transformation of International Transitional Justice Advocacy." *International Journal of Transitional Justice* 6 (1): 106–25.

———. 2014. "Bargaining Justice: A Theory of Transitional Justice Compliance." In *Transitional Justice Theories*, edited by Susanne Buckley-Zistel, Teresa K. Beck, Christian Braun, and Friederike Mieth, 127–43. London and New York: Routledge.

———. 2015. "Truth, Justice, and Reconciliation on the Ground: Normative Divergence in the Western Balkans." *Journal of International Relations and Development* 18 (3): 361–82. doi:10.1057/jird.2015.13.

Teitel, Ruti G. 2003. "Transitional Justice Genealogy." *Harvard Human Rights Journal* 16: 69–94.

———. 2008. "Transitional Justice Globalized." *International Journal of Transitional Justice* 2 (1): 1–4.

Thornton, Chris. 2014. "The Rocky Path from Elections to a New Constitution in Tunisia: Mechanisms for Consensus-Building and Inclusive Decision-Making." Oslo Forum Background Papers. www.files.ethz.ch/isn/195956/The-rocky-path-from-elections-to-a-new-constitution-in-Tunisia.pdf. Accessed 3 August 2021.

Torfing, Jacob. 2005. "Discourse Theory: Achievements, Arguments, and Challenges." In *Discourse Theory in European Politics: Identity, Policy and Governance*, edited by David Howarth and Jacob Torfing, 1–31. Houndmills, Basingstoke: Palgrave Macmillan.

Travouillon, Katrin. 2015. "Speaking to an Imagined Community: How the Paris Peace Agreements Shaped Ideas of the New Political Order in Cambodia 1992–93." Dissertation. Philipps-Universität Marburg.

Truth and Dignity Commission (TDC). 2019. "The Final Comprehensive Report: Executive Summary." www.ivd.tn/rapport/doc/TDC_executive_summary_report.pdf. Accessed 17 December 2020.

Tsing, Anna L. 2005. *Friction: An Ethnography of Global Connections*. Princeton: Princeton University Press.

Tunisie14.tn. 2014. "La Liste Officielle des membres de L'instance 'Vérité et Dignité.'" https://tunisie14.tn/article/detail/la-liste-officielle-des-membres-de-l-instance-verite-et-dignite. Accessed 22 June 2018.

United Nations. 2010. "Guidance Note of the Secretary-General: United Nations Approach to Transitional Justice." https://www.un.org/ruleoflaw/files/TJ_Guidance_Note_March_2010FINAL.pdf. Accessed 3 August 2021.

United Nations Security Council. 2004. "The Rule of Law and Transitional Justice in Conflict and Post-Conflict Societies: Report of the Secretary-General." S/2004/616. 23 August.

Vatthauer, Jan-Philipp. 2015. "Introducing a Data Set on Socioeconomic Contention in Post-Revolutionary Egypt and Tunisia." Paper Prepared for the Middle East Studies Association Annual Meeting, Denver.

Vatthauer, Jan-Philipp, and Irene Weipert-Fenner. 2017. "The Quest for Social Justice in Tunisia." PRIF Report. https://www.hsfk.de/fileadmin/HSFK/hsfk_downloads/prif143.pdf. Accessed 3 August 2021.

Wiebelhaus-Brahm, Eric. 2010. *Truth Commissions and Transitional Societies: The Impact on Human Rights and Democracy*. London: Routledge.

Willis, Michael. 2014. *Politics and Power in the Maghreb: Algeria, Tunisia and Morocco from Independence to the Arab Spring*. New York: Oxford University Press.

Wolf, Anne. 2017. *Political Islam in Tunisia: The History of Ennahda*. London: Hurst & Company.

———. 2018. "'Dégage RCD!' The Rise of Internal Dissent in Ben Ali's Constitutional Democratic Rally and the Tunisian Uprisings." *Mediterranean Politics* 23 (2): 245–64. http://dx.doi.org/10.1080/13629395.2017.1287629.

———. 2019. "The Myth of Stability in Algeria." *The Journal of North African Studies* 24 (5): 707–12. doi:10.1080/13629387.2019.1647899.

Yakinthou, Christalla. 2018. "Reframing Friction: A Four Lens Framework for Explaining Shifts Fractures and Gaps in Transitional Justice." In *Transitional Justice, International Assistance, and Civil Society: Missed Connections*, edited by Paige Arthur and Christalla Yakinthou, 177–208. Cambridge: Cambridge University Press.

Yakinthou, Christalla, and Sky Croeser. 2016. "Transforming Tunisia: Transitional Justice and Internet Governance in a Post-Revolutionary Society." *International Journal of Transitional Justice* 10 (2): 230–49. doi:10.1093/ijtj/ijw004.

Yohannes, Dawit, and Meressa K. Dessu. 2020. "National Dialogues in the Horn of Africa: Lessons for Ethiopia's Political Transition." https://issafrica.s3.amazonaws.com/site/uploads/ear-32.pdf. Accessed 17 December 2020.

Yousfi, Hèla. 2015. *L'UGTT, une passion tunisienne*. Tunis: Edition Med Ali.

Zimmermann, Lisbeth. 2017. *Global Norms with a Local Face: Rule-of-Law Promotion and Norm Translation*. Cambridge: Cambridge University Press.

Zvobgo, Kelebogile. 2020. "Demanding Truth: The Global Transitional Justice Network and the Creation of Truth Commissions." *International Studies Quarterly* 64 (3): 609–25. doi:10.1093/isq/sqaa044.

Index

Note: page numbers in bold indicate tables and the suffix n following a page number indicates an end-of-chapter note.

Abdellatif, Ibtihel 154
accountability 88, 118–19, 140
accountability norm 54–5
Algeria 22–3, 181
Amami, Aziz 109, 123n.62
amnesty 73, 86–7, 96
Amnesty International 71
Amor, Abdelfattah 91n.12
Amor Commission (Commission for the Investigation of Corruption and Embezzlement Affairs) 74, 79, 91n.12
Arabic language 23
archives
    presidential archives 152, 165n.125
    of victim testimony 153
assassinations 37, 106, 115
Assembly of the Representatives of the People (ARP)
    friction with TDC 151–2
    reconciliation law 142–3
    TDC mandate renewal 3, 12, 39, 132, 137–8, 167–8
    see also National Constituent Assembly (NCA)
Avocats Sans Frontières 147, 148

Belaid, Chokri 37, 115
Ben Achour Commission (Fulfilment of Revolutionary Goals, Political Reform, and Democratic Transition) 76, 85, 91n.12, 92n.29

Ben Ali, Zine El Abidine
    commissions of enquiry and reform 72
    coup 28
    exile 28, 35, 38
    extradition not prioritised 72, 91n.10
    human rights violations 29–30
    livre noir 103, 115
    nepotism and the 'market of power' 30–31
    petition on standing for 2014 election 86, 93n.54
    rumoured return 104
    trial and sentencing 71–2, 95, 105
    violence and repression 28–30
Ben Jafar, Mustapha 36, 106
Ben Nejma, Oula 117
Ben Sedrine, Sihem
    changes to final TDC report 154
    friction with Essebi 152
    friction with fellow truth commissioners 154, 175–6
    Makhlouf accusations 153–4
    rumours over personal integrity 104, 136–7
    unavailability for interview 161n.45
Ben Youssef, Salah 24, 25, 26
Borsali, Noura 118
Bouazizi, Mohamed 1, 34–5
Bouderbala Commission (Investigation of Abuses Registered during the Period from 17 December 2010

until the Fulfilment of Its
    Objective) 79, 90n.6, 91n.12, 96
Bourguiba, Habib 24–5, 25–8
Brahmi, Mohamed 37, 115
Bread Riots (1983/4) 27

Carthage Agreement 144
Central African Republic, lessons for
    transitional justice 182–3
Centre de Tunis pour la justice
    transitionnelle 74
Chahed, Youssef 141, 144
Chammari, Khemais 116
Chennaoui, Henda 156
Chiboub, Slim 128
civil society
    discontent with transitional justice
        project 156–7
    exclusion from truth commissioner
        selection 112, 116, 117, 175
    friction with state 87–8, 155–7
    incompatible with political activity
        52, 67n.22
    internal friction 88
    and international actors 112, 175
    international funding 84
    National Dialogue 37–8
    transitional justice 112
    transitional justice dialogue 97
    under Ben Ali 28–9
    under Bourguiba 25
    see also protests
civil trials 71–2, 75
Colombia, transitional justice 185
colonial rule 22–3, 183, 186
commissions of inquiry and reform
    72–3, 75, 79, 91n.12, 96
    see also Truth and Dignity
        Commission (TDC)
Communist party 24
compensation measures 72–3, 96, 98,
    129
conflict *see* frictional encounters;
    protests
Congress for the Republic (Congrès
    pour la République; CPR) 36
consensus 63
constitution
    ambitious one-year timeframe 101,
        115, 125n.94

compromise 102
negotiations 36, 102
negotiations deadlocked 37, 101
Coordination nationale pour la justice
    transitionnelle 74
corruption
    Amor Commission 74, 79,
        91n.12
    Ben Ali regime 30–31
    INLUCC (Instance Nationale de
        Lutte Contre la Corruption) 74,
        75, 91n.21, 96
    post-Ben Ali continuation 134
    public hearing 135–6
    Trabelsi family 30, 71–2, 135
criminal trials 70

'deep state' 75, 78, 81, 91n.24, 181
democracy, transition paradigm 46
design phase 95–126, **100**
    ad hoc measures continuation 95–6,
        100
    adoption of transitional justice law
        97–8
    conflict and friction 114–18, 119
    international connectedness
        110–114, 173–4
    National Dialogue on Transitional
        Justice 96–7
    non-linearity, trends and counter-
        trends 105–110, 172
    planned and unplanned measures
        101–4, 170
    Truth and Dignity Commission
        98–100
Destour party 23
Dignity Fund 98, 130, 153, 154, 186
Dilou, Samir 73–4, 88

economic growth 32
economic situation 32–3, 38
education
    and employment gap 32
    French influence 23
Egypt, coup 37
elections
    (2011) 36, 72
    (2014) 38, 86, 130–32
    (2019) 39, 138–9
    free and fair 1

Independent High Authority for
    Elections (ISIE) 76–7, 86, 154
  vetting 77
electoral law 38, 76–7, 85–6, 106–7
Elias, Norbert 9, 10, 77, 79, 139, 168
embezzlement 30, 71–2
Ennahda
  ambivalence over draft
    reconciliation law 133
  ambivalence over transitional justice
    project 143–5, 157
  anxiety over political intentions
    170
  civil society discontent 156
  coalition government 143–4
  constitution negotiations 36
  discontent with Ben Achour
    Commission 85
  electoral success (2011) 36
  internal friction 115
  myths and rumours 77–8, 103–4
  National Dialogue 37–8
  relations with Nidaa Tounes 115,
    143–4
  reparation measures 73
  troika government 36
Essebi, Beji Caid
  absence from public hearings
    141
  lack of interest in transitional justice
    133
  Minister of the Interior 27, 74–5
  president 131
  prime minister 35–6
  relations with Ben Sedrine 152
  relations with Rachid Ghannouchi
    115
Essid, Habib 144
Ethiopia, lessons for conflict resolution
    182
Ettakatol (Democratic Forum for
    Labour and Liberties) 36
expertise
  appreciation 68n.31
  criticisms 51
  international expertise 83
  legal drafting 112, 173
  and politics 53
  Tunisian experts marginalised 58
  see also international professionals

Fakhfakh, Elyes 39, 141
foreign investment 38, 141, 150
France
  colonial rule 22–3, 183, 186
  independence negotiations 24
French language 23
frictional encounters
  Ben Sedrine/Essebi 152
  design phase 114–18
  drivers of change 7–8, 62–4
  initiation phase 85–8, 175
  Islamist/secularist divide 78, 88,
    117–18
  performance phase 151–7, 158
  productive or disruptive 7–8, 62–4,
    174–6
  TDC internal friction 117–18, 119,
    150, 153–5, 175–6

Gafsa
  TDC regional office 154–5
  uprising (2008) 33–4
Gafsa Phosphate Company, workforce
    cuts 32
The Gambia, transitional justice 185
Ghannouchi, Mohammed 35, 72, 73,
    74–5
Ghannouchi, Rachid 28, 115, 143,
    144–5, 168

Hammami, Ayachi 141
holistic approach 48–50, 113–14,
    125n.83, 184
human rights, scholarship 45
human rights violations 25, 26, 27,
    29–30, 40, 150
  see also Bouderbala Commission
Human Rights Watch 71, 82, 150

ICTJ *see* International Center for
    Transitional Justice (ICTJ)
IMF (International Monetary Fund) 27
independence 23–5
Independent High Authority for
    Elections (Instance Supérieure
    Indépendante pour les Élections;
    ISIE) 76–7, 86, 154
initiation phase 70–94, **75**
  ad hoc measures 16–17, 70, 78–9,
    88–9

conflict and friction 84–8, 175
early measures 71–4
international connectedness 82–4,
    89, 173
non-linearity, trends and counter-
    trends 78–82, 171–2
planned and unplanned measures
    74–8, 88–9, 169–70
INLUCC (Instance Nationale de Lutte
    Contre la Corruption) 74, 75,
    96
international aid 84
International Center for Transitional
    Justice (ICTJ)
    early involvement 83–4
    knowledge hub 56
    knowledge transfer 148, 173–4
    opposition to reconciliation law
        149–50
International Criminal Court (ICC),
    Tunisia formal accession 72,
    83
international financial institutions,
    economic reforms 32
international interconnectedness
    challenges 106
    criticism 112
    design phase 110–14
    and domestic actors 57, 67n.28
    global/local interaction 179–80,
        179–81
    importance 173–4
    initiation phase 82–4, 89
    performance phase 147–51,
        158
    role 3, 111–12
international professionals 10–11,
    50–1, 54, 148–9
ISIE (Independent High Authority for
    Elections) 76–7, 86, 154
Islamists
    beneficiaries of amnesty 73
    public sector recruitment 91n.18
    speculation over intentions 89
    victims of old regime 30, 80
    violence 37, 109
    see also Ennahda
Islamist/secularist divide 78, 88,
    117–18, 170
Islamist values 59

Jebali, Hamadi 36, 75
judiciary 30–31, 81, 172
justice industry 50–51

Kacem, Rafiq Haj 95
Kamour Movement 157
Kasserine 147, 154–5, 190n.6
Kilani, Abderrazak 142
knowledge transfer
    circulation 56
    discursive resources 56–7
    early adoption 83
    insights from Tunisian transitional
        justice 176–84
    international support 110–113,
        173–4
    overseas visits 111
    power relations between actors 57–8
    workshops and training 56–7, 97,
        110–11, 147
Krichi, Khaled 117

Laarayedh, Ali 37
Lamine Bey 25
Lawyers' Order 121n.24
Lebanon, protests and the ruling class
    181
leftists 27, 87, 144
liberal democracy 46, 47
Libya
    border activities 34
    instability 38
"Livre Noir: le système de propaganda
    sous Ben Ali" 103, 115
local transitional justice 58–62
LTDH (Ligue Tunisienne des Droits de
    l'Homme) 37, 55, 83
lustration
    abandonment 106–7, 115, 118–19,
        143, 175
    introduction 70, 72
    military 25

Mchichi, Hicham 39, 141–2
Makhlouf, Zouheir 146, 153–4
Manich Msamah campaign 134, 135,
    146, 156–7
marginalised regions 26–7, 32–3, 40,
    98, 147
    see also regional offices (TDC)

'martyrs and wounded of the revolution' 72–3, 91n.14, 95, 96, 105–6, 108–9, 129
Marzouki, Moncef 36, 103, 115
Mebazaa, Fouad 35
MENA (Middle East and North Africa) region, lessons from Tunisia 180–82
middle classes 23
military, prohibited from political activities 25
military tribunals 71, 75, 81, 95–6, 105–6, 129
military violence 27, 29, 35
Ministry for Human Rights and Transitional Justice 73–4, 82, 87–8, 96, 97, 141, 175
Ministry of the Interior 27, 75, 91n.24
Ministry of Justice 96, 132
    chargé de mission 96, 140
Ministry of Relations with Constitutional Bodies, Civil Society, and Human Rights 3, 39, 138, 168
Morocco 22, 111
Morsi, Mohamed 37
Moussi, Abir 168

National Constituent Assembly (NCA)
    consensus committee 38, 121n.28
    constitutional agreement 38–9
    electoral law vote 106–7
    post-uprising membership 36
    restricted mandate under Ben Ali 42n.40, 121n.26
    suspension 101, 106
    TDC selection committee 103
    transitional justice law (Organic Law) (2013) 3, 98, 107
    vetted membership 77, 115
    see also Assembly of the Representatives of the People (ARP)
National Dialogue 37–8, 102, 115, 121n.24, 140, 170
National Dialogue on Transitional Justice 56–7, 96–8, 120n.7
National Instance to Fight Corruption (Instance Nationale de Lutte Contre la Corruption; INLUCC) 74, 75, 91n.21, 96
NCA *see* National Constituent Assembly (NCA)
Neo-Destour party 23–4
nepotism 30–31
NGOs (Non-Governmental Organisations) 74, 83
    see also civil society
Nidaa Tounes
    election losses (2019) 138
    election success (2014) 131–3
    former RCD members 38
    government coalition 143–4
    internal conflicts 144, 163n.74
    National Dialogue participant 102
    political power changes 139
    relations with Ennahda 115, 143–4
    scepticism over draft reconciliation law 133
norms of global justice
    accountability norm 54–5
    circulation of values packages 55–6
    global values package 79–80
    knowledge circulation 56–8
    local understandings 58–60
    perspectives 7–8, 10, 54–6

Office of the High Commissioner for Human Rights (OHCHR) 83, 149, 173–4
Organic Law on Establishing and Organising Transitional Justice (2013) 3, 98, 107

performance phase 127–66, **131**
    conflict and friction 151–7, 158
    international connectedness 147–51, 158
    non-linearity, trends and counter-trends 138–52, 172–3
    planned and unplanned measures 130–8, 158, 171
planned change, interplay with unplanned
    challenges 9–10, 183–4
    design phase 101–4, 170
    initiation phase 74–8, 88–9, 169–70
    performance phase 130–38, 158, 171

pointage (duty to report to police
    station) 29
political polarisation 36–8
political prisoners 27, 29, 72–3, 117
power
    changes in political landscape
        138–42, 157, 171–2
    exclusion of old-regime elites 102
    and knowledge 58
    rumours and conspiracy narratives
        103–4
presidential archives 152, 165n.125
problem-capacity nexus 17, 119,
    179–80
process-concurrent research 12–13, *13*,
    15, 178
prosecutions, measure of success 52
protests
    against interim government 85
    Bread Riots 27
    Fech Nestanew? (What are we
        waiting for?) campaign 156
    food prices 27
    Gafsa uprising (2008) 34–5
    general strike (1978) 27
    Kasbah sit-ins 116, 125n.97
    Manich Msamah campaign 134,
        135, 146, 156–7
    post-revolution 36–7, 38, 43n.42,
        106, 156
    see also uprising (2010/11)
public-sector employment 73, 86,
    91n.18, 96, 156

Qalb Tounes 146

Rassemblement Constitutionnel
    Démocratique (Democratic
    Constitutional Rally; RCD)
    ban on public office 35, 74, 79
    ban on public office lifted 106–7
    former members gaining political
        seats in parl 38
    former members ineligible for
        election 85–6
    internal discontent 80
    liability of former members 133
    party dissolved 38, 72
reconciliation law 133–4, 135, 142–3,
    149–50, 160n.31, 168

regional inequality 26–7, 32–3, 40, 98,
    147
regional offices (TDC) 128, 154–5,
    159n.1
reparation measures 72–3, 86–7, 98,
    157, 186
    Dignity Fund 98, 130, 153, 154,
        186
research
    data collection and analysis 14–15
    future avenues 184–6
    interpretive 13–14
    process-concurrent approach 12–13,
        13, 15
rumours 77–8, 103–4, 104, 136–7,
    145

Sahbani, Mohsen 96
Saied, Kais 39, 139, 141
Salafists 73, 109
Saudi Arabia, Ben Ali exile 28, 35, 72,
    91n.10
scholarship, on transitional justice 8,
    45–6, 56
secret police, 'deep state' 75, 78, 81,
    91n.24
security forces 27, 35, 95–6
Seriati, Ali 95–6
sexual violence 154
socio-economic concerns 45, 50,
    98
strikes 27, 109

TDC *see* Truth and Dignity
    Commission (TDC)
terrorist attacks (2015) 38, 150,
    165n.115
Tolbert, David 149
torture 27
Trabelsi family 30, 33, 71–2, 135
Trabelsi, Imed 135
Trabelsi, Leila 30, 41n.23, 71–2
training 56–7, 97, 110–11, 147
transitional justice
    broader understandings 46
    conceptual origins 44–50
    definition 6
    failure, reasons for 52
    goals and outcomes 4–5, 47–8,
        65

holistic approach 48–50, 113–14,
    125n.83, 184
interdisciplinary field 44
measures and practices 47
normative perspectives 7–8, 10,
    54–6
perceived omissions 49
phases 44–5
political dynamics 9–11, 53, 65
practices 47
professionalisation 10–11, 50–1,
    54
scholarship 8, 45–6, 56
shifts over time 10
technocratic/political entanglement
    11, 51–3, 90, 171, 178–9
teleological perspective 46
voluntary setting 179
see also Tunisian transitional justice
Truth and Dignity Commission (TDC)
arbitrage cases 128
archives of victim testimony 153
budget 151, 165n.119
challenges 130–33, 151–3, 158,
    172–3
closed hearings 188
composition 103
conflict with government and
    parliament 151–3, 155, 158
criticisms 135, 168
defections 118
dossiers 128, 188
establishment 3
internal friction 117–18, 119, 150,
    153–5, 175–6
international support 147–9
mandate extension 39, 132, 138
mandate extension denied by
    assembly 3, 12, 39, 132, 137–8,
    167–8
mappings 41n.17, 188
negative public perceptions 145–7
preparatory work 99–100
presidential archive access 152,
    165n.125
press coverage 129, 189
public hearings 129, 135–6, 141,
    144, 146, 189
regional offices 128, 154–5, 159n.1
report *see* below

rumours and conspiracy narratives
    103–4, 136–7, 145
specialised chambers 129–30, 146–7
statement takers 188
sub-commissions 99–100, 117–18
truth commissioners' selection 98–9,
    112, 116–17, 175
truth commissioner vacancies 132,
    151–2
urgent cases 188–9, 190n.6
Truth and Dignity Commission (TDC)
    report
on colonial era 22
inconsistent quality 186
international help 147
missing chapter on sexual violence
    154, 186
not approved by all commissioners
    154
publication in official gazette (2020)
    3–4, 139, 141, 168
publication on website (2019) 139,
    168
retrospective changes 186
submission to 'three presidencies'
    39, 138
Tunisian Confederation of Industry,
    Trade, and Handicrafts (Union
    Tunisienne de l'Industrie, du
    Commerce et de l'Artisanat;
    UTICA) 37, 121n.24
Tunisian Human Rights League (Ligue
    Tunisienne des Droits de
    l'Homme; LTDH) 37, 55, 83
Tunisian Order of Lawyers 37
Tunisian transitional justice
changing understanding of 107–8,
    111, 118
diverse ministerial responsibilities 132
early engagement 70–74
historical overview 2–4
holistic approach 113–14
institutionalisation 73–4, 87–8, 100,
    147
legal or cultural recognition 98
measures of success 52
optimism for the future 173
Organic Law on Establishing and
    Organising Transitional Justice
    (2013) 3, 98, 107

outlook 186–7
perceived delay 89–90
political measures 72–3
problem-capacity nexus 17, 119,
    179–80
socio-economic concerns 45, 50, 98
technocratic/political entanglement
    90
three phases 9–11
timeframe (1955–2013) 98
transferability to other regions
    180–3
see also design phase; initiation
    phase; performance phase

unemployment 32–3, 35
Union Générale Tunisienne du Travail
    (Tunisian General Labour Union;
    UGTT)
fight for independence 24
general strike (1978) 27
National Dialogue 37, 121n.24
political activism 67n.22
protests over draft reconciliation
    law 133
strikes 109
support for uprising (2011) 35
TDC public hearings 144
Union Tunisienne de l'Industrie, du
    Commerce et de l'Artisanat
    (Tunisian Confederation of
    Industry, Trade, and Handicrafts;
    UTICA) 37, 121n.24
United Nations
Special Rapporteur for Truth,
    Justice, Reparations, and the
    Guarantee of Non-Recurrence
    111, 113
transitional justice policymaking 49
United Nations Development
    Programme (UNDP) 112, 149,
    173–4

United Nations Human Rights Council
    73
uprising (2010/11)
causes 26–7, 31–3
deaths and casualties 35, 71, 90n.6
events 34–5
precursor events 33–4
UTICA (Tunisian Confederation of
    Industry, Trade, and Handicrafts)
    37, 121n.24

vernacularisation 60–2, 83, 111
vetting for political office *see* lustration
victims
Dignity Fund 98, 130, 153, 154,
    186
empathy for 79–80
General Authority of Resistance
    Fighters, Martyrs, and Wounded
    of Revolution and of Terrorist
    Operations 142
identification of 30, 40, 108–110
testimony archives 153
see also 'martyrs and wounded of
    the revolution'
violence 27, 29, 35, 37, 109

What are we waiting for? (Fech
    Nestanew?) campaign 156
women
Ben Ali 'progressive image ' 29
and sexual violence 154, 186
World Bank 27

young people
in transitional justice 109, 123n.59
unemployment 32–3
as victims 109
Youssefi Movement 24, 26–7, 40,
    41n.17

9 781526 155382